Yalkut Ya'akov

Lessons from Bereshit

Insights, Reflections and Divrei Torah
from the Book of Genesis.

Rabbi Jack Tauber

Yalkut Ya'akov

Lessons from Bereshit

**Insights, Reflections and Divrei Torah
from the Book of Genesis.**

Rabbi Jack Tauber

ISBN Number 1-57087-517-0

Library of Congress Catalog Card Number 00-131052

Professional Press
Chapel Hill, NC 27515-4371

Ordering Information:

Book Clearing House
46 Purdy Street
Harrison, NY 10528
1-800-431-1579 — Fax: 914-835-0398
E-mail: bookch@aol.com — www.bookch.com

Manufactured in the United States of America
00 01 02 03 04   10 9 8 7 6 5 4 3 2 1

For Our Parents

Rabbi Jack Tauber
Roslyn Tauber

יַעֲקֹב אָבִינוּ לֹא מֵת.
מַה זַרְעוֹ בַּחַיִּים – אַף הוּא בַּחַיִּים.

"Jacob our Father did not die, for as long as his children
live by his values, he will live." (Ta'anit 5b)

מִשֶּׁרָאָה אֱלִיעֶזֶר שֶׁכָּל־כַּךְ מוּפְלֶגֶת רִבְקָה
בִּגְמִילוּת־חֲסָדִים, רָמַז לָהּ גַּם אֶת שְׁנֵי הָעַמּוּדִים
הָאֲחֵרִים, תּוֹרָה וַעֲבוֹדָה, שֶׁעֲלֵיהֶם הָעוֹלָם עוֹמֵד.

"When Eliezer saw just how much benevolence Rivkah
possessed, it was apparent to him that she also possessed
the characteristics of Torah and Sacrifice, thus possessing
all three of the pillars on which the world stands." (Gur
Aryeh to Genesis 42:22)

v

Contents

GLOSSARY

BIBLIOGRAPHY

Editors' Preface

As a pulpit rabbi for nearly half a century, Rabbi Jack Tauber was confronted on a regular basis with the practical application of Torah ideals to daily life. As a scholar, he was at home with both Maimonidies and Einstein, with Judaism and science. He did not try to reconcile the two because he saw no contradiction between them. Science and secular learning were part of God's creation and can be appreciated for the insights they bring to the workings of God's universe, but it is Torah which provides direction and meaning.

These philosophies are reflected in Rabbi Tauber's teachings on Torah study, and particularly in this volume *Yalkut Ya'akov,* dealing with *Genesis, Bereshit.* Themes of creation, evolution and scientific knowledge are explored in a manner which provides a new understanding of the basic foundations of Judaism. Torah values of faith, Divine purpose, relationships between man and his fellow, love of Israel, loyalty, steadfastness are all shown to be eternal values for all societies, including our own.

Nearly forty years ago, Rabbi Tauber, z'l, published his commentary *Chazon Ya'akov* which examined and explored Maimonidies's *Hilchot Talmud Torah, Laws of the Study of Torah,* which forms part of his great codification of Jewish law, *Yad HaChazakah* which is one of the foundations of Rabbi Yosef Karro's, *Shulchan Aruch,* the definitive code of Jewish law. Rabbi Tauber himself noted an apparent oddity in Maimonidies's work, namely, that it contains "the laws we observe today concerning the study of Torah and also the rules of *Cherem* and *Niddu,* excommunication and the ban, which we generally do not observe today." *Chazon Ya'akov* does not avoid mention of the incongruity but faces it head on. Why did Maimonidies combine two such disparate subjects, education and excommunication? *"Patach beTorah veseyem beniddui,"* "He begins with Torah study and closes with excommunication!" How apparently odd. But, Rabbi Tauber explained, the two topics are actually one, because the Rambam introduces the topic of excommunication and the ban with the discussion of the relationship between the people and their Rabbis, between Rabbis and their students and the severe penalties for improper respect. In short, *ain Torah beli derech eretz,* There can be no proper Torah study without respect.

In deciding to write on this subject, which in the author's words, was abstract with no practical value, Rabbi Tauber cited Rashi's advice, that one should spread teachings which are otherwise neglected. With hindsight, we can see another motivation, that of a visionary who could see beyond his times. When *Chazon Ya'akov* was written, postwar orthodoxy was in its infancy, still building an infrastructure. Who could worry about particular guidelines about Torah study or how the people would relate to Torah scholars? The fear at the time was whether there would be Torah study and scholars at all. Rabbi Tauber could see ahead, to the next generation, when Torah study would again flourish, and the need for the constructive and respectful airing of halachic differences and understanding of the required respect for Torah scholars would become acute. As Rabbi Abraham Herschberg, chief Rabbi of Mexico City pointed out in his *haskama,* introductory tribute to *Chazon Ya'akov,* "Respect for the Rabbis and Torah scholars is of greater importance than honoring the Torah itself, for without the existence of the teachers and scholars of Torah, the Torah itself would be lost."

The teachings and Torah commentary of Rabbi Tauber were also ahead of their time and express an area of study and philosophy which has been neglected but is sorely needed in our day. The disciplines of Judaism and secular study are separated and compartmentalized. The non-orthodox either ignore *Halachah* and Jewish values, or subjugate them to secular goals and perspectives. At the other extreme, the secular world is all but ignored except for its functional aspects. The Centrist or Modern Orthodox actually compartmentalize modern society and Torah values, creating an almost schizophrenic personality. Rabbi Tauber however, was a truly integrated personality, the embodiment of *Torah u'mada.* As a young man he embraced the Zionist Revisionist philosophy, serving as the great leader Ze'ev Jabotinsky's personal secretary and assisting the Irgun. He did so not out of a sense of extremism but recognition that this philosophy of Zionism provided a realistic view of the world and the problems facing Jewish life, and that its promotion of Jewish rights and the Jewish right to *Eretz Yisrael* was consonant with the three fold Torah values of *Am Yisrael, Eretz Yisrael VeTorat Yisrael,* the Nation of Israel, the Land of Israel and the Torah of Israel. As part of the *Vaad Hatzalah,* the Orthodox rescue organization which was singularly responsible for the rescue of thousands of Jews during the War years, he demonstrated there was a time for study and a time for action.

Rabbi Jack Tauber was a pulpit rabbi. He served his temple for 43 years. When we were young and spent our summers in the Catskills, we often wondered why he so often took the Greyhound back and forth to and from the city. Unknown to us was that there was always a *shiva* call to be made, a hospitalized person to visit, a wounded person to comfort.

Rabbi Jack Tauber was a husband and father. In the cold of winter, he would carry a blanket to the school bus stop to wrap us in as we waited. He walked in front of us, to block the wind. When our mother took ill, he prepared our lunch for school. When job offers which would have provided greater name and money were offered, he rejected them so his wife could remain near her physicians. He never lacked giving hugs and kisses. He sang and made up stories as he mesmerized his children. He loved his wife and children with "every fibre of my being," he was never afraid to show it, he was never ashamed to say it.

Rabbi Jack Tauber was brilliant. He would lay in bed at night and teach himself languages, four, six, eight, we eventually lost count at how many he knew. Religion, science, philosophy, history, literature, he knew it all. He was brilliant, but never condescending. He once stated that he wished to write a book, *"Doro shel Abbah,* My Father's Generation," all about the brilliance of his father's generation. In his humility, all he knew, the languages, the Bible, the Jewish Law, the science and philosophy, when compared to his father, he claimed to know nothing.

We've often felt that his life made for "....a Wonderful Life," for truly he was a man who touched so many others. A federal Judge who grew up under his supervision, called him "a powerful force for good in my life." At his funeral hundreds of his congregants pushed and shoved to touch and kiss his coffin.

Maaseh Avot siman lebanim, the deeds of the Fathers are guideposts for their children. For those who knew him, this adage was a constant theme of our Father Rabbi Tauber. The lives and teachings of our forefathers provide the guidance to all of Israel to

face the challenges of the day. Rabbi Tauber's life and his exploration of the meaning of Torah are guideposts to his children and
to the Jewish People of today as well.

Stuart, Laurence, and Kenneth Tauber

Bereshit

— 1 —

בְּרֵאשִׁית בָּרָא אֱלֹהִים אֵת הַשָּׁמַיִם וְאֵת הָאָרֶץ:

"In the beginning God created heaven and earth."
(Genesis 1:1)

IN THE BEGINNING...

As we begin the reading of the Torah, we find ourselves fascinated by the same words that have attracted the best minds of Biblical commentators among Jew and non-Jew alike.

"In the beginning God created heaven and earth."

Time and again, we are compelled to remind those who seek to compare the cosmology of the Bible with the latest scientific theories, that the Torah is not a scientific textbook, although its cosmology is reinforced with the passing of time. It is always fascinating to compare Aristotle and Platonic concepts with Biblical intimations interpreted by our Sages. It is a thrilling adventure to consider the scriptural word along side the latest scientific advances and observe how majestically the Holy Writ stands firm.

1

Primarily however, the Torah contains social truths and philo-
sophic-scientific attitudes which time can not destroy nor the human mind deprecate. As the centuries roll by, and the accepted
proof of yesterday becomes discarded antiquated fantasy, we cannot help but appreciate the words of Ben Bag Bag who said: "Turn
it and turn about it, and within it shall you look, and grow old and
gray over it; for there is no better portion for you than this." (Ethics of the Fathers 5:25)

"Torat Hashem Timimah,"
"The Lord's Torah is perfect." (Psalms 19:8)

Fundamentally, when we recite this Psalm, we do not mean
that its modernity is such that we can find diagrams for jet planes
or other contemporary mechanical devices in it, but that in the
words of the Midrash, the words of Torah are compared to water
(Gen. Rabbah 66:1), for just as water refreshes the human body,
so does Torah refresh the human soul. This is true because the
attitudes expressed or implied by the Torah are applicable in all
times and generations, regardless of the century within which its
readers have lived. The fundamental truth of Torah was the same
in prehistoric times, an era of time apparently conceived of by our
Sages long before Darwinism became popular, because we read in
the Midrash that before the period of Abraham, men's counte-
nances had the appearances of apes (Gen. Rabbah 23:6). The truth
of Torah was real centuries later when the Roman Empire was at
its height. The truth of Torah is untouched today in the age of the
atom.

It was the Greek-Jewish philosopher Philo who indicated
that "*Bereshit*," "In the beginning," has nothing to do with time,
as we human beings can conceive of that feature in our lives, be-

cause as modern science and ancient philosophy have taught, time is associated with movement. Einstein made that clear to even the least scientific of us when he said that time is relative. Time, space and movement are connected with each other, because time means living or moving or occupying space. Philo indicated that with *Briath Haolam*, the creation of the world, there came into existence time. And that is what the word *Bereshit* means.

The Torah starts with that great *Bet* in the word *Bereshit*, which in numerology indicates two and second. To compel us to focus our attention on what that word really means to us, it seeks to remind us of that which was before time, that which came first. Before there was anything, there was God. For a doctrine which wishes to speak to all men, the simplest among us who are not great philosophers and scientists, is it not strange that the Torah should wish us to concentrate our thoughts on what is obviously such a deep thought? But perhaps we can understand this problem if we consider the teaching of Rabbi Yitzchok ben Moshe Arama, in his commentary *Akedat Yitzchok,* who states that the Hebrew Scripture of the Bible says, "In the beginning created God," to teach all of us an undeniable truth. That no matter how much we learn, how many atoms we study, how much we learn about the structure and composition of matter and energy, we are constantly being driven to the realization that we cannot comprehend the nature of God.

Throughout the centuries there have been deeply educated minds which have dissipated their energies and their brilliance by seeking to discover what God is and thereby they have wasted time and strength which might have been better used for less abstract problems and utilized instead in attempts to make this world a better place to live. Torah sought to solve this problem by forcing our attention on the creation and creative forces operating within the universe. Why bother your head on abstract problems concerning God? God created the world, and by studying the universe we can best learn to appreciate the greatness of God.

Unlike other schools of thought, Judaism doesn't ask one to delve deep into mystic interpretations that seek to define the makeup of our Heavenly Father. Judaism says to each of us: Don't be ignorant, use the Divine intelligence that has been planted within you. Do you wish to know the greatness of God? Look about you. You examine an automobile and are impressed by the ability of the mechanic who first constructed it. You are impressed by the assembly line that set the parts together. Now look at the great harmony that is called the universe and think of the Creator, the architect who first drew the blueprints for so vast mechanism. Think of the natural forces that were set in motion so that this world could come into being with its land, its oceans, its mountains and living creatures. Think of that stupefying sun, a ball of fire so far away from us which supplies us with heat, light, and all the energy for life itself. Think of the delicate organism called a human being, whose nervous system and brain work quicker than any computer system man has devised. Think of the human heart and the emotions it can build up within us.

Think of the food we develop and which was first planted and grown before mankind made its appearance. Think of the perfect order by which the universe functions and you will at least know enough to realize that no man can see God and live. But that each of us can at least recognize what he is and it is this thought which the Torah wants to start its entire philosophy with. For once you have accepted that pretense, it is easy for you to understand Torah. Once you start out life with the realization that "In the be-

ginning God created the heaven and earth," you can understand
that the world was empty and void.

Non-Jews have always criticized Jews as being a people filled
with avarice. We are purported to be greedy, money-mad, to think
only in terms of business, and adding to our worldly possessions.
Each of us has come across the anti-Semitic caricatures of the Jew
wherein he is portrayed as a notorious creature, a Fagin. Yet it is
the very first lines of Torah, which dispel that lie about us by laying the foundation stones of our faith, our philosophy, our attitude
towards life. In the words of one of the Sages, when a Jew begins
life by understanding that God created heaven and earth, then he
understands immediately that:

"*Haaretz hayetah tohu vavohu*,"
"The earth was unformed and void." (Gen. 1:2)

Realizing that all earthy mundane things are empty and void,
he no longer places all his effort upon amassing world goods only.
He does not think all of life's happiness rest in becoming rich. He
cannot help but realize that there are other values, spiritual wealth
to be achieved by each of us. Philosophy cannot help but change a
person from a grasping greedy beast into a human being, conscious
of his destiny and filled with a desire to live a life of good works.

Bereshit instructs us that as we consider the way of all flesh,
it should be clear that we are different from other creatures. We
are people with souls; people stamped in the true image of God
who must seek not to concentrate only upon the material, but to
seek the higher, spiritual aspects of life as well.

Beginning life this way, creates a new attitude towards life
which makes us desirable human beings who must play proper

roles as husbands and wives, fathers and mothers, sons and daughters, and fellow human beings.

RELIGION AND SCIENCE

Several decades ago, the academic world vehemently criticized Genesis as a book of legends that had absolutely no value as compared with the scientific opinion, regarding the age of our planet. Furthermore some scientists asserted that no one could take the Bible seriously since it postulated the creation of the world in six days, a declaration which brought smiles to the faces of the learned ones. After all, it was claimed, in this modern day and age, everyone knew that the planet had emerged from a piece of a nebula which had been severed and after a period of cooling, eventually established conditions which were conducive to the emergence of life. Today we find that the opinions of the scientific world have changed and some of this fury has diminished in time, but now it has been resurrected in the argument between the evolutionists and the creationists.

Each group makes the statement apparently documented on scientific observation, to disapprove the opposition or to defend itself. What is very sad is the failure of both groups to look carefully at the Bible and try to understand what the Bible really teaches. On one hand, we have a scholar like Ernst Haeckel, who points out that science actually follows the Biblical pattern that teaches us that in the course of creation, there were various stages wherein life was created. The later stages indicated higher advanced forms of life, culminating in the creation of a man. If someone wants to simplify evolution and the arguments about many ape like ancestors, we can find some support, as we noted earlier, in the ancient

Midrash that asserts that before Abraham our Father, man looked like a monkey and had a tail. (Gen. Rabbah 24:10)

But as we were saying, both the defenders and the detractors have missed the important implications of Genesis. The Bible is really not concerned with scientific theory at all. It is not particularly interested in ascertaining the results of some laboratory experiment, to know whether the rearing and observation of many generations of fruit flies for example, prove or disprove the possibility of mutations or explaining evolutionary assertions. What all these people have overlooked is the fact that the Bible wants us to understand what we mean when we pray. We bless God for fashioning light and creating darkness, for making peace and creating everything.

The story of Genesis is concerned with laying the foundations of the most central teaching of our faith, that it is an absolute *Weltanschauung*, a philosophy of life, in which all things are due to one Creator, the First Cause, the Omnipotent, the Omniscient, the one and only Lord God, whom we can never understand because we are so limited in our reasoning and finite in our intelligence. The Midrash indicates that just as furniture was made by a carpenter, cloth by a tailor, building by a stone cutter, etc., the world was created by a Creator who alone is eternal. And if there are certain natural laws that exist, a phenomenon that cannot be ignored, then it is suggested that there is also a moral law upon which mankind must depend and which alone can ensure our continued existence, even as natural phenomena depend upon their laws.

Now what is the outline of this moral law? The first observation is that when this world was made:

"*VeRuach Elokim merahchefet al pe'nai hamayim,*"
"The spirit of God hovered over the face of the deep."
(Gen. 1:2)

And how does that great Sage Rashi explain this spirit of God? "You hear, when God created this world, he immediately integrated within its form, the messianic spirit, a potentiality to redeem and deliver all things, all life from those forces and pressures which might impede its development or threaten its survival." The ancient Rabbis, characteristically, understood this tremendous insight to mean that within the material resources of our globe there are factors, elements, impulses, and even material compositions with intimations of redemption. Thus they taught, that before God imposes evil, whatever the blow may be, he first fashioned the cure for the difficulty. Can a human being become ill with diabetes? Well somewhere there are chemicals like insulin that can treat this sickness. Is there heart disease? Then there are herbs that can produce digitalis or other medications. Is there such a terrible disease like cancer? Well, rest assured that in this world of ours, there are specific chemicals, plants or genetic aspects within man which can cure this disease. But ours is the duty to search for them. Even in its original state the Garden of Eden required care; the Bible says:

"*Vayekach Hashem Elokim et haadam, Vayaneechahu*
***be'gan aden leavdah ohleshamera,*"**
"And God took man, placed him in paradise, to work at
it and to guard it." (Gen. 2:15)

Even a Garden of Eden, if not watched and cared for properly, will deteriorate, be covered by weeds, and become a worthless wild jungle. So, too, does the Bible imply to us, this world was created magnificently indeed far beyond your original comprehension and as you progress and advance, as you toil and watch the knowledge that you accrue to yourselves, you, too, will find the solutions to your problems within it.

So what will happen, you may ask, if some scientists are correct, that the sun may grow colder and one day in a very distant future, it may grow so old that it will radiate no heat upon the earth and then we shall all die. To such fears as what will happen millions of years in the future, the Prophet comes and gives us a word of comfort and advice. "For thus speaks God, He created the heavens, He is the Lord who fashioned the earth and made it, He has established it. He did not create it in vain, He formed it to be inhabited by man," (Isaiah 45:18) and the world has a future. Don't worry about the sun getting colder, worry about the foolishness of man that may threaten his existence and that of the world.

We live in a troubled world. Consider the problems that assail us. The greatest problem is war. We see humans engaged in a wild fury of killing other humans. Everyone says, we are intelligent and it is clear that war is not inevitable, everybody should work for peace.

Meanwhile, in our own land for example, there are politicians who would diminish and reduce our support for the ill, the aged and the handicapped, and are instead concerned only with tremendous expenditures for military offenses. Meanwhile, the fear of blasts and burns from atomic and nuclear weapons fills the atmosphere everywhere in the world. What is horrifying is the realization that traditional madness, cruelty, bloodline and vileness of war have been intensified in unprecedented measure due to the scientist's thoroughness and efficiency. The next great evil, all social observers note is presented by man's failure to control his new powers. We have achieved a fabulous control over physical matter. We can create for our children an undreamed wealth of living. Man's brain has gone from triumph to triumph in building machinery, in attaining new magical skills, in mass production that gives wide diffusion of rich comfort and ease, in scientific agriculture in removing distances, and yet, when we look out at this world today, we see paralyzing fears in our hearts and the terrifying inadequacy of the human material in whose hands is entrusted this world of marvelous potential power and beauty. Look at the economic world that troubles us so deeply. Class warfare, racial antagonisms, crippling strikes, economic nationalism, propaganda against freedom of thought, speech and spirit, threats of concentration camps, and instead of a moral rule, the rule of immorality prevails. The murder of innocent men, women and children who are shot at when they leave synagogues. Coveting the land and territory which others make blossom with sweat, sacrifices and blood. Swearing false witness against anyone and everyone who ventures to question the correctness of bloody tyranny. This is what threatens the world everywhere, in Europe, Asia, Africa, South America and even our own country.

To a humanity which is engulfed by these problems, the Bible comes and speaks simple words, eternal words, and immortal teachings.

"Vayevaraich Elokim et yom hashiviee vayekadesh ohtoe,
ki vo shavat mekol melachto asher barah Elokim
la'asot,"
"The Lord blessed the seventh day and sanctified it, for
on it He rested from the world of his creation."
(Gen. 2:3)

The Rabbis tell us that this means that God having created this tremendous world, with all of its cures, with all its promise of richness and exalted living, now expects man to do things to become partners with God in creating the world and in creating the future world, the world of tomorrow. That is the outline of the *Weltanschauung*, philosophy of life of Genesis. And when all discussions do not recognize or include that philosophy, then all the polemics are just empty words. In the original Hebrew, the last letters of the first three words of the Bible form the word "*Emet*" which means truth. And this is the greatest truth of the Bible, which no other teaching in the world will ever surpass. And that truth is the only hope for the entire world. When the Bible proclaimed the truth that there is only one God it also proclaimed the corollary that there is only one humanity. The day will come when all men will be ready to admit that. On that day of the acknowledgment of God's unity with man, there will be established man's unity with God. And then wars, hatred, illness and pain will disappear, because then man will redeem himself and subsequently the world as well.

MEN OF SCIENCE

For a person who wishes to consider the intellectual ferment which exists all about us, it becomes increasingly clear that what we have classified as religious reasoning, is a mental discipline which nobody should dismiss. One day, while reading the newspaper, I could not help but realize that truth. A review of a study on art quoted a most prominent authority of the 20th century, that art is a thing of the mind. Therefore, "the scientific study of art must incorporate psychology." Ernst H. Gombrich in his classic *The Story of Art* declares: "There is no such thing as art, there are only artists."

Obviously, all of us can infer from this that the personality of the artist, his *Gedankengang*, pattern of thought, will color his art.

On the other hand, there is science that deals with events as they occur in the external world of objects, and which obviously, works to eliminate the projection of personality in its observations. The scientist must be an observer. He investigates an event, he watches, compares, relates events to each other, but he himself must not, cannot, be a participant in that event. The scientist studies the universe, and by astrophysics, which is the study of the stars, may come to the conclusion that star explosions provide us with evidence that entire galaxies act as engines of chemical evolution, building simple atoms into more complicated atoms within the stars. When stars exploded, carbon atoms that are built out of helium atoms were scattered throughout the areas between the stars. All life here on earth, they inform us is then based on the carbon atom. Certain giant stacks that exploded provided us with the heavy atoms that we know as gold here on earth. Even before this, there was a cosmic fireball which existed during the first few minutes of the expansion of the universe and this created Hydrogen, which is known to most of us through H_2O (the formula for water of which most of the human being is composed). So through the study of these atoms, we see that the earliest history of the universe is woven throughout the structure of matter. From this, we may infer that everything is related to each other. The piece of gold, the living fish, the growing plant, the running animal, and the observing human being are all related, especially to the extent that they exist or live in the same world.

However, we humans, by virtue of our intelligence, our potential creativity are so different, compared with the rest of creation, that we invariably do project our personalities into every encounter we have, and thereby must determine when we are so participating. But did I not indicate just a moment before that the great thinking human being, who is a scientist is determined to be a great observer, but not a participant in the event he investigates? How can there be hope for human society if man will not be a participant?

In reading a New York Times book review by Timothy Ferris of *Never at Rest*, a biography of Isaac Newton by Richard S. Westfall, I was reminded how everyone knows how great Newton was, and how he has entered into our early education. He is always presented as the man who discovered or clarified the law of gravity during the incident when, while sitting under a tree, an apple fell and hit him on the head. When we were children we asked certain questions, "why does the apple fall down? Why don't the stars fall out of their orbits?" We reflect some of that wonder when we repeat the ancient prayer "*Toleh eretz al beli mah,*" the earth is suspended on nothing." Yet, this great scientist was a man with a human personality that did project itself in life.

Similarly, Albert Einstein has emerged to most of us as the great scientist whose mathematical equation $E=MC^2$ indicated that matter can be transformed into energy. Even if we all do not understand the details of this advanced labor, we do know that it led to the creation of the atomic bomb and we do not have to discuss the details to admit what this means. But also this same Einstein entertained certain sensitivities towards both events in the universe and happenings among human beings.

Physicists seeking a unified theory of nature's forces have considered the problem. Where did the universe come from? That question may be unanswerable by science. It may be unanswer-

able period. But scientists do try to investigate it and their speculations deepen our appreciation of the nature of science, whatever
they may tell us of Genesis. Among the most provocative and promising of these are theories proposing that the universe sprang into
existence from little or nothing. Of course to traditionalists this is
nothing new, because long ago Sages were telling us that the earth
was created *"yesh miayin,"* a material universe from non-mate-
rial. However, the essay goes on to quote the physicist, Heinz R.
Pagels whom in his book, *The Cosmic Code* writes, "Nothing contains all of being. All of physics, everything we hope to know...is
waiting in the vacuum to be discovered..." and then the essay continues "...so we are invited to imagine that uncertainty was present
at creation." What the universe began in chance, just as it has been
subject of chance even since in its 20 billion-year tumble down
the sluice gates of time... To see the universe as evolving like life,
like thought, as subject to change, just as our lives are subject to
change, "is to deepen our sense that we have a rightful place in
nature."

It is here that science reaches its limitations and the scientist
would suppress the creative artist with us. We are able to go beyond, to search for the new frontier. Nowhere does the scientist
pretend that he does not see cause and effect everywhere he speaks
of sparks and explosions of expansion and growth, but only at the
very beginning of phenomena he sees nothing and cannot admit,
except that the very start of the cosmos came from chance. But the
religious personality is far more courageous and more dazzling
and more attractive. He is not afraid to gaze into the heavens, recite the Psalms and say:

"Barchi Nafshi et Adonai,"
"Oh my soul, bless the Lord (Psalms 103:1)."

That is because unlike the scientist who fears personal involvement with the event because such a projection may upset his data, the individual with a religious outlook becomes like an artist who is dealing with an encounter, with a reality that is not only extraneous to him, but also relates to the inner world of his reality.

He can absorb himself in the Psalm of which Alexander von Humboldt wrote, "That we are astonished to see within the compass of a poem of such small dimensions, the universe, the heavens, the earth thus drawn with a few grand strokes."

This person sees the relationship between the plant, the beast and man in the one and same world. He perceives his relationship to the seas and its inhabitants; he visualizes his relationship to the sun and moon and because he sees this he is not afraid to approach the scientist and listen carefully to the latter's search for the controlled, repetitive experiment. But he can go further. The essay ends by quoting the American physicist John A. Wheeler of the University of Texas, "We find that the world is strange, but what is strange is us. It seems to me that we don't yet read the message properly, but in time to come, we will see it in some simple, single sentence. As we say that sentence to each other, we'll say, oh how beautiful, how could we have missed it, all that time?"

But the man of faith knows the sentence and does not miss it. He reads the sentence "In the beginning God created the heavens and the Earth" and can only respond, "Oh my soul, bless the Lord." Not chance. Because the man of faith now has a personal encounter with God, he knows and recognizes his responsibility to life and the universe and so he can end by proclaiming "Let sinners cease out of the earth and let the wicked be no more. Bless the Lord, oh my soul hallelujah."

It may indeed be questioned whether science really assures us of our rightful place in nature, especially in a world of nuclear decay. But the Bible repudiates the uncertainty, the insecurity and anxiety of chance, because it proclaims the encounter of a people with God, an encounter at Sinai, an encounter in the desert and on its sacred soil through the prophets. And in that we can each find true security and a real hope.

THE GENERATIONS OF MAN

The Torah starts its tale and cosmology in what is the most scientific form, its approach to humanity is the only one that can save man from complete annihilation, it is the only attitude that can keep this world and mankind alive.

Most religions initiate their doctrines by a reference to their founders, a Nazarene, Mohammed, Confucius, Buddha, or Zoroaster. The great Sage, the Vilna Gaon, indicated that the history of the Jewish people as a nation really commences with *Shemot,* the Book of Exodus. Rashi noted that the Bible should properly begin at Exodus, which is the first commandment imposed on the Jewish collective. (Rashi to Gen. 1:1) At most we may say that our origins as a faith begin with the story of Abraham. But Genesis begins not with a Jew, Christian or Moslem. This sacred document which is the root of our complete national philosophy, which gives us the foundations of our national history, which makes us conscious of what the word Jew means, does not start by speaking of the Jewish people, nor does it start by imposing ritual obligations of religious nature. It opens its fascinating narrative with the creation of man. Let other creeds seek their beginnings in Jesus, Mohammed, Confucius, Buddha, or

Zoroaster. The Jewish mind first began to spin its philosophy by beginning with the creation of man.

This is evidently what the Rabbis had in mind when they postulated principles of faith. Rabbi Akiba taught: "And thou shall love thy neighbor as thyself, that is a great principle of Torah." Whereupon Ben Azzai responded with the verse: "This is the Book of the Generations of man and is even a greater principle." Rabbi Akiba's insistence that one verse was due to the concept that the essence of Judaism is found in love and compassion for ones fellow man. Love and generosity said his colleagues are his broad patterns of Judaism. The Torah opens with the narrative in which God clothes the naked by dressing Adam and Eve, and it closes by reminding us that the Lord buried Moses. This is indicative of generosity and compassion. Ben Azzai, however, was dissatisfied with Rabbi Akibah's contention, because he found a greater philosophic truth in the verse "and this is the book of the generations of man on the day that God created him." He saw broader and deeper implications in this verse. Social relations must not only result from generosity and compassion, but from respect and honor. Every human being is created in the Divine Image, every human being possess great significance. Everyone merits our respect and consideration. No man should be humiliated, insulted, or emotionally wounded because in owning a soul he stands at the very top of creation. It is that which makes each of us an individual world, an entity that reflects the rest of mankind. To protect and respect the personality of every human being constitutes the alphabet of true civilization. Freedom, equality, and alienable human rights are derived from that unprecedented concept.

Hermann Cohen called Judaism the religion of reason and it is in the first chapter of Genesis that we prove our merit of this title. For when all mankind looked with fear and distrust on the stranger, a sentiment which has not disappeared today, a primitive unreasonable fear which still is the basic cause of many of our foreign policies, which still is the cause of international crisis, wars, and bloodshed, the Torah taught us that man was created in the image of God, and only one man was created. As the Gemarah teaches: Why could not God create many men? To teach us that no man can rightly say, "My linear descent is greater than yours" (Sanhedrin 37a) There are no superior or inferior races. There is no pseudo moral justification for the exploitation of so-called backward peoples, rather a stark reminder that all of us come from the same stock and are subject to the accidents of flesh, the same pangs of hunger, the same illness, and the same death. Men are equal in their alienable right and they are equal in their importance. God spoke to Adam and Eve, to Abel and Cain, and Noah long before he spoke to Abraham. From the very beginnings of time, as soon as man realized that he was in the image of God, that he was more than just a lump of chemical matter, more than just a beast in the field, the voice of God, his conscience thundered to him, to do what was right.

The Bible speaks of man, not a famous man, a clever man, a wealthy man, but an average man. Every man who thus becomes a link in the golden chain called creation. It is important, for as the Rabbis teach, "Destroying one man means destroying a world, preserving one man means saving a world."

That is the great lesson of Genesis that makes it the greatest document of all time. Let the scientist do all the research he wishes to. Let him add theories about the creation of the world. Let him revise his calendar a hundred times after he makes more geological discoveries or archaeological excavations. It is *Bereshit* that remains the unchanging truth. It is *Bereshit* that insists upon the respected and consideration due every human being regardless of race, color, or creed. When all men will realize that truth, when all of us can feel that we are more than beasts, that life must mean more than the amassing of wealth, that we are all children of the same source, and that we are created in the image of our Creator, that we have been endowed with certain rights and privileges and duties, only then shall the world be able to maintain itself safely. Only then will the hatred of strangers, individuals, and nations alike disappear, only then will we create the true united nations of the world.

BERESHIT BARAH ELOKIM

The more we explore it, the more we realize that the Torah lesson of *Bereshit* will continue to be ever old and ever new. No matter what scientific or philosophic innovations or new discoveries in *Bereshit* may portend for the cosmogonies we entertain, there emerges an insight on world and man that will continue to hold, regardless of the cycles of time, which pass over our heads.

A Chassidic attempt to grapple with questions considered during the ages alerts us to some startling perceptions of man and time. *Bereshit bara Elokim*, in the beginning God created. *Lamah nivrah haolam bebet*? Why was the world created with the letter bet, which is the second letter of the Hebrew alphabet and in numerology has the value of two? Should not logic dictate that the Torah begin with an aleph, the first letter of the Hebrew alphabet?

The responses to this question, while superficially strange are no less intriguing than the question itself. With an aleph it would have become a world of curses, since the Hebrew word for curse *"arrur"* begins with an aleph. But with bet, which is the first letter of the Hebrew word for *bracha*, blessing, it has the opportunity to become an *olam bracha*, a world of blessings, so that we may exert an influence for the good among all the nations of the world. (Gen. Rabbah 1:10)

Some of our earliest traditions, considered in the light of contemporary science imply what constitutes the blessed world which each of us seeks today. As we noted, bet stands for the number two. *Halo shtei hayu be'briath haolam*, there were two manifestations of creativity. The first was *briat hachomer,* the creation of matter. Afterwards, the second creation was the creation of *hitpatchuto*, the development. The order of creativity was gradual, almost evolutionary. God created Adam, Man, from the dust of the earth. Afterward he breathed the soul of life into his nostrils. First the form, the structure, and then the development of life with its intelligence, aesthetics, philosophies, sciences. Therein lies our blessing.

Here is a suggestion, that were there only one immediate form of creation, every result would have meant a perfect complete form. What if everything had been formed immediately with its full potentiality or even perfection? What a curse that would be. Imagine life so dull, so stagnant. To feel no need for improvement, to be unaware of the impulse of creativity in our own existence. How flat life would be, how uninteresting to be deprived of all stimulation, all provocation, all challenge, to have no need for labor and toil, no exploration, no discovery, no novelty, to be as stale as any inorganic substance, not to feel the sting of indignation, not to respond to the prodding of compassion, not to reach out in friendship and companionship, never to experience the need for affection and love. What a cursed world that would be.

Perhaps a single creation would have robbed us of the diversity that abounds in nature, or impeded the evolution or development of the various species that enrich the globe with their profusion and multiplicity. Long ago we began to understand that were all the trees of the world to consist of only one perfect type, we might gorge ourselves with apples or pears as the case might be. But overall, we would be the losers; deprived of the beauty and the fascination which nature offers us.

But what if *hitpatchuto*, the development of matter does not apply solely to the evolution which most of us accept by virtue of the universality of scientific assertions? What if the development of the phenomena really refers to man as a partner of God? After all, in various ways, our faith has always sought to remind us that man is a *shutaf bemaase Bereshit*, man is a partner in creation. But to what extent?

Consider the implication that God alone created the *chomer*, that which the world is made of, because He is the creator of all that exists. Man, however, can develop the world, since he was created the Torah tells us, *Betzelem Elokeem*. Translations of *Betzelem Elokeem* that man was created "in the image of God" are not wholly proper. *Betzelem* in Hebrew does not actually mean image, but rather means a semblance, a derivation. A camera is the device that produces a likeness, but not the original. A photograph conveys a sense, a reflection of man, but it certainly is not man himself. Indeed this nuance is reflected in modern Hebrew, which utilizes the term *tzelem* as "photograph." *Betzelem Elokeem* in no way means the puerile, silly notion that we are images of God, or that He resembles us in some physical way, namely that he has eyes, hands or feet. Or that He is subject to the accidents of flesh as we are. The word *tzelem* has a second meaning. It is also used to mean an idol and therein lies the total depravity of man's deterioration, morally and spiritually. "Oh, come now," says contemporary man, the modern personality who has been subject to the progressive, advancing world, wherein science and technology have combined to create an almost utterly, new world. "No modern person worships idols today." But this is not true. Man does continue to worship idolatry, perhaps not the statue of wood and stone that overwhelmed our primitive ancestors. Perhaps not the idolatry so graphically portrayed in Kings, where Mesha the King of Moab took his crown prince, his son who should have one day reigned in his stead and threw him into the flames as a sacrifice unto his idol. Perhaps not the idolatry of Terach, the father of Abraham who had to sustain the shame of having his own son smash the idols which he produced for the worship, or if you will, to deceive and con those gullible willing to pay money for the idol. No, idolatry today is of a different nature.

There is tremendous admonition in the Psalms, which finds its way into one of the weekly prayers:

"*Lo ye'hyeh becha kail zar, velo tishtahchaveh lekail naichar.*"
"Do not let any strange god within you. Do not worship any foreign god." (Psalms 81:10)

What idolatry could this refer to today? First and foremost is the idolatry of the self. For 1500 years, we considered as correct a theory of the solar system promulgated by Claudius Ptolemy an Egyptian astronomer. But today we know he claimed to have performed certain astronomical measurements that he did not. No less a person than the founder of the scientific method, Galileo Galilei, exaggerated the outcome of experimental results. Johann Bernoulli, the man who refined calculus, plagiarized his own son's discovery. Gregor Mendel, the father of genetics, has been accused of publishing statistics that were too good to be true. And even Robert Millikan, the great American physicist and winner of the Nobel Prize, was accused of not mentioning that unfavorable results were omitted in the publication of his studies.

What is it that drives people to act in this manner? Money, careers, pressures from interests concerned vitally with scientific advances? Or is the other side of the *tzelem* not here? The idolatry within man, the false god, the ego, and the self which he worships and which he wants the rest of the world to defy.

When modern man claims that we no longer have a King Mesha to burn his own child, Emil Fackenheim the great Jewish philosopher will quickly remind us that in our modern world, Nazis were idolaters, who in their worship of the pathologic, destructive demonic mentality of Hitler, followed Mesha's example. Only they did not throw their children onto the flames. They threw Jewish children.

If the insistence that a pharaoh is the reincarnation of a sun god, is an idolatrous paganism to be relegated only to antiquity, what then is the cruelty, brutality, and repulsive violence imposed by a Saddam Hussein, if not the age old paganism, ascribing characteristics of a god to a man? How striking are the words of Sociologist Will Herberg, "Idolatry is the root source of our sin and wrongdoing. Ultimately, all idolatry is the worship of self, projected and objectified, in proclaiming as ultimate the ideas and programs to which we are devoted. We are but proclaiming the work of our minds to be the final truth. In the last analysis, the choice is only between love of God and love of self, between a God-centered universe and a self-centered one." That is why this Torah beginning will always endure, because God created the matter. Man, at best may be involved with *hitpatchuto*, with its development. But man must be cautious. He has been created "*Betzelem Elokeem,*" thus he does possess some tremendously Divine inspired traits and may seek to develop this world but he must be very careful. Lest he forgets who he is and who created him. Man may think that he is a *tzelem*, an idol, a false god, and that he can supplant Him who created all *chomer*, the matter and all that really exists.

Forever and ever *Bereshit* teaches us, Man, go and develop that which God has created. "*Maleh ha'aretz vekevashta,*" "fill the earth and conquer it," develop it, but never forget, you are man, the great developer, you are man, but are not God. *Bereshit barah Elokeem.*

OUT OF THE BET AND INTO THE FUTURE

We possess another tradition that declares the reason why the Torah begins with *Bet* the second letter of the Hebrew alphabet. A practice that is also followed by the Talmud, is to emphasize that no matter how much we may study, we never reach the *aleph*, or the very origin of knowledge. This observation assumes a special significance when we consider the very first words of Genesis, *Bereshit*, In the beginning, *Barah Elokim*, God created the Heavens and Earth. Cosmologies, theories, interpretations, explorations of natural phenomena to explain the universe or the emergence of life and man on our planet continue to fascinate us. Despite the current polemics engendered by Christian creationists who accept the literal translation of the Hebrew Bible's narration of Genesis, scientists have dismissed such strategies as indicative of blind faith rather than the pursuit of truth.

This, so to speak, muddles the waters of dialogue, because while we Jews continue to uphold the sanctity of scruples, we have done so imbedded with a conviction that "*Totem shell Hakadosh Baruch Hu Emet,*" "The seal of the Almighty is truth." (Sanhedrin 94b) Hence, we listen to scientists, savants and scholars with respect, and in disagreement, without rancor or hatred. But we are in a rather unique position, because our Sages have not just accepted literal translations of Torah, but have analyzed its teachings, assisted by the insights provided by *Lashon HaKodesh,* the Holy tongue, and bolstered by the vast sea of *Torah sheh be 'al peh,* the Oral Law which unfortunately is unknown to the other peoples who profess loyalty to and claim absolute knowledge of the word of God, as found in our Torah.

Thus we find the Talmudic Sages looking at the very first letter of the Torah, the *Bet,* and they are intrigued by what they see. Consider this letter, outlined by a line on top and a line on bottom connected by another line at the right side, leaving the left open. Whereupon we hear them comment, "Do not seek solutions for human relationships by looking above, or below, or behind, but go forward" (Gen. Rabbah 1:10.) Yet, the scholars, whether engaged in the natural or social sciences, pragmatically, look above or below or behind.

For example, consider the theories of a prominent scientist, Stephen Jay Gould, who is a Harvard Professor of Biology and Geology. In his study he is concerned with the catastrophe which buried loads of strange creatures a half billion years ago. These remains have been revealed in a slab of rock, named the Burgess Shale in Yoho National Park in Canada. Dr. Gould belongs to that new school of scientists who say that the usually accepted concept of evolution, that we gradually evolved from some monkey looking ancestor, is all wrong. What he and the scholars who agree with him claim is that we are an accident of nature and catastrophic events which have eradicated many species of life on this planet and could have wiped us out as well. Studying the fossils of the Burgess Shale, says the Professor, makes us realize that the previous scientists were wrong in assuming that those creatures were the original, less complicated forms of life, from which we have descended. Now, we are told, they were wiped out by some catastrophe. With this view, Gould would have us understand that from the millions of species of life on this planet, it is purely an accident that one should have developed conscious intelligence. So with such an appraisal, there is little predictability about our ability to continue here, before another accident wipes us out. That is a view revealed by looking below, into the very soil which allegedly has preserved for us a record of the Genesis. (Incidentally, it is interesting to observe that Dr. Gould has declared other scientists were wrong.) What will happen if new evidence, 10 or 20 years from today, will persuade other scientists that Dr. Gould is wrong. This sensitivity to other opinions is manifest in the Talmud, where despite the announcement that the *Halachah*, Jewish law we uphold is based upon the opinion of one authority, the opposing arguments of other scholars are included, since we must realize that what has been rejected today, may very well be deemed correct in another decade.

Now, there are those who look and explore the vastness of space which is both intriguing and awesome simultaneously. Some of us know of the anecdotal report on the query, what is man when compared to the overwhelming picture presented by astronomy and physics? Little fragile man, little puny man, vulnerable man, dispensable man, mortal man, standing before the expanding universe with its galaxies of possibilities which are mind staggering. As the world of science continues its studies of the stars and the gases between them, as we hear more and more of electromagnetic forces, radiation and cosmic rays, quasars from which emerge enormous quantities of energy which equals output of hundreds of galaxies, pulsars which beam radiation, black holes in which matter falls and eludes our study, a universe forever accelerating at an increasing pace, the travel of light over the vast differences of space and time, the incredible results of our space and satellite studies, before this awesome spectacle of astronomy and physics, what is man? But the answer is simple. Man is the astronomer and the physicist. Insects may be the largest species numerically, but roaches, bedbugs and lice do not ponder problems of astronomy.

And what is the view of those who would look behind? The picture we are confronted with does not particularly enhance the prominent or should it enlarge the contemporary arrogance of prejudices of the scientist. If we pretend that the unpleasantness and the grievances of the past were due only to the ignorance of the primitive man arising out of the superstitions and the fears of the unknown, and were due to the lack of progress as we humans like to define semantic, what shall we say when we look at our own 20th century, and tremble before the bestiality, inconceivable brutality, the deterioration of the conscious intelligence we call man?

When such horrifying words like genocide, crematoria, concentration camp, totalitarianism, gulag, torture, imprisonment, lamp shades of human skin, have become part of our current vocabulary, *Bereshit* teaches us, says *Torah Sheh Be'al peh*, that there is no need to surrender to panic at catastrophic upheavals of which professor Gould warns us. Have we not been taught, "*Barah Hakodesh Baruch Hu Olamat umackivin Otam*," "God created many worlds and destroyed them," (Gen. Rabbah 12:4) *"Shehaya Mabit BaTorah Ubarah Et Haolam,"* until he peered into Torah and constructed our world? Is there some retention in the archetype of human mentality that preserves such record? Carl Jung maintained that somewhere in the human subconscious each of us carries the history of the entire human race. Is that why we retain tales of ancient Atlantis? Or the narrative of Noah and the flood which receives support from studies of an ice age or the destruction of Sodom and Gomorrah which certainly is not far fetched to us, who have experienced earthquakes, volcanoes and other catastrophes? And how many times have we humans boasted of our culture and civilization, only to witness how crime, violence, war, financial disasters, and human stupidity which are man made and not natural catastrophes have shattered our illusions?

Looking above to the stars, looking below to geological evidence, looking behind to history are apparently no guarantees of the progressive advance of our life here on earth. Yes we may not be able to reach the aleph, or as Robert Oppenheimer that great Physicist admitted, "We shall never know everything," but one thing we may know and that is to go forward, outward from the bet, toward the potentiality which man does have. A potentiality, a capacity and skill and talent which arises from the recognition, that *"Bereshit, Barah Elokim,* In the beginning God created." That our presence here is not an accident, that even as God *Hayah Mabit BaTorah,* as our Creator looked into Torah to fashion this, our world, we too must look to Torah, towards God's moral imperative for the proper life. "What is Man" may be a mocking cry on the part of a scientist, but the question "what is man," enosh, the cry of Psalmist, is answered by the Torah. Man is created, not as the gentiles literally translate *Betzelem Elokim,* in his image, (Gen.

1:27) but reflecting his shadow of capabilities, talents and intelligence transcending other forms of earthly existence.

Man's intellectual progress is to be encouraged, but his achievements will fail unless they are accompanied by the will to go forward, as life created to fulfill a moral imperative of divine sanction.

Accident means no purpose. No purpose means no reason. No reason means no ethics. No ethics means humanity is nothing but another chance of expression of some blind force and can not be expected to live with compassion, sensitivity, justice and love. Are not the Rabbis correct, *Ain Dayan Ain Din*, if there is no judge, there functions no justice, no God? Why ask me not to kill, rob, and oppress, when nothing counts and we expect to stand before no judgment? *Dah lifney Me atah omed*, know before whom you stand (Berachot 28b) is not only the cry of the Rabbis, but the *shibboleth* of him who recognizes *Bereshit*. We may not pretend to know God's mind but we realize that he knows ours. And with that realization comes the only hope for humanity to go forward, out of the *bet* into the other stages of progress of existence. To go forward, unintimidated by above, below, or behind, secure in the faith that we are unique, not because of fortuitous chance but because of deliberate choice by that creative force of all. And that is our only hope for salvation and the retention of our unique status on this planet or elsewhere in the universe.

IN HIS IMAGE

Bereisht brings us to the beginnings of our faith, our philosophy of life and our sensitivity to all phenomena in our existence, as it impinges up our very lives here on Earth.

While most people when discussing the book correctly and oratorically refer to it as the Book of God because it does declare *"Bereshit barah Elokim,"* in the beginning God created heaven and earth, the Bible itself uses another phrase which is poignant and fitted with meaning, *zeh sefer toldot ha'adam,* this is the book of the generations of Man. (Gen. 5:1) What does the Bible tell us about ourselves?

There are some insights into the inner life of man, which are impressed upon the pages of the Bible and upon our contemporary researchers.

In this Biblical lesson, we find that we are introduced to a scene in which it is reported that the Lord spoke and said:

"Naaseh adam Betzalmainu kedemutainu,"
"Let us make a man in our image, after our likeness."
(Gen. 1:26)

But further on, we read:

"Vayivrah Elokim et ha'adam Betzalmo" and
"God created man in his image." (Gen. 1:27)

Is there not a slight contradiction or change from the original plan? Does it not seem that God's intent was perhaps to create the perfect being as the image of God would imply. But notice, if you will, the phraseology of the actual creation. *Betzalmo,* in his own image, often read to mean in God's image, may be read as in man's image. A human image is not perfect. Had man been completely in God's image, he might have been the perfect creation, perhaps even as immortal as God is. Also notice, the Hebrew expression which is used, *"adam,"* man. The Hebrew expression *ish,* which is more commonly used in the language, might have been used to designate man, so why the expression *adam*? The word *adam*, incidentally, has no plural in the Hebrew language. Therefore we know that each man is a creation unto himself, thus a *Betzalmo* means a man in his own form. Indeed, we are not completely Godly, rather human, mortal and imperfect. Each man is an individual in his own, completely different from his brothers and sisters, our sages tell us. Just as there are no two exactly identical faces, so too, are our thoughts, different. There are no two human beings physically or mentally alike.

I remember trying to argue this with a physician. He reminded me very quickly that while we were talking about two identical twins, the fact remained that their finger prints were different, their aesthetic tastes were different, their opinions about people and events were different, and what is more, their problems even when dealing with similar phenomenon were totally different as they explained them. No, said the physician, we must admit the fact that no two human beings are exactly alike, physically or mentally. Each of us is a creation in himself. As a result, we, to a large extent, can shape our own destiny. Each man has the capacity and God given right to think differently to preserve that adam, that individuality in his pursuit of life. How do we apply this knowledge?

You have often heard people emphasize their alibis in life, by saying: if this is happening it is because God wants it to be so, what can I do? The power of life is in God's hands. But we are not left without *bechirah*, choice in our daily lives. Man was made *Betzalmo*, in his image and therefore man is what he makes of himself. Man is what his experience teaches him to be. The choice is with him. He can develop and grow in maturity and spiritual strength, or he can deteriorate and wither. Our creation is not complete. It is up to us to interpret our own aims for our own improvement. Let us closely continue to examine the text and we shall come upon another interesting phenomenon. As God created this universe we find with each separate creation, the expression. And God saw that it was good. However, this expression is not found after the creation of man. Man was given a mind to be able to think and choose. Whether or not this creation of *Adam,* person is good, depends upon the *bechirah,* the choice of each and every *adam.* For the miracle of the creation is repeated with each and every birth.

Thus you will notice something strange, Jewish people do not commemorate the day of birth of their ancestors, but rather the *yahrzeit,* the day of death. Only at the end, can we evaluate the life of each individual. Each day, until the final hour of our existence, we are faced with a *bechirah,* a choice as an individual person. To make something of ourselves, to make this universe a little better than we found it. This a basic Jewish concept which is of tremendous importance to every one of us.

Modern psychiatrists are trying to interpret the latest scientific developments and are speculating as to the hidden unconscious reasons for man's yearning to reach the beyond, to conquer space, to embark upon policies and programs we once assigned only to science fiction. Some are coming to a conclusion that as a whole, people are frustrated to the point where man cannot live with man. For that reason, they claim, we search for a new and different world. Can you understand how confused such thinking is? The emerging countries are frustrated with the continued existence and strength of capitalism, so they are determined to demonstrate that they can out do the West in weapons of destruction and ruin. The West, feels that the only chance for salvation lies in conquering space or in science. In star war programs, in outdoing any other experiments. But people overlook the fact that we do not lack space, we lack values, we lack morals. Look at the world in which we live. After the Holocaust, and after the second world war which resulted in murder, torture, persecution, humiliation and mass massacres of millions and there are such psychopathic frauds, people deliberately lying to pretend that this insanity never existed. Much of your personal development and your contribution to society as large will depend upon your choices. Once when a pupil in my class complained to our teacher, in a crooked world, what is so important if I shall be honest. And the teacher replied, at least there will be one crook less to make people unhappy. And your goodness will help make others happy. Of course this means that you will have to be alert to problems and how they affect others.

There is a rather interesting incident recorded of a Rabbi who was asked to help provide food and clothing for a very poor family. The wealthiest man in town was a miser who simply refused to help. Whereupon the Rabbis left very early in a cold winter's morning and rang the miser's doorbell. The man was still asleep, but he ran downstairs in a thin robe to open the door and when he saw who rang the bell, he invited the Rabbi in, but the Rabbi said that he was in a hurry and had to state his business immediately. Quietly putting his foot into the door so that it remained open, he bean to speak about responsibilities, sympathy and compassion and making the right choices. Meanwhile the wind and frost were blowing against the miser who was getting colder and colder. Listen Rabbi, my teeth are chattering, my bones are frozen I can't take it any longer. Wow, said the Rabbi, if you can't stand this cold for just a few minutes, how do you expect a family of six children with no food, no woolen clothes and no quilts to stand this cold all winter. The miser looked at the Rabbi and said: I think I have to make a definite choice and pulled out a great contribution.

Perhaps we all have to feel the pinch of others in order to make the proper choice. We have seen others make choices and self sacrifices for other peoples welfare. People have demonstrated their sense of morality. We must all follow these good examples and indicate that as an *adam*, a human being, we are determined to improve ourselves, by our character, our compassion for others, our sensitivity to justice and our determination to make this world a better place. That will prove our individuality and make us a credit to our people and to the community in which we live.

Noah

— 2 —

שֶׁמִּצְוָה גּוֹרֶרֶת מִצְוָה, וַעֲבֵרָה גּוֹרֶרֶת עֲבֵרָה;

"*Mitzvot* and evils produce their own kind."
(Ethics of the Fathers 4:2)

ONE MITZVAH LEADS TO ANOTHER....

T he story of Noah always has attracted the attention, analysis and even speculations of scientists and scholars whose
academic disciplines lie outside Biblical studies or cre-
dence. It is a story of fascinating tale, full of appeal to the adventure and stimulation to our imagination. Even in our own day and
age, a depiction of a world drowning is so full of implications that
we cannot help, but be overwhelmed by the narrative.

The visions which the Torah depicts of mankind drowning
in an unprecedented *mabul*, deluge has always conjured comparisons with possible effects of an ice-age, glaciers, earthquakes or
even cosmic disturbances produced by some collisions between
earth and other planetary influences. When the late Immanual
Velikovsky in his highly controversial volume, *Worlds in Colli-*

sion, first suggested that some of the Biblical events like the flood, or the Israelites crossing the Red Sea, or Joshua's victory in Gibeon, (which all ended with an interference in the natural movement, i.e., setting of the sun) were all really due to some catastrophic influence which the planet Venus exerted upon the earth, hordes of laymen were intrigued by this idea. But it soon developed that many scientists entertained opinions and theories regarding such catastrophic events that, they believed, determined the manner in which all life increased or was threatened. Thus while once, such assertions were laughed at by the scientific community, today, we find serious scholars in various fields speaking about such possibilities.

No one dismisses the narrative as a figment of the imagination of primitive man. Today, science has accumulated for us data that indicates how true and valid is the *Dor hamabul,* the generation of the flood. We know that large sections of our planet were subjected to deluge, and it is calculated that a Mediterranean civilization that boasted a population of forty million people was wiped out by a deluge.

Indeed, we have an entire school of thought known as catastrophic science that certainly is cognizant of disasters, from volcanic eruptions to earthquakes, to collisions of cosmic significance, as meteorite or comet impacts with subsequent devastation.

These are truly fascinating and intriguing observations. The Torah, however, is not concerned with geographical, geological, or even graphic descriptions of the past. What constitutes Torah concern is a narrative of moral analysis and the moral implications in the background of the account.

Thus, the story of *Noah,* basically is not a *maaseh,* occurrence about a *mabul,* a flood and people who drowned.

The story of Noah is essentially a moral lesson about human conduct, its failure to maintain proper, moral standards and to strive for righteous, social relationships. It is in this dimension that we should consider the Torah portion of Noah.

One of the great lessons of our faith is the recognition that actions and events invariably can influence upon our fellow man to the extent that either good or evil may be duplicated, continued, and even expanded to our probable deterioration and even punishment. The *klal,* general principle is:

"*Mitzvah goreret mitzvah* and *avehrah goreret avehrah*,"
"*Mitzvot* and evils produce their own kind."
(Ethics of the Fathers 4:2)

This applied in the days of Noah, as it does today. The continued deterioration and transgression does not have to be productive immediately of flood or some type of violence.

Long before Adolf Hitler achieved the ability to utilize state power and physically force human beings to be thrown into mass graves while alive or subject them to the searing flames or noxious gases, he inaugurated these policies with the book *Mein Kampf* and his constant uninterrupted vitriolic hatred against Jews, Slavs, Gypsies, and others. What we should have learned from this incredible horror, is to be aware of the waves which one wrong may expand upon our little world.

How aptly do the commentaries see it, when viewing the punishment of the flood that destroyed an iniquitous world in which Noah lived. On the verse:

"*Key malah ha'aretz chamas me pe'naihem*,"
"For the earth is filled with violence" (Gen. 6:13),

Rashi notes, "The legal decision (i.e. the divine decree to punish them) was sealed only because of robbery." (Sanhedrin 108a)

The Midrash asks, what were the habits of the generation of the flood? And answers, that if a man possessed a basket of peas, he would soon be attacked by a mob. Each attacker would steal a small amount, worth less than a *pruta*, until the basket was empty. The victim would be unable to bring his case to court because each of the accused could claim that he was not subject to punishment because the amount taken was so legally insignificant. (Gen. Rabbah 31:5)

One of the anthologies includes the following comment. In the Talmud (Baba Matzia 44a), we find that the Sages ordained that a person who did not fulfill his word in the course of business, even though he had as yet not obligated himself in writing, is to be brought before the court, which would rebuke him saying: "He who punished the generation of the flood and the generation of dispersion, He will take vengeance of him who does not stand by his word." Why such a reference? It would appear that our commentators throughout generations understood it to mean that such a person might say to himself, I have not robbed my fellowman from anything save a word, and speech in itself is no action.

It is nothing specific. It is nothing specific that I have deprived my fellow man of. However, though the mere dishonest expression constitutes no ordinary violation of law, the police cannot jail us for speaking dishonestly, the courts do not sentence us to jail for the dishonest word, but once we begin robbing each other of words, we must invariably be prepared for robbery and violence on a greater scale. Hence he is reminded, consider this, an entire world was destroyed because of activity which was of no great substance. Since robbery is still robbery, even if the damages and injuries amount to less than a penny, our ethical heritage seeks to caution us against the resort to speeches dealing with it as of passing, insubstantial consequence.

Not standing by our words may not make subject to police action, but it does mean that we prepare the way for flood to deluge man. Noah saw a generation corrupting itself before God. Its members abandoned the spirit of God by embarking upon dishonesty with each other, and would soon deteriorate where violence filled society. Violence to our bodies, violence to our souls, to our feelings, and to our hopes. And the world would drown. It was then that Noah realized that he had to save himself with the *taivah*, the ark.

Rabbi Shimon Ben Eliezer also related how small transgressions can lead to lasting damage. He told how he was walking across a field when a young girl called to him, "This is a privately owned field." When he answered that he was walking on an existing path, the girl replied that the path was blazed by "robbers like you." (Lamentations Rabbah 1:19) Thus small wrongs pave the way for much greater ones. In short, *averah goreret averah.*

SAINT NOAH

"*Eleh toldot Noach, Noach ish tzaddick*,"
"These are the generations of Noah, Noah was a righteous man." (Gen. 6:9)

One of the most magnificent aspects of the Hebrew Bible is the tremendous honesty with which the Torah evaluates its personalities whose experiences, convictions and faith constitute the origins of the awesome spiritual heritage which is Judaism. Throughout our tradition, we find that the human personality is not exaggerated to the heights of angels. No, on the contrary, cognizance is taken of the weakness, the defects, the failings, and the foibles of mankind. We are never permitted to pretend that our forefathers, Abraham, Isaac and Jacob are other than ordinary humans. True, they are inspired by Divine revelations, they are encouraged by their faith in God to pursue objectives of social justice, compassionate relations with others. They are bidden to bring freedom to the oppressed, nurture to the hungry, comfort to the suffering, but they are always human. That is why, we find that in Talmudic discussions, the Rabbis criticize even Abraham, when they think he has fallen behind his own standards.

On Yom Kippur when we read as part of the afternoon service, the Book of Jonah, one of the great lessons of that book is to alert us to the need of compassion and understanding. God makes Jonah understand that the city of Nineveh that has embarked upon a policy of oppression, idolatry and immorality deserves to be cautioned and urged to return to the path of proper living. Even the prophet Jonah finds himself subject to Divine criticism. God planted a large tree that gave Jonah shade and then made it wither quickly. And when Jonah suffering heat and hunger was disgusted with himself and the very tree, God rebuked him saying "You feel pity for a tree for which you did not work...and do you expect me not to be concerned for the welfare of the people of Nineveh, among who are children who do not know what is right or wrong?" (Jonah 4:11) This magnificent narrative reminds us of the necessity for human compassion and understanding. This issue is the focus of Rabbinical discussions concerning Noah.

The Torah lesson of Noah deals with the narrative that was disseminated in ancient times among all peoples, namely, the story of a flood that erased a civilization. In the Babylonian epic of

Gilamesh, the story is related how the Babylonian gods decided to wipe out mankind with a flood because men were so noisy and bothersome, they interfered with the rest of these divine beings. Only the Babylonian Noah was saved because he was friendly with one of the gods. In contrast to the Babylonian story that provides us with no guidance, the story of Noah is a source of moral lessons that are applicable to our own lives and problems that confront us today.

The Rabbis were quick to note the obvious emphasis upon him. The Torah portion begins:

> **"*Eleh toldot Noach, Noach ish tzaddick,*"**
> **"These are the generations of Noah, Noah was a**
> **righteous man." (Gen. 6:9)**

Why the repetition Noah, Noah? Could not the verse be condensed into only one mention of his name? These are the generations of Noah the *tzaddick*? The Rabbis interpret this repetition to indicate the basic decency of Noah in his relationship to God, as well as in his relations with his fellowman.

But what does it mean to be a *tzaddick*, a righteous individual, or as some would say a saint? Is the Hebrew conception the same as that of the rest of mankind?

To determine whether such an assertion is valid, naturally, requires consideration of the various people who have been acclaimed as saints in our civilization and culture. An item from a newspaper indicated that a guru had been acclaimed as a saint, because he was totally unconcerned with the pragmatic demands of daily life. He found the purpose of his existence to be best expressed by a continual meditation in which he divorced himself from reality and sought union with a higher force.

Some defined saintliness as the ability to deny the body pleasures and instead, through extensive fasting and uninterrupted
prayers, to elevate the soul into higher spheres. The history of
religious doctrines invariably indicates that for many, saintliness
has meant the deliberate suppression of what we today call normal expressions of human needs, physiological, emotional, or hygienic. Thus in Christianity, Paul proclaimed celibacy as the best
way of life, but consented to permit marriage as a concession to
human weakness. This type of sainthood was not restricted only
to Christians.

About 1800 years ago, Appolonius rejected marriage, ate no
animal food, walked barefoot and participated in other restrictions.
Two hundred years later, Neoplatonism, a great school of heathen
philosophy, also taught that the soul must be freed from becoming
subject to the material world. Sometimes the asceticism of these
Saints arose from the belief that the world was soon coming to an
end. Those who believed that Jesus had suffered on the cross in
order to redeem humanity from sin, easily were convinced that
sainthood meant suffering, self denial, and even martyrdom. Such
doctrines later found acceptance among followers of Mohammed.
Although Islam did not proclaim asceticism as the basis of its faith,
yet, there have been Islamic Saints who became hermits, living in
the desert, caves and even cemeteries.

In Asia, important religions like Buddhism and Hinduism
also had their share of saints. Westerners on occasion will smile at
the depiction of a Buddhist Saint almost hypnotizing himself, isolating himself from the world about him and aspiring to achieve a
high spiritual level of self. Hinduism also boasts of Saints who are
known as Sanniyasi, people who have deserted their families,
thrown away their business and material possessions, and become

hermits, with no friends, no homes, living in the woods, eating whatever edibles they find, and begging for food and water. This becomes the highest level of sainthood and holiness.

And what about our *tzaddickim* and what about our fasts? Is Judaism with its fasts any different in its emphasis on self-denial? However, as we began to analyze our own restrictions, we quickly began to wonder whether we could boast of saints, as do other faiths. After all, if we do find here and there, an attempt by Jews to be so ascetic and withdraw from the world, they never represent the Jewish norm. If a Nazarene pledged himself to refrain from wine or other permitted joys, despite the sanctity with which his pledge was associated, nonetheless, Torah commands him to bring a sin offering upon completion of his pledge period, because by abstaining from the pleasures which are permitted, he sins.

Many think of Chassidim as those who seek *kedushah*, holiness by withdrawing from worldly pleasures like television or movies. The fact remains that this segment of the Jewish people believes in the verse:

"Ivdu et hashem besimchah"
"Worship God in joy." (Psalms 100:2)

The founder of Chassidism, the Ba'al Shem Tov, rejected excessive fasting and warned his followers not to forget the admonition in Talmud (Masehchet Shabbat 92a), "The Divine Spirit rests only on a wise man, a strong man..." And the Prophet Isaiah, has in the High Holyday *haftarah*, given us an enduring message for Yom Kippur. The emphasis of the day is not fasting and self-denial. Rather it is a day to motivate us to let the oppressed go free, to share bread with the hungry, to invite the homeless into our homes, to cover the naked and not hide ourselves from our people in need.

This term *tzaddick* is applied to one who does good to his fellow creatures, for the term is derived from the Hebrew word, *tzeddeck*, which means justice, righteousness. The *tzaddick* is not one who hides from humanity, but is concerned with it.

It is in the Torah portion Noah that we first are introduced to the *tzaddick*,

> **"*Eleh toldot Noach, Noach ish tzaddick*,"**
> **"These are the generations of Noah, Noah was a righteous man." (Gen. 6:9)**

He was a person who towered among his neighbors in his generation. They had all become very corrupt. They imposed violence upon each other. They robbed. They seized by force or dishonest legislation, whatever another possessed. They were immoral and lost their entire perspective on what really constitutes a proper society. And the Lord repented that He had created man and decided they would be eradicated, extinguished from this planet. Consider Noah, one man, whose environment was that of a society of theft and oppression, seething with moral depravity, where love had been supplanted by desire, bestial passion to an extreme that apparently corroded the entire earth. Corruption, falsehood, prevarication and violence continued to increase.

And one man, in the eyes of our Sages as we shall see, not the greatest man who ever lived, do not believe for a moment that he was always saintly towards God, or on the other hand, always saintly towards men, no, but one whose decency provided perspective, he was complete in his generation with his contemporaries, in his human relationships, he walked with God, He who exercised an influence over his household, and stood firm by convictions and faith, was divinely inspired to launch a family project, the construction of a box-like structure which could float on an anticipated deluge and thus lead to the rejuvenation of the planet and the survival of the species. (Gen. Rabbah 26:1)

Noah was a righteous man and so the Midrash reminds us, God told him to build for himself and his family and samples of the creatures of the earth an ark, a ship that would rescue him and the rest of his family from the flood. Rashi reminds us of the Midrashic tale that Noah labored for one hundred and twenty years to build that ark. (Rashi to Gen. 6:14) And that period was given to him by God in the hope that people would consider why Noah was building such a vessel, and that contemplating the answer they would be efficiently impressed to change their ways, repent and be saved. But instead they laughed and jeered at Noah, considered him an impractical, wild-eye idealist, romantic fool, someone who was a little touched in the head. (Gen. Rabbah 30:7) And thus, any attempt to arouse humanity to repent for its cruelties, its barbarism, its violence, its hatred and bigotry, failed, and an entire civilization was wiped away in the flood.

The Rabbis are very practical in their understanding of Noah. They, too, try to evaluate him as a human being. He is not an angel, he is not a divine figure who has come down from heaven, he is a normal human being and they try to understand him. And so we find that when Rabbi Yochanan reads the Bible verse today, Noah was an *ish tzaddick*, a righteous man, and God said,

"*Ohtechah raiti tzaddick bedor hazeh*,"
"I have seen that you are righteous in this generation."
(Gen. 7:1)

Rabbi Yochanan says: "*Bedorotov*," "In his generation," Noah was an outstanding good man, "*velo bedoro acharev*," "but not in another generation." But had he lived in another generation, where people were not so corrupt and ugly, he would not have been considered a saint. Thereupon another commentator replied, "*Bedorotov kol sheken bedoro acharev*," "Why if the man could be decent in his generation, when bestiality, viciousness and hypocrisy surrounded him, just imagine how saintly he would have been in another generation where good people could have surrounded him?" (Rashi to Gen. 6:9) The Rabbis realize what vast implications there are in the Biblical tale. So in the Midrash, they refer to a legend amongst our people to show that Noah too, had his defects.

They do this by depicting Noah meeting Moses in the true paradise. And in the conversation, Moses refers to some of his hardships that he encountered trying to rescue the Jewish People from the slavery of Egypt, whereupon, Noah displays arrogance, false pride, and perhaps lack of sensitivity towards Moses. Noah declares! "What, you think you had hardships because you had to save the Israelites? What is that compared with my mighty accomplishments? I was so good that the Lord saved me when the entire world drowned, and from me sprang again humanity after the flood. Why, if not for me, Moses where would you be? You are small in your achievements as compared with mine..." Apparently, Moses was hurt, or better we may say, the Rabbis were trying to prove a point, so they had Moses reply by saying: what kind of a saint are you? I knew that I had to rescue my people who were crying and suffering, who were humiliated and beaten by the enslaver, Pharaoh. And when I took them out, it was because I shared their sorrow and suffering. And when we escaped and they had to fight the wicked Amalekites who attacked us, I prayed for their victory, and sat upon a large, hard and uncomfortable rock, because I did not look for a moment of ease or comfort when the people were suffering. But you, you were satisfied to be saved. You sat with your family in the ark, and looked out as humanity was drowning, dying, watching husbands and wives cry for each other, watching mothers cry for the children who were swept to their death before their eyes. What kind of a saint are you that you could face the sorrows of mankind that easily?

In this story, the Rabbis were not denying the positive qualities which Noah may have had, but they did not close their eyes to the fact that this man who was certainly righteous when compared with his neighbors, this man who did not kill, rob, torture, and betray humanity and was certainly righteous alongside others, was not exactly the greatest kind of a saint which mankind could offer.

Yitev Lev, ponders a peculiarity in the Noah narrative:

"Tzaddick tamim hayah bechol hadorot shelifney hamabul"
"In all these generations of evil and iniquity, of violence and crime and hatred, he is called a *tzaddick tamim*,"
"a perfect or wholesome saintly man." (Gen. 6:9)

But when the deluge comes, after the destruction, the massive upheaval which will destroy communities, wiped out human society, inundate all vestige of civilization, we find Scriptures saying, *"Key ohtechah raiti tzaddick lifanai bador hazeh,"* "I have seen that thou were righteous before me in this generation." (Gen. 7:1) Just righteous? What happened to *"tzaddick tamim?"* Why this sudden withdrawal of perfection and wholesomeness?

"Et HaElokeem hithalech Noach,"
"Noah walked with God." (Gen. 6:9)

The commentary sadly observes, oh yes, Noah was a good
man, he walked with God, with God whose attribute of justice is
incorporated in the term *Elokeem*. Ah yes, God said Noah you
want to wipe out this lousy generation? O.K. they are no good
Lord, as you have declared. And I thank you that you are going to
let me and mine live. Noah, *hischeem lamidat hadin sheyavo mabul
leolam*, he immediately agreed with the sentence that the world
should be flooded *veloh hitpallel levatel hagezeirah*, he did not
even pray in an attempt to have this harsh sentence on all humanity nullified. (Zohar Chadash A 67) What tremendous insight, we
are afforded by our sacred tradition. We should recognize the truth
when society both from above and below become corrupt, when
men lose their sense of decency and become totally inconsiderate
of others, they are begging for the flood. But the child of the eternal God, who has been created by our Heavenly Father for a purpose of goodness and higher pursuits, even when the entire world
loses its sanity, must stand firm in his faith, in his supplications, in
his prayers, in his deeds always attempting to save humanity.

This measure of true religiosity as envisioned by the Torah
portion intimates a definite awareness of others. For example, we
are taught that in the construction of the ark, Noah hears the divine injunction:

"Tzohar ta'aseh Lataivah"
"A light shalt thou make to the ark." (Gen. 6:16)

The Rabbis differ in their explanations. One opinion holds
that *Tzohar* was a *yahalom*, a light that illuminated the interior of
the ark. Midrash Rabbah says *margoli,* a precious stone. Some
meforshim, commentaries *comment that Tzohar hu ehven taivah
hame'erah lahem, Tzohar* is a precious stone which illuminated

the Ark. (Rashi to Gen 6:16) Rab Aba bar Kahanah said *"Challon,"* Rabbi Aba the son of Kahanah said, "It was a window." This Sage holds that *Tzohar* was a window that would permit Noah to survey the world and observe what was transpiring. The Tractate (Berachot 34b) declares: *"Al yitpalel adam elah bebayit sheyesh lo Chalonot,"* "A person should not pray save in a room which has windows." To which some added in order to have a view of heaven. To think of the *mitzvot Beyn adam leMakom*, to be aware of the relationship between man and his creator.

But another commentary holds that this is proper, in order for a person to be able to see what is happening to his fellow creatures and thereby be compelled to ask himself, if he is responding properly to their needs. Without downgrading Noah, without joining those who reduced his own decency and righteousness, it is clear that there are categories among the righteous, too. For do we not see how Moses reacts at the suggestion that his people will be wiped out and removed from the arena of history, and from him there will go forth a new nation? Instead of accepting this decision of Providence, Moses immediately and passionately manifests his total concern for the welfare of his people. Wipe me out from your books of coexistence, if you persist in bringing the downfall of my people. In fact, the Gemarah (Berachot 32a) places Moshe in a stirring stance before God. *Amar Moshe lifney Hakadosh Baruch Hu, "Ribono Shel Olam Vilo od, elah sheyesh bi boshet may avotai, achshav yomru, riu parnes shehemid aleyhem, bikesh gedulah liatzmo, vi lo bikesh rachameem,"* Moses said before the Holy One Blessed be He, Master of the Universe.... "And not just this, but I will be ashamed before my forefathers, (if I will consent to the destruction of Israel and agree to God's offer that I be the founder of a new people,) people will say, look at the

leader that was placed over the Children of Israel, he asked God
for the greatness for himself but did not ask for mercy for his
people."

Apparently, Providence understood that under the circumstances, Noah was the best in character in his days, and since there
were none better than he, he qualified to be the leader of that generation. However, the greater qualifications for leadership emerge
from the character within. Noah started his career as an *ish tzaddick,*
a righteous man. *Et HaElokeem hithalech Noach,* Noah walked
with God. (Gen. 6:9) His religiosity his frumkeit was basically
proper. But he did not exert himself sufficiently in behalf of everyone. And the result is that after the Deluge as we shall see, this
righteous man transformed into an *ish adamah,* a mundane drinking man with only material objectives.

Moses, on the other hand, appears in Midian as *ish mitzri,* an
Egyptian. (Exodus 2:19) He wears Egyptian clothing. He speaks
its language and expresses himself in its cultural medium. He is
thoroughly a product of Pharaoh's palace training but the emotions which impelled him to attack the Egyptian taskmaster prevail, when he protects the daughters of Jethro, and that same
compassion makes him feel sensitive towards the little lamb who
flees from a lion, in the pursuit of water. And the result is that the
ish mitzri, the Egyptian ends up as an *ish Elokim,* a man of God.
While some may preach Noah as a lesser man, when compared to
an Abraham, the Rabbis see him starting as a decent person. It is
the Torah that subtly reminds us that too often we end up with
lesser credit, than we first began because of our own targets in
life. How many of us have thrown away the idealism of youth?
How often are we motivated by what is known today as the bottom line? How often do we forget that tremendous insight of the

Torah? *Lo al halechem levado yichye haadam,* Man does not live by bread alone (Deut. 8:3), and with the passing of time, we lose some of our original greatness. That is what happened, alas, with Noah. But Moshe continued to advance, to go from height to height, to pursue constantly higher objectives, but always because his concern was always for his fellow Jew.

Today we recognize some people who followed Noah's policy. These were the people who said they believed in democracy, who said they did not agree with Hitler's policies of depriving others from free speech and torture. People who disagreed with his policies of robbing people of their property and their material riches for which they worked and sacrificed lifetimes, only to be told that it was confiscated because the fuhrer denies the rights of those who are Jewish, or gypsy, or believers in another church. He denies their rights to have property. Oh, no, these people compared to Hitler were good people, and yet, they closed their eyes to the murder and torture of millions. They refused to bomb train tracks that led to the concentration camp by saying they were too human, they would not think of perhaps hurting some innocent people on the trains. These were the good people who refused to permit ships loaded with Jews fleeing from Nazi Germany to let land, who returned them to Germany so they could all be murdered. These are some of the righteous people of our day who are so concerned with the holiness of life, that they did not demonstrate when Jews were burned alive and buried alive by the Germans.

Ah, you may very well say, let us not permit our passions to get away with us because Moses was correct in his criticism of Noah in that Midrashic legend. The fact remains that Noah is called by the Bible a righteous man, granted in his generation, but, nonetheless, a righteous man and the Bible does not mean that to be taken in a sarcastic or ironic vein. Well, what gives Noah the right to be counted as a righteous man? A Rabbinical source supplies us with one of the answers. The Pesikta Zutratha declares he was a righteous man because he fed and supported the animals in the ark.

You may note that Joseph is also known as the righteous one, because although he was sold by his brothers, still when he came to power in Egypt, he took care of his family as it is written, "and he supported and provided food for his father and his brothers." Another Rabbinical commentary turns to the *Tanchuma* and says, he was righteous, because he fed Gods creatures and thus emulated God. As it is written, "God is righteousness because he loves righteousness." (Psalms 11:7) A person deserves that title whenever he does good to other creatures. Note that during the ten plagues, when God threatened the slave master with hail: God declared: "I shall bring a terrible hail upon the earth so that men and beast that will be caught in the field shall die. (Exodus 9:18) Therefore, hurry up and get your cattle out of the field and bring them to safety." (Exodus 9:19) Observe God wanted innocent cattle to be saved, because He had mercy on them. And only because of the guilt of Pharaoh and his nobles were innocent animals doomed to die. And when Pharaoh cried to have the plague removed he said, God is righteous and my people are wicked. That is God is righteous because He had mercy, even upon the cattle, and my people and I are wicked, because, we had no pity.

Thus it is clear is that the Hebrew *tzaddick*, is not the same as a saint as the world understands the concept. Whatever errors and mistakes our ancestor Noah may have made in his life, one thing is clear. He demonstrated *tzidkut*, saintliness when he went out to the world, and as the Midrash would have it, worked at building the ark before the eyes of everyone, warning them, *Kach amar miarey dealmah dihu meyte mabulah al almah*, I have been told to do so by the master of the universe who will bring a flood upon the world. And the world laughed at Noah and cursed him, (Gen. Rabbah 30:7) But the Midrash comments at this point that Noah was not only a *tzaddick*, but an *ish tzaddick*, which means both a *tzaddick umumchah*, that is a saint and an expert. And the commentary has it that: *nikrah tzaddick, mi shehu tzaddick befney atzmo, umumchah, mi shehu moreh derech lerabim lehitnaheg bederech hatov vehayashar, tzaddick* may be a righteous man for himself, but *mumchah* is he who teaches many to comport themselves with decency and righteousness.

Noah reminds us today that we need *tzaddickim*, righteous people, not simply saints who may impress animals. But those who try to influence humans to be humane; who do not hide from mankind, but who are ready to warn us of the deluge, floods that threaten us, and perhaps arouse us to follow those paths that lead to decency, goodness, truth and peace. Let others enjoy their saints, let us seek out our *tzaddickim*.

PRODUCTIVITY

The previous chapter discussed Noah, the *tzaddick*, the righteous person with his merits and shortcomings, but a *tzaddick* nevertheless. But after departing from the ark, Noah falls from this lofty station.

Unfortunately, he planted a vineyard and Rashi asks, "what did he do? "*asah atzmo chulin*," he made himself the antithesis of *kodesh* which is holiness, he profaned himself by planting a vineyard. (Rashi to Gen. 9:20) The Radak in his commentary tells us

Noah was the first one to plant a vineyard for the purpose of making wine. They had grapes before the flood. The grapes were eaten as a regular fruit, but no one had taken grapes and pressed them, processed them, and refined them with the intention of drinking wine and getting drunk. Unfortunately that is exactly what happens to Noah.

> ***"Vayaiysht min hayayin vayishkor,"***
> **"And he drank from the wine and got drunk.**
> **(Gen. 9:21)**

and the story which evolves from that incident is a most debasing one.

His son the youngest, Ham, unfortunately, castrates his father. He is afraid when he looks upon the first man who wants to rebuild the world. He says: "My goodness, Adam had two sons, they couldn't get along, we have three already and I am afraid that Father is going to have more children and there is going to be more strife." It is incredible what the Son does. And the Torah tells us that Shem and Japhet go in a most honorable, respectful fashion. They cover the nakedness of their Father and they tend to their Father in his state of trouble, in this horrible state of being drunk and having been attacked. But it is interesting if you note the text, the Torah does not tell us that *Vayikchu*, they took, but rather *Vayikach*, and he took. (Gen. 9:23) The Rabbis tell us in their very careful reading of the text, the motive of the two sons and their behavior towards their Father. Shem who took the *talit*, prayer shal and covered his Father did so because he was concerned that his Father's basic identity as a human being was violated, man being created in the image of God. Shem was rewarded with the *mitzvah* of *talit*, *midah keneged midah*, measure for measure. Just as he realized that man had been defiled, and in that state he was uplifted with the *talit*.

Jefet the second son was not concerned with the religious aspect, the image of God in his Father being defiled, rather he was disturbed from a cultural perspective.

The Rabbis tell us says Shimshon Raphael Hirsch, according to the Midrash Tanchuma, that he was rewarded by having his descendants being granted the precept of *kevurahm*, burial rather than being left on the field to decompose as was often the case in primitive times, again the idea of the dignity of man. And Ham, we know was punished. This happened when Noah unfortunately chose the route of being an *ish adamah*, a man of the field, planting the grape for a vineyard, enabling Ham to commit his act.

What we learn from Noah is that man has to be constantly creative. Man constantly has to see how he can better and improve the world. At the very end of the *"Vayechulu"* paragraph in the Torah, (Gen. 2:3) it describes how God ceased his work after six days and *ki vo shavat mikol malachto*, because on this day he rested from all his work which he had created *asher barah Elokim laasot*. (Ibid) The last word of the paragraph is *laasot*, to be done. What does the word *laasot* there mean? The Rabbis tells us that God intentionally did not create a perfect world. Whatever He created was perfect but he left room for man to complete every aspect of creation including man himself, whereupon the Rabbis tell us symbolically that is the *mitzvah* of *milah*, circumcision, by which man completes the human being himself.

The Mishnah tells us:

"Kol Torah she'ain emah melacha sofa betaila
vegorehret ahvon,"
"All Torah study that does not have work

**accompanying it, must in the end come to nothing and
bring sin in its wake." (Ethics of the Fathers 2:2)**

And so it is in every single aspect of life. God made it that
man becomes a productive partner in creation with God Himself.
But sad to say Noah chose the wrong route. He chose the route
whereby he could glorify himself. He chose the route of personal
fun, pleasure but no productivity. And when such a situation occurs only ruin comes to the world. We are told in the Masechet
(Ketubot 63a) that man may try to support his wife on as fine and
as high an economic plane as he can afford. He may even provide
her with one hundred servants, but she must still produce because
whenever a person is idle, it leads to *zeema*, lewdness.

A person constantly has to be productive. The Mishnah tells
us that a gambler, a person who makes his livelihood from gam-
bling is *pasul le'aduth*, unable to testify. (Sanhedrin 24b) One
whose lifestyle, whose vocation is one of a gambler, one who occasionally sits together with the boys, such a person cannot testify
in a court of Jewish law. Why? Explains the Gemarah because
eyno oseh beyeshivut haolam, such a person is nonproductive. A
person has to be constantly productive and sad to say, Noah chose
the sinful path. At the end of the Torah portion, Noah demonstrates how he is not a productive man, and therefore the Rabbis
have the right to question the true *tziddkot*, the true righteousness
of Noah.

Very interestingly, they contrast Noah to Moshe Rabbanu.
As we noted previously, Moshe is first known as an *ish mitzri*, an
Egyptian man (Exodus 2:19) and then is known as an *ish Elokim*,
a man of God. (Deut. 33:1) Noah is first known as an *ish tzaddick*,
a righteous man (Gen. 6:9) with so much potential, and unfortunately in the end he is categorized as an *ish adamah*, simple man,

man of the earth (Gen. 9:20), who unfortunately could not raise himself. Let us remember that the greatness of Moshe was that all his life, he was productive and on his last day, he says to the people:

"Lo uchal od latzait ulavo,"
"I can no longer go out to lead you." (Deut. 31:2)

Not because he was physically tired, not because his legs hurt him, not because his eyes were not functioning, but because as the Rabbis tell us, he no longer grew in spirituality, in his performance of *mitzvot*. And once a person does not grow, then it is time for a person to take leave.

Unfortunately after the Flood, Noah does not grow. He goes down hill and therefore Noah is judged by later generations with a questionable point or view. I pray that we are going to follow the examples of the person to whom Noah is contrasted. To follow the example of Abraham to reach out, to follow the example of Moses and to constantly grow, and to never be satisfied as Noah, as to stop and plant a vineyard. To never say now I will drink to my success, to my survival and not be concerned with the future.

THE EARTH BECAME CORRUPT

"Vatishachet ha'aretz lifney Elokeem,"
"The earth became corrupt before God with idolatry and immorality" (Genesis 6:11)

This Torah lesson, like so many other narratives in Scriptures, fascinates us, not only because of the powerful simplicity by which these literary masterpieces have been transmitted to us as part of our own cultural and spiritual heritage, but because they have an incomparable validity which rings true in the human experience, regardless of the era in which we live, or the kind of groups which read and attempt to absorb them.

Consider the account of Noah and the flood, an experience which humanity has sustained in various forms, whenever society has declined, deteriorated and depressed itself from living as befits the highest form of intellect that we recognize here on earth, and instead reduces itself to primitive expressions of existence that we delineate as the law of the jungle. Here was Noah and his contemporaries, people who were advancing in certain areas of technology and astronomical studies, losing their perspective, acting towards each other in outbursts of immorality, theft and violence. Men were casting aside their religious beliefs. The heathen gods were becoming impotent before the machines, and the descendents of Adam who might have considered and worshiped the creator of their forbear, no longer could find him. The contemporaries of Noah had forgotten the Midrash which reminds us that every generation of wrong doers drove God further away from earth until they completely lost touch with him. Having forgotten Him, having rejected God, they quickly embraced new attitudes away from the moral principles that dictated relations. How do such horrors develop in society?

In the ancient homilies of our Sages, we find that the Rabbis in the Midrash were concerned with the same inquiry. They were discussing the plagues which had smitten Egypt, when divine justice was outraged by the cruelties and barbarism, the terror and violence, the pain and torture which man was inflicting upon his fellowman, during the period of the Egyptian enslavement of the Israelites. Some Rabbis felt that of all the plagues, the one that best characterized the terrible situation was that of *choshech*, darkness, where one human being simply did not see the other. Despite the Egyptian advances in civilization, progress which today is often considered by some scholars as to have been so advanced that we moderns underestimate its power and influences, yet this society became cruel and dark. From where did this darkness come?

In their discussion we read that Rabbi Judah says, "*Michoshech shel maalah,*" "this darkness came from above," but Rabbi Nehemiah declares, "*Michoshech shel matah,*" "It came from darkness below." The Rabbis with their characteristic incisiveness were discussing and analyzing a sociological theme: the reason why life had become dark was due to the fact that the masses of people were contaminated by the predominating philosophies of the day. The common people accepted the ideas of slavery, they felt if they suffered why should they feel any compassion for others. Perhaps it even made them feel better to think that somewhere in their society, a group was treated worse than they were. Perhaps it was some kind of false comfort to their own poverty, their own degradation to feel that they could terrorize, humiliate and hurt others under such conditions. Argued Rabbi Nehemiah, "It was not surprising that Egyptian society should crumble." On the other hand, Rabbi Judah argues that this sad state of affairs emerged from the deranged, corrupt, power-lusting upper classes. The learned, intelligent, educated leaders, rulers, masters of legislation and law, the judges and nobles, they had become so corrupt in their pursuit of power, they were so totally hedonistic, that they simply had lost emotions of compassion and pity. In their cruelty and viciousness they were responsible for the terrible destiny that struck their land and people.

The discussion of the Rabbis might very well have applied to the era of Noah. Consider how this social collapse originally started. At the end of the Genesis Biblical lesson, we were introduced to a rather strange social phenomenon.

> *"Vayiriu b'nai elokeem et bnot ha'adam ki tovot, heynah,*
> *vayikchu lahem nasheem mikol asher bacharu,"*
> **"And the sons of the rulers saw the daughters of man**
> **that they were good, and they took unto themselves**
> **wives from whoever they chose." (Gen. 6:2)**

This shocked commentators among our people and with justified reason, too. Here are the upper classes, the sons of the judges and rulers who were obviously responsible for the maintenance of law and order, justice and decency, right and wrong. These men came along and were attracted to women they saw and they acted not only immorally and indecently. But they seized any woman they found attractive. And one of the Rabbis suggests that they took anyone they choose meant they did not care whether she was married, or the mother of a family. They had power that others could not resist and their lewd activities, their wildness, their lack of restraint, their total abandonment of human dignity and right, naturally, affected the lower strata of society.

> *"Vatishachet ha'aretz lifney Elokeem,"*
> **"The earth became corrupt before God with idolatry**
> **and immorality" (Gen. 6:11)**

Thus we find that the Torah portion of Noah tells us, that a corruption contaminated the very soil and all animal as well as human life. When man acts like an animal, we should not expect beasts to act normally.

> *"Vatimaley haaretz chamas,"*
> **"And the world was filled with violence and robbery."**
> **(Ibid)**

The social fabric had been torn asunder, force and lawlessness became the characteristic of that society. Darkness descends when no one sees his brother, when people do not understand the first great lessons of *Bereshit*.

When Cain asks:

"*Hashomer achi anochi,?*"
"Am I my brother's keeper?" (Gen. 4:9)

Yes, you must help each other because out of the creation by the one eternal God, all humanity are brothers.

AND ALL THE EARTH WAS OF ONE LANGUAGE

"*Kol ha'aretz safah ehchat udevarim ahchadim,*"
"And all the earth was of one language and of one speech." (Gen. 11:1)

Scholars have observed that the Biblical lesson of Noah that introduces us to the personality of Noah refers to two tremendous catastrophes that erupted in the world. The first occurred when mankind became violent, immoral, corrupt, and betrayed each other to such an extent that the creator perceived there was no future for such humanity. Punishment was poured over the sinful earth through the flood that wiped out an entire sinful civilization.

Scarcely three centuries later, the world again experienced a tremendous upheaval. This occurred when

"*Kol ha'aretz safah ehchat udevarim ahchadim,*"
"And all the earth was of one language and of one speech." (Gen. 11:1)

People decided to construct a tremendous tower that would reach the very heavens. But God confounded their speech, found them incomprehensible one to the other and thus scattered humanity over the face of the earth. That superficially is a very strange story. It is true that there are philologists who claimed that originally humanity might have spoken a language with common roots. Why should this unity have been disrupted?

But our ancient homilies and Rabbinical sages provide us with deeper insight. The Jerusalem Talmud comments on the Biblical phrase, "And all the earth was of one language," by having Rabbi Yochanan and Rabbi Eliezer discuss it. One said that unity was maintained because people spoke seventy languages, and the other claimed they all spoke one universal language, the Holy Tongue. What happened? The Midrash explains further that the Tower of Babel was intended to be a launching pad for some device to reach the moon and thus control the earth. In plain words, it was an attempt to create a totalitarian society and government where everyone would be subject to those who wanted to obtain power by controlling space. Men would lose their freedom, because they would be subjects or slaves to the government, the state and the military forces then in power. But Rabbi Eliezer asks, do you think they were all united in speaking to each other? What really happened was that they all spoke one language, the Holy Tongue, everything they said was proper, and their words were honorable because their intentions were honorable. But as the desires for power overcame their original integrity, they began to employ a profane language. Whatever they said was an attempt to conceal their dishonesty, falsehood, lack of responsibility, loss of compassion, sensitivity and humane response. All society began to decay. Social deterioration let cruelty, bigotry, prejudice and hatred begin to predominate, and those who dreamt of power forced everything and everybody to be subject to their mad ambitions.

Unfortunately, they had not really learned the lesson of the flood. This is really not such an ancient tale. Is it?

Scarcely several decades ago, we all shouted that we would never again forget the lesson of the Second World War blood bath, which began when Hitler dreamt of building his own tower, a German Reich which would last for a thousand years and rule and control all the world. And this rule would be accompanied by a terrible carnage of the Holocaust where six million of our people, innocent women and children were slaughtered in an insanity, a bestiality and repugnant disgusting viciousness hiding behind human forms. And that same insanity spread, as it always must, and resulted in the death of tens of millions of human beings in all countries and of all nationalities.

But we learned nothing. The world proclaimed to speak one language, the language of truth, justice, honor, righteousness, peace, compassion, sensitivity, and humane understanding. But we did not learn. The language of unity we have heard continues with onslaughts of words against the very principles we swore to uphold, against the very ideals for which millions died and against the very victims who we pledged never to forget. The United Nations remains the center of a vituperative assault on the rights of the Jewish People and the integrity of the State of Israel. The result, a Tower of Babel in our midst, where diplomats and politicians, the masters of words speak lies, treachery and betrayal. Where words are corrupted so that lies becomes truths, and truth is ignored. And such a world courts only one result, disaster, wars and extermination. The Biblical lesson of *Noach* warns us against the misuse of words, as the Jewish tradition repeatedly warns us about our speech.

Certain people never care about their words, they spread gossip and vile slander. In a few moments they can destroy the reputation of a person who has driven an entire lifetime to acquire it. The Rabbis despised such people. They tell a little story in the Midrash where a serpent was once asked: "A lion tears an animal in pieces in order to satisfy his hunger; so does a wolf, but what possible pleasure do you derive from injecting your deadly poison into the body of a person? Surely that does not satisfy your hunger?" The serpent slyly answered: "Why ask me? Ask the gossip, the scandalmonger, and the spreader of untruth, his poison is far deadlier than mine for I can poison only the person whom I touch, whereas their venom spreads for many miles." How true this is. Even King David who as a boy was not afraid of Goliath, and who fought armies, hated and feared vile people who slandered others. We find him imploring God to help him against slanderers. Do not say nasty things about others. Avoid gossips and careless talebearers. Don't listen to gossip or scandal because the Rabbis say the person who receives the gossip is as guilty and as wicked as the one who brings it. Learn to speak well and to think well of everyone you know. Treat them, as you would have them treat you, honestly, squarely, and above board.

The Torah teaches us that the purpose of all mankinds is world improvement. The Torah doesn't start with the *mitzvot* which are binding on the Jewish People, or stories about the redemption of the Jewish People from Egypt, because Torah teaches a lesson to all humanity. Everybody must be creative and improve the world. Stamp out gossip so that you may be a fine specimen of clean living, clean thinking and generous manhood. Be careful of your words.

Lech Lecha

— 3 —

לֶךְ־לְךָ, מֵאַרְצְךָ, וּמִמּוֹלַדְתְּךָ וּמִבֵּית אָבִיךָ

**"Go for yourself from your land from your birthplace,
from the house of your father." (Genesis 12:1)**

FATHER ABRAHAM

In this Biblical lesson of *Lech Lecha*, we are introduced to the very beginnings of our people, the Jews, a nation which developed as defined by Baruch Spinoza, into a God-intoxicated people.

Religion today, presents us with many intriguing aspects. To illustrate, a controversy with legal ramifications has arisen, because some Indians claim that they must use peyote as part of their religious rituals, probably to obtain some exhilarating enthusiasm. Religion among certain Asiatics has influenced them to reduce the significance of this world through contemplation, or seeking nirvana, a state of mind in which the world would not intrude upon the spiritual.

65

Catholics partake of a ritual called transubstantiation, where they believe that a sip of wine and a piece of unleavened bread, a wafer, is miraculously or symbolically transformed into the blood and body of the deity they worship.

Anthropologists continue to study various tribes of primitive cultures who reach out to spirits operating within nature and which have to be propitiated by some form of offerings.

The two predominating religions in our civilization "kindled their fires at the altars of Judaism." Both Jesus and Mohammed did not claim that they were original in the messages they preached.

The first claimed that he had not come to inaugurate a new religion but only to revive the true faith of Abraham. We should not forget that Jesus did not worship at St. Patrick's Cathedral, but at the Temple in Jerusalem. It is an historical fact that Mohammed and his followers first turned their faces eastward toward Jerusalem when they prayed. This ritual was changed after Mohammed understood that the Jews would never voluntarily agree with his new religion. And so he commanded his followers to pray toward Mecca, where a huge rock, the Ka'aba, originally associated with an ancient idol practice, was now said to have been founded by Abu Ibrahim, Father Abraham.

So great a personality is Abraham that the Church often presents its followers with the idea that as true Christians they are his sons. Muslims are also proud of their lineage with Abu Ibrahim and they, too, like to think of each as an Ibn Ibrahim, a son of Abraham. Much to the consternation of the majority religion in our part of the world, its followers are often upset, because they cannot convince us of their alliance with Abraham. Even as our Arabic cousins in Islam pretend that we have emulated the stories of Abraham by copying their account, although every knowledgeable person in all western civilization knows that we and Torah were around long before Mohammed's discovery of Allah gave rise to the Koran.

Our people developed a conscious purpose in life, which rotated around the idea of constant service to the one eternally living creative God, and for this idea, we are forever indebted to our forefather Abraham who is introduced to us in the Torah lesson of *Lech Lecha.* Abraham, who is a truly gigantic iconoclast, who smashed the idolatry of his day and hence he continues to serve as a teacher to all who would smash idolatry everywhere and in every age.

Abraham apparently felt like a contemporary observer in speaking of religious faith. It has been observed that one of our problems is that very few of us have developed a distinctive personal life. Everything about us seems secondhand, even our emotions. In many cases we have to rely upon secondhand information in order to function. I accept the word of a physician, a scientist and a farmer on trust. I do not like to do this however; I have to because they possess vital knowledge of living of which I am ignorant. Secondhand information concerning the state of my kidneys, the effects of cholesterol and the raising of chickens I can live with.

But when it comes to questions of meaning, purpose and death, secondhand information will not do. I cannot survive on a secondhand faith in a secondhand god. There has to be a personal word, a unique confrontation, if I am to come alive. This apparently is what happened with Abraham. Tradition has it that at an early age, he pursued what Einstein might have called cosmic religion. He slowly but surely realized that the phenomena of the universe, which we call nature, or natural law, had to be the product of an all embracing eternal force.

In his personal pursuit of this all-comprehensive belief, he rejected the rather hypocritical idolatry of his Father, who manufactured idols and was shocked when his son, Abraham questioned their efficacy. He also repudiated the accepted prevailing philosophy of his time and found himself in opposition to everyone about him because of the doctrines which he espoused and which he insisted upon explaining to anyone who would just listen. And with the passing of time, he too, began to experience a unique, personal relationship with the idea and force, which totally controlled him.

If an aura of mysticism hovered about, who of us does not realize that everyone is possessed of some mysticism? When we confront the tremendous scenario of man and the universe, when we consider the attraction which astrology and horoscopes still possess for contemporary modern individuals, that mysticism did not transform him or his beliefs into an unintelligible, deliberate withdrawal from the pragmatic existence which we call daily life or relationship with other human beings whom moved in his orbit.

And who knows what other decisions for which we must pay tribute to the patriarch Abraham, who was a gigantic pioneer in teaching us that the celestial bodies were not divine, but merely instruments yielding to the laws which the almighty instituted in the operation of the universe.

However, although the Jews are those who have introduced the world to *Avraham Avinu*, Abraham our Father, it would appear that our tradition does not think that the circumstance of birth is sufficient to adorn us with the glory of Abraham. The Rabbis taught that the true disciples of Abraham could be recognized by three characteristics. They are *rachmoniim, bashonim* and *gemelut chasadim.*

The first, *rachmoniim*, means mercy. The Rabbis teach, "*Me shemirachem al chavero, beyadua shehu mezerah Avraham Avinu, vechol me shehaiyno mirachem al chavero beyadua shehaiyno mezerah shel Avraham Avinu*," "Whoever is merciful to his fellowman is certainly a child of Abraham, but whoever is not merciful to his fellowman is certainly not of the children of our Father Abraham." (Beitzah 32b)

Second, *Talmidei shel Avraham Avinu*, the true disciples of Abraham are those who are *bashonim*, modest. In our tradition, we have always been proud of modesty. In our personal lives, we have tried to display to the entire world, our adherence to modesty.

The Midrash tells us that when Bilaam was hired by the King of Moab to curse the Jews and try to tar their image before the entire world, he was himself overcome when he looked down upon the Jewish home and saw how *tzniut*, modesty reigned in our households. In public life this modesty is a great treasure.

Finally, the disciples of Abraham practice *gemelet chasadim*, acts of benevolence and charity. The English word charity is derived from the Greek word caritas, from which we get similar terms like caro, dearm, in Italian, or cher in French, carus, etc. Charity means that you are kind because you are a dear, human being yourself who is moved by pity for the unfortunate plight of another. But *tzedaka*, charity in Hebrew is derived from the word *tzedek*, which means justice. A Jew gives *tzedaka* because it is just that he shares his good with another. Because *tzaddick hashem bechol derachav*, God is just in all his ways and we have to be able to emulate Godlike qualities in dealing with each other.

We find a fascinating aspect of his personality depicted in which all of these traits are exhibited, when there arose a controversy between his household and that of his nephew Lot. Rather than quarrel with the younger man, he suggests that Lot take first choice of the territory he would prefer, while Abraham declares that whatever his nephew chooses will be agreeable and he will simply turn in the opposite direction. Naturally, the greedy young man selects the richest area, that around the community of Sodom, where theft and violence, torture and murder were accepted socially. Soon thereafter, both Lot and his personal possessions were taken captive by invaders. Learning of this, Abraham does not respond as many would: "Good for that pig of a nephew who was so greedy and could not live at peace with me." Instead, he organizes his own militia and liberates both Lot and all the other people who were captured with him.

Now consider the rest of the narrative. Returning victorious he is naturally welcomed by the defeated king of Sodom, who is now also rescued from future possible difficulties by Abraham's victory. And so the King said to Abraham:

> *"Ten li hanefesh, veharichush kach Lecha,"*
> **"Give me the people, and you can keep all the loot and booty." (Gen. 14:21)**

It seems to be a normal gesture, one whereby he paid homage to Abraham. But look at the humble response of Abraham who says:

> *"Harimoti yadi el hashem, aile elyon, koneh shamayim va'aretz"*
> **"I lift up my hand to God the most high, maker of heaven and earth." (Gen. 14:22)**

"*Im michut viad sroch naal...Lo tomar he'ehsharti et Avram*"
"That I will not take a thread or a shoelace from you, that no one should say he has made Abraham rich."
(Gen. 14:23)

There also is here, another apparent implication. Abraham is saying "I don't want anyone to think I went to battle just for wealth, rather than liberating human beings." My father, of blessed memory, a long time ago called my attention to these verses. Although, the sages give various interpretations to these lines, my Father was fascinated by the conversation. Abraham says that he refuses the wealth, but he says nothing directly about the people. Even in his commentary, Chief Rabbi of the British Empire, the late Dr. J. H. Hertz noted that in those days, Abraham could have kept the people, made them his salvation sold them into bondage. He did imply another aspect of Abraham's faith. I can give you the wealth we have captured, but I cannot hand over to you human beings, as if they were chattels, as if they were objects, as if they were animals. "*Ten li hanefesh*" you said, which means, "Give me the souls." (Gen. 14:21) And Abraham does not say "O.K.," because souls are to be cared for, souls are to be protected, Human beings have souls and are not to be thrown back into the hands of tyranny and murder, as the whole world did to the Jewish people.

Even our own beloved United States of America could stain our history forever with the cruelty of refusing shelter and haven to the frightened, terrorized adults and children, fleeing from Hitler on the Ship, St. Louis, only to be returned to the Nazi hell they sought to escape. Herein lies the beginning of the Jewish philosophy of life, in which under in our search for life's purpose and meaning, there it stands that there are two relationships, one between man and his God, and the other between man and his fellowman. Throughout his life Abraham provides us with many illustrations of that lifestyle.

Oh sure, we all know and have read and have heard of those who congregate in their houses of worship on one day of the week, and then continue to exploit, rob, oppress, take advantage of and increase the misery and unhappiness of their fellowman. The very next day Abraham's deeds demonstrate that is not the true path of religion. Praising in hymns to God on one day and imposing hardships on his creatures the next cannot be accepted within the Jewish way of life. In a moment of mystic vision, Abraham enters the *brit beyn habtarim,* a covenant with God, (Gen. 15:18) and in it he was granted the insight to know that his descendants will eventually be enslaved and mistreated in a foreign land, but that they will be liberated and leave with great wealth. (Gen. 15:13,14) In view of Abraham's basic teachings that form the foundation of our faith, we may even question what those riches were. Which of Abraham's descendants would take it with them on their emancipation from Egypt?

As we consider the awesome personality of Abraham, it should be clear that the wealth our forefathers took with them did not consist simply of gold and silver, of precious gems or material commodities. But rather the increased knowledge on how to live with people and act towards others; the enslavement taught us to sympathize and empathize with the downtrodden, with the impoverished, with the ailing and elderly, with the lonely and alienated, with all the handicapped physically or emotionally. That was our greatest wealth. The prophet in the Bible calls upon us to be *ohr lagoyim,* a light unto all the nations. (Isaiah 42:6) Abraham who is acclaimed by western civilization, who is called the father of the church by Christians, the Father of Islam by the Muslims, continues above all to be *Avraham Avinu*, Abraham our Father. And we wait for a confused and turbulent world to accept his precepts, namely that the confrontation with God must mean the loving embrace of all humanity. Abraham's eventual victory will be achieved when justice and peace will become the shared inheritance of all mankind.

THE GOOD AND EVIL EYES

"Maaseh Avot Siman LeBanim"
"The narratives and activities of our Patriarchs are supposed to serve as guiding posts for their descendants."

This week's Torah portion introduces us to our Patriarch Abraham, regarded as the founder of our people and faith, the first Jew from whom we call ourselves Jewish. Granted that we, who regard ourselves as Jews, continue to look upon *Avraham Avinu*, Abraham our Forefather, the progenitor of our people and faith, as a personality whose influences continue to reverberate in our midst. That his stature hovers over our civilization and culture, despite the passing of the centuries, is a feature most of us rarely consider, until we suddenly must confront the various doctrines and assertions of Christianity or Islam, which claim him as Father Abraham or Ibrahim, each contending for the glorious status as his children.

It can not be denied that Abraham was a radical in the finest sense of the word. It was he who stood against his entire contemporary world proclaiming the principle of the one eternal God. And that challenge was of such propensities that he has caused us to bear the historical yoke of being both a part of humanity, as well as apart from it. That his was and is a revolutionary doctrine is apparent when we consider the hundreds of millions of people who are still steeped in idolatrous practices and beliefs, as well as recognizing that a large part of humanity contends that it has accepted this principle for which millions of our people throughout the ages have laid down their lives, but which others have diminished or reduced by assimilating acknowledgments of other manifestations of the deity with the monotheistic principles we proclaim every day with the *Kriyat Shema*, the Shema prayer.

When the Rabbis of old declared that Father Abraham observed *mitzvot,* commandments long before the Torah was transmitted to Israel at Sinai, they were not only referring to his iconoclastic nature and his struggle unceasingly against paganism, but also indicating the moral stature of the man, whose character and ideological principles became standards of behavior for his physical and spiritual descendants, the Jewish people.

The commentary has it when discussing the well known assertion in Talmud (Pesachim 117b) *Bechah chotmin ve'aiyn chotmin bahem,* namely that in the *amidah* prayer, where we refer to the God of all three Fathers, Abraham, Isaac and Jacob, because each possessed a special excellency in serving God, each of them was an innovator in the path of Judaism.

The Divine states and "I shall make of thee a great nation, and I shall bless you and make thy name great." Resh Lakish taught: I shall make thee a great nation refers to the benediction which one recites for the God of Abraham. I shall bless thee refers to the benediction one recites for the God of Isaac. And I shall make thy name great refers to the blessing one recites for the God of Jacob. Hence we might imagine that we can conclude the blessing of the *Shmoneh Esrai Amidah* prayer with the names of all three. However, tradition has taught us that the blessing is concluded not in the names of all our Fathers but only in the name of Abraham.

The benediction, closes with "*magen Avraham*," "Shield of Abraham," and does not include the other Patriarchs. Rav Yehuda Leb bar Dov Ginsburg in his commentary, *Yalkut Yehuda* interprets this to mean that since Abraham is the symbol of *chesed,* kindness and *gemelut chasidim*, benevolence towards humanity, those characteristics exalt him above the other Patriarchs.

Isaac truly represented the service, the *Avodah* in the ancient Temple because he was truly representative of the sacrifices, for he offered himself at Mount Moriah as a perfect burnt offering. Jacob was known as the *yoshev oholim*, the dweller of tents, and of course this means he who sat in the tent of Torah study. That is what we mean when we say the benediction should be concluded by alluding to all three names, because each of these characteristics equal each other.

But the Talmud emphasizes Abraham's role, because the *Yalkut Shimoni* declares, that already in Genesis, in the paradise incident with Adam and Eve, *lishmor et derech etz hachayim*, that 20 generations that preceded him made *derech eretz* proper, which means that human relations precede Torah. Why? Because *derech* means *derech eretz*, human relations, *etz chayim* of course refers to Torah, and *etz chayim* comes after *derech eretz.*

Second because, *gemelut chasadim,* benevolence toward humanity, emerges as even a more significant attribute than Torah and Avodah, therefore we end with a reference to Abraham.

In our faith, therefore, it is clear that the human relationship takes precedent over the other rituals, important though they be, hence we are taught that Yom Kippur cannot forgive our sins before God until we reconciliate ourselves with our fellow man.

Perhaps it is just that teaching which enabled the sages to denote the distinction between the disciples of Abraham and those of Balamm, the distinguished and talented prophet of the idolaters. In comparing Abraham with Balamm, discerning which attributes reprise the best in each personality we find the *Perek* associates Balamm with the *ayin harah*, evil eye, while Abraham's praise is implied by his possession of *ayin tov*, an eye for good. What is it that makes the evil eye so horrendous and threatening to humanity throughout the ages? When human behavior plays havoc in our lives it can be destructive to individuals and families, nations and societies. Our Sages were very sensitive to this negative attribute.

We have read and heard about the powers of the evil eye; primitive superstitions attributed many kinds of witchcraft to this organ, Dracula, Rasputin, the Dark Side of the Force, beasts of various types had one thing in common, the evil eye, which could control, inspire fear, inflict pain and eventually kill a poor victim. It is the evil eye which is associated with that insight of the *Perek*, "Arrogance and misanthropic attitudes take a man out of this world."

The High Holyday *Machzor* refers to *memshelet zadon*, the governments of malice, while *rishut*, this inescapable evil that contaminates human relations, sorely tried their hearts and minds. Freud discerned opposing forces in human existence, forces that embraced life and others that sought to destroy it. The first he called "eros," the life instinct, and the second, "thanatos," the death instinct. The latter impulse, says our contemporary thinker, obtains so much help from the evil eye that projects greed, envy and often hatred of its victim. And here, again, we cannot help but perceive his closeness to the ancient Sages who proclaimed

"*Hataavah, vehagaavah vesnoth habriyoth motzeim ha'adam min haolam,*" "Lust arrogance and misanthropy remove a man from the world." Throughout the ages, both primitive and more advanced humans have been aware of the dangers inherent in the eye that regards others with evil intent, malice, and envy. To the Romans this was the oculus fascinus, the Syrians called it aina-basa, my Italian neighbors still shudder at the malocchio, and our people recognize the term *ayin harah*, which was ascribed to Balaam and rejected by Abraham's *chesed* and *gemelut chasadim*.

The evil eye has that great propensity towards envy. Envy does not have to have a logical reason, although its basis may be produced by intrinsic factors. Does not the Talmud quote Rabbi Akiba to the effect that when he was ignorant and unschooled he hated every Talmud *chacham*, scholar? Is it not a fact that young Polish barristers, just out of the university, protested that Jewish attorneys were taking their positions, even when the latter had begun practicing long before the former were born.

And do we not know how envy polluted the German mentality that wanted to supplant the Jews as the chosen people, except that when Israel was chosen to propagate morality, decency and justice under the fatherhood of God, the deity of Nazi Aryanism, Hitler, declared Germans the *herrenrasse* of mankind through murder, torture and repulsive bestiality.

If we shall look once more at the Torah portion of *Lech Lecha*, we shall perceive the malice of envy at work. Consider Lot, the nephew of Abraham. He has been welcomed into the fold by Abraham, probably considered as the child he and Sarah did not have, the probable heir of Abraham's inheritance which unfortunately for Lot, consisted of both material substance and spiritual riches. But the obvious disinterest that Lot felt for the latter heritage comes to the fore in the strife between the shepherds of Abraham and Lot. True, the Torah does not reject the possibility of a grazing area too impoverished to support both. However, the reading of the Bible opens deep insight into their relationship. Lot prospered, he certainly was not deprived, but Abraham was *kabed miod*, very rich in cattle, silver, and gold. (Gen. 13:2) Furthermore, he has only the good eye:

> *"Hepared nah mayalai, im hasimol veamenaw veim hayamin veahsmeelah,"*
> **"Separate yourself from me, if you go left, I will go right, if you go right, I will go left." (Gen. 13:9)**

Take whatever area you prefer, and I shall go elsewhere," is Abraham's reply, with no restrictions, no conditions, and no stipulations to restrict the others advantage.

And Lot, of the envious eye selects Sodom, totally unconcerned with the moral climate of that community. In fact, *Yalkut Yehuda* suggests that in making this judgment, many scholars have been too lenient upon Lot. Perhaps because he was attracted to their standards. Because he silently yearned for a release from moral restrictions, because a life of licentiousness, gluttony, hedonism, and xenophobia's which totally repudiated the good eye of Abraham vis-a-vis all humans, because these really appealed deeply to him, was he in such a haste to demonstrate his preference.

However, consider Abraham, our Forefather, accepting Lot's decision with grace, continuing his mission in life, and bearing neither ill will nor malice towards an ungrateful relative. The moment he learns of Lot's capture by the combined forces of local rulers, he embarks immediately upon a military venture to free

him and the unfortunate residents of Sodom who have fallen into
the hands of the enemy.

It is in his victorious return, however, that we see the good
eye in all its glory. Met by the defeated King of Sodom who should
have been only too happy to emerge whole from the slime pits, in
which he had fallen, Abraham still confronts the shallowness of
his contemporary culture. The King plays the game of being mag-
nanimous. After all, to the victor belong the spoils. "Yes, you,
Abraham, have smashed the enemy and all the booty belongs to
you.

> *"Ten li hanefesh, veharichush kach Lecha,"*
> **"Give me the people, and you can keep all the loot and
> booty." (Gen. 14:21)**

Take it all, just leave me the people..." Not only the King of
Sodom, but it would appear our own commentators have been surprised by Abraham's response.

> *"Harimoti yadi el hashem, aile elyon, koneh shamayim
> va'aretz"*
> **"I lift up my hand to God the most high, maker of
> heaven and earth." (Gen. 14:22)**

> *"Im michut viad sroch naal...Lo tomar ani he'ehsharti et
> Avram"*
> **"That I will not take a thread or a shoelace from
> you...that no one should say I have made Abraham
> rich." (Gen. 14:23)**

Father Abraham, how wise you were. You immediately understood the envy, jealousy, malice, prejudice, and hatred, which
would ensue, every time the king would think of your wealth. He
would not say that Abraham won these riches, fair and square. He

took great risks and freed our people. No, he would only see with the evil eye, mine is the wealth of Abraham.

Why does Abraham not say that he has taken an oath? The answer supplied by a chassidic preacher is derived from that incident in Torah when Amalek first attacked Israel. Then Moses sat on a rock with his hands uplifted towards heaven, and when Israel saw that pose, they were inspired to fight. When physical fatigue compelled Moses to lower his arms, Israel lost its courage and the enemy began to prevail. Justly do the Rabbis ask, "*Vi chi yadav shel Moshe asah milchama?*" "Was it the hands of Moses that waged war? *Elah lomar lechah,* but this incident teaches us:

"*Kol zman shehayoo Yisrael mistaklin klapey maalah, umishabdeen et libahm liavihem she-bashamayim, hayoo mitgasbreem...*"
"So long as Israel kept their eyes (thoughts) lifted upwards and subjected their hearts to serve their heavenly Father, they prevailed, but otherwise they fell." (Rosh Hashanah 29a)

So, too, does Abraham now proclaim his unceasing declaration of faith: victory comes from the Lord, my inspiration and courage comes from my faith, as does my wealth. You shall not say, "I have made Abraham rich."

Abraham is saying, neither my hands wage war nor smash enemies, only when my heart is channeled towards heaven, then my victory is due to God. In God's benevolence and goodness he has enabled me to defeat the enemy; and restore your people and property. I have achieved my goal, Lot is liberated and I have no intention of having you declare that you have made me wealthy. I do not intend to then be conducive towards encouraging you to be an evil eye and regard me with envy, and using a rationale that it was you who have made me wealthy and hence have the right to covet and take it away from me.

It would also do us well to consider what Abraham is not quoted as saying. He does not say, "Take the people" and therein, I humbly suggest we may again find the good eye and conduct of the Patriarch. Yes, you speak of the people I have liberated, as though they were chattels, nothing more or less than the other part of the loot and booty. But I and my household of whom Torah will appraise through the "*nefashot asher asu beCharan,*" the souls they redeemed in Haran, (Gen. 12:5) the many they converted to the faith of the one and only eternally living God creator of heaven and earth to whom we all belong, we cannot evaluate the people as you do. I return the booty to you, and implied are the sentiments, the people belong to *aile elyon, koneh shamayim va'aretz*, the most high God, maker of heaven and earth. (Gen. 14:22) The people must be free, even as I am free to speak to them of the God who has given me the victory and who inspires me to regard all mankinds as his children.

When we consider the results of the evil eye in our own lives, attributes of jealousy, greed, and envy, nurtured by the evil eye, we may take pride indeed, in the principles of Father Abraham and his declarations in behalf of the good eye, which spells the repudiation of arrogance, false and distorted prides, superiorities which exist only in the sick minds of the evil eye. How fortunate are we that we may truly exalt and say:

"*Habitu el Avaham Avichem*,"
"Look unto Abraham your Father." (Isaiah 51:2)

COMMON LANGUAGE

As we noted, this portion of the Torah introduces us to the founder of our people, Father Abraham, whose character and attitude towards life became apparent according to Rabbinical tradition in the earlier days of the Tower of Babel. From the Midrash we learn that Abraham was a constant opponent of the generation which was aspired throughout the world. They looked upon him as one who was completely unsympathetic to their principles and goals.

They were a generation which was dedicated to unity, an ideal that has always sounded beautiful to the ears of men and which constitutes a theme that is uppermost in our minds today. Who of us does not hear the statesmen of the world constantly speaking of the necessity for human unity, cooperation and harmony? It seems strange that Father Abraham of all people, a man to whom God promised that through him all the nations of the world would be blessed should oppose the unity of peoples.

But if we look at the Midrash we shall find the Rabbis teaching us that although the Torah does tell us what constituted the sin of the generation of the flood "*Key malah ha'aretz chamas me pe'naihem*, "For the earth is filled with violence" (Gen. 6:13), it does not specify why the builders of the tower of Babel were dispersed throughout the earth.

But if we compare our world with its various ideologies with that primitive world, we shall find points of great similarity and coincidence. In our generation, we see that the great problems facing international solution are the unity of mankind and the desire of each nation to create for itself a great name as a great civilization and a great culture and a stable economy. To attain that goal, each country uses all the scientific skills and technical knowledge it can muster. That apparently was the state of conditions in the ancient world. Now certainly that is not bad when nations seek to improve their status by building towers, i.e. the symbol for their material wealth and strength and power. Certainly each nation has the right to strive to make itself as great and as superior as it can. Also, uniting the forces which men have at their disposal to attain such ideals are also good and positive and should not be criticized.

But there comes a time when we must be careful of how we are building and for what. An ancient Midrash tells us that after a while, the people forgot they were just building a tower to better themselves, but that the tower itself became the goal of their lives. When a man fell down to his death while working they were unconcerned, but if a laborer lost a brick in the process of building they were unhappy and they wept.

It sounds very much like the anecdote told by the British Prime Minister Winston Churchill. He relates a tale of a staff conference that took place during the First World War after the British had suffered some of the worst defeats in the beginning of the struggle. Lord Kitchener was very upset and he walked up and down the room moaning and groaning. When someone tried to say some sympathetic words concerning the terrible slaughter of British manhood, this military leader shouted: "I'm not thinking of the casualties, I'm thinking of the loss of shells."

Abraham was shocked at this state of affairs where building material had supplanted the value of human beings. The tower that was supposed to help and benefit mankind had now become more important than mankind itself. The holiness of human life had become forgotten.

And the unity that the generation of the dispersion represented was not the unity that Abraham sought. Unity is art provided it is a unity devoted to a sacred purpose and not to a profane goal. The tower had become the new religion; it became the new god. It aspired to reach the heaven, which was the ideal that was uniting that generation.

There has been unity that did not help mankind. The Germans were united behind Hitler, although Chancellor Adenraod pretends in his so-called peace offering to the Jews that only the Nazis were responsible for Jewish atrocities, but it is a fact that the Germans were united behind the Nazis. They did not show any great revolt versus the inhumanity of the dominating power that they had put in power and permitted to remain there. Unity is a great ideal provided it is the unity of the righteous; it is a danger when it is the unity of sinners cooperating with each other to achieve the top of the Tower of Babel from which they can extend their supremacy over the world.

The Bible does not have to tell us what their sin was specifically. The mere fact that they united to wield their combined powers not for the good of mankind, but to secure supremacy speaks for itself.

Abraham fought those people because he saw in their activity the danger to themselves and the rest of man. Today too we can say, if men only spoke the same language and unified their efforts, what a wonderful world this would be. Yes, provided that unity was devoted to the sanctity of man and the acknowledgment of God.

Just convening a conference of United Nations does not mean that we ensure the peace of the world. When men unite to build towers of Babel, the great symbols of the material aspect of generations without considering humanity, it is inevitable that their unity will not last, that their tongues will become diversified, hostilities will result, and from their differences in speech there results the victims of violence and war. Today we have the leaders like Nimrod of old who sought descendants and dominion through that unity which was subservient to his wishes. Today we have leaders who seek a unity of nations provided others speak their language and support their demands for power.

Like Abraham of old, we must oppose that unity. We must oppose those policies which begin speaking about the benefit of man and the liberation of man from exploitation, but soon end by making man subject and slave to the government and state. As much as we pray today for unity and for the combined effort of all nations in the material economic spheres of man, let us first be sure that it is a unity dedicated to righteousness and a combined effort devoted to man.

Like Abraham, let us go forward to the land and the goals that God shows us. Those goals which consecrate humanity as well as our efforts to holy living, and then all the nations of the earth will be blessed with true unity to which we will last, because when all men will speak the language of God, then we shall have real peace.

IT'S IN YOUR HANDS

This Torah lesson also inaugurates the blessings of Jewish history. Until the present portion, the Torah has been telling us about the origins of man. It has reminded us that humanity comes from a common source in spite of the differences in race, skin pigmentation, or varying creed. It reminds us how conflict developed among men and how humanity dissipated its strength in unity for false ideals.

Now the Torah veers towards its main theme, the development of Israel as the people who were chosen by God, because they chose God. This is the story of a people whose primary contribution to the human race whether in social relations, political growth, natural, material or intellectual aspects of life, have developed from the one God idea which was first pronounced by Abraham our Father. The personality of our progenitor is projected upon his descendants in every phase of our history. Rightly does the Midrash say: God said to Abraham "go and conquer the path before your children." You will find that everything that has been written about Abraham is applicable to his children. For of Abraham it is written, and he went forward to his journey. And of the children of Israel it is written, and these are the journeys of the children of Israel.

What is the great journey of life that Abraham blazed for his descendents? What great pattern did he leave behind him to guide us in our journey through life? Abraham was born, we noted earlier, during the *Dor haflagaah*, the generation that tried to build the Tower of Babel. But the Bible introduces him to us at that moment when God tells him to start on his great journey of life. "*Lech Lecha*," "Get thee hence" (Gen. 12:1) says God. Start on your way and it will be for your own benefit. It will be a pilgrimage of blessings, for God says:

> "*Ve'esicha legoy gadol va'avarechecha va'agadlah shemehcha veheyai baracha*,"
> **"I will make of you a great nation, and I will bless you, and I shall make your name great, and thou shalt be a blessing." (Gen. 12:2)**

Well, asks the commentary, why all this constant repetition about blessings? Rashi explains this by saying that God is saying to Abraham "I will bless you with the specific good that you need." Now, you are being called upon to travel, but if you are constantly on the move such things may interfere with the growth of a family and I know that you want a family, so I will bless you with a family. And traveling may also interfere with your amassing money because you might not be able to stay in one place and do as much business as you can or as much as you would like to, so I shall bless you with money. I know said God that a rolling stone gathers no moss. If you do not stay in one place long enough many people may not have an opportunity to meet you and get to know you and you will not be able to build a good reputation for yourself and enjoy the benefits of a good name. So I assure you, said God, that you will have a good name. You will have all three, children, wealth and a name. And thou shall be a blessing. Before this, the blessings were in my hand, but now on they are placed in yours.

Now all of us are engaged upon a great journey of life. Each of us is told *Lech Lecha*, get thee hence. We would never make any progress if we did not get out, if we stayed in one place and did nothing. But the implications in this verse are many because many people have a family, many people have wealth, many people have a name, but do they follow the path first cut out by Abraham?

Many people have families, but their children unfortunately are not blessed nor do they bring blessings. There are children who are deprived of proper religious influences, there has been no attempt on the part of the parents to mold their young personalities and teach them the finer things of life. Too often, these children are not like Abraham, they are neither blessings to themselves or to their parents.

God promised Abraham material prosperity. Now many people have a great deal of wealth without associating it with any spiritual purpose. The Midrash (Gen. Rabbah 16:2) in discussing the opening verses of the Bible and God's creation of the world quotes some of the sages who say that gold is a wonderful metal. It can be stamped and minted into coins and easily carried on our person everywhere and thus utilized for barter and exchanged for the various commodities that we produce. One of the Rabbis however, considers the evils, the terror and the suffering that has been brought into the world just because of this money. After due thought, he declares that the world does not deserve it, it is not worthy to use this precious metal. Why then was it created? And the answer given by this wise Rabbi is that gold was created because of the Temple. God knew in advance that gold would be needed for the construction of the Temple. What the Sage meant was that though gold has brought us difficulties, it was made to be primarily utilized for sacred purposes. This sometimes means the building of a temple for worship or other holy building, e.g. schools, hospitals, shelters for the aged, the weak, the orphaned, etc. Many people have money, but they do not use it for socially constructive purposes. God assured Abraham that his wealth would be a blessing, because he would use it for the good.

You will have a name, promised God. Superficially, there is nothing great or strange in this statement. Nearly all of us have names. Dillinger had a name. The men who engineered the Brinks Robbery certainly have a reputation. In fact, so do all the people whose pictures are plastered over the circulars that appear on the walls of prisons, courthouses, post offices or certain television programs as being wanted by the police. These men have names and reputations. God reminded Abraham of all these things, "be thou a blessing" said God. Yes, I shall make of you a great nation, I shall bless you with money. It shall make of you a great nation with many descendants but be thou a blessing. See to it you use these treasures properly. See to it that your children, that your wealth, that your reputation become sources of blessings. These blessings were all in my hands before, now I place them in your hands. I have caused this goodness to be given unto you, but how you use them is up to you, it is all in your hands. This charge that Abraham received from God is of course given to each of us in one form or another. "It is now up to you." Whether your family will be a nice one, whether your children will be blessed depends upon you. Your conduct and actions will determine whether your parents will reap hardships or pain from you or whether they will harvest love and happiness. Through your work and their ideals you will pursue. You will show what you can do with your material possessions. Will you waste them for idle treasures and senseless pursuits? Or will you use them for charity, for socially constructive purposes, for making out of this world a temple dedicated to God and the realm of the spirit?

What will you do with your name? Will it signify disappointments to people? Will it stand for someone who hurts others or who causes fear and antagonism and hostility to arise within their hearts, or will you use your name properly so that it becomes a blessing? Will people associate it with love, kindness, understanding, and generosity with others? There are many blessings in the offering as you embark upon a new path of life, but always remember, the blessings are in your hands, it is up to you.

Lech Lecha, get thee hence, go out into the world and reap blessing, but be certain to bring others happiness, glory and pride.

PEACE AMONG OURSELVES

When some of us were very young, we were quite attentive to our Rebbe who once startled us by saying that the Rambam or some similar authorities entertained an opinion, that just translating a scriptural verse literally meant misunderstanding it. He then went on to introduce us to those concepts of *pardes*, that every word, indeed every letter of the Torah, is to be interpreted on several levels, *peshat*, explaining its plain meaning, *remez,* allusions to additional matters, *drash*, its traditional meaning in the various Midrashim, and sod its still deeper hidden meaning. The Rambam elaborates on the idea that no word, not even a single letter could be taken at its face value. No, some ideas might be rather obvious, but other meanings were concealed, hidden from the superficial reading, and therefore, ours was the obligation to study and ascertain the wealth of instruction found in "*lernen*."

Once, verses in the Torah portion of *Lech Lecha* were assigned to us, and mine was that little, clearly obvious sentence, "And there was a quarrel between the shepherds of Abraham's cattle and the shepherds of Lot's cattle. And the Cannanite and Peruzite dwelt then in the land." And so I continued to look ahead and read about the generosity of Abraham who permitted Lot to be first in choosing what areas he would prefer. And so, I first considered the fact that by telling us that the Cannanites and the Peruzites lived then in land of our ancestors, we could perhaps determine historically the time when this narrative took place. My Rebbe listened quietly, as he was wont to do and then asked me if I would not consider reviewing my homework and perhaps searching for further explanations, of a moral nature, whereupon I went home and finally found an explanation along the lines of the Hertz commentary. I returned to the class and reported that although it would appear that the Cannanites and the Peruzites occupied the land, there still were other areas that were attractive. And here I added what I thought was a *chidush*, new interpretative light on the verse. You see, I told the Rebbe, it is like the Jews and Arabs in *Eretz Yisrael*, then known as Palestine. There are areas on which the Jews can work and others to which Arabs might go. Here I thought, I was demonstrating a capacity to be a political scholar, a fervent Zionistic and also a *chacham*, scholar who would please my Rebbe. But all my Rebbe replied was, "it is an improvement, but you have to give the verse more thought, study and consider other commentaries." In addition to deflating me, it also encouraged further homework and after a while, it opened my eyes to understand how the verse displays an insight into both history and guidance for us, even in our own day.

As time progressed, we managed to get involved with the Rebbe who invariably indicated a *kushye*, a question or a *stirah,* conflict or a *plugta*, a polemic. And not because we were just *"ipcha mistabra,"* contrary minded, or because we were children of an *"am peziza,"* rash or impulsive, but because dissension is part of our civilized manner. And as we gathered insight into the mentality of gigantic thinkers, we learned to respect opinion, contention, convictions of differing analysis, but always aware that each was not only due to inner convictions, but always concerned with the heritage, the traditional claims and the needs of our people. That is why, we perceived how sensitive were these holy teachers to the solidarity of our people in confronting the external, prejudiced world which seethed with hatred and persecution against us, and how quick they were to react toward inner betrayal or menace. How they quivered at the words of the prophet Isaiah:

"*Miharu banayich, miharsayich umacharivayich mimaych yetzayu*,"
"Thy children shall make haste, thy destroyers and they that made thee waste shall go forth from thee."
(Isaiah 49:17)

How frightening it always has been to watch Jews who have not been dedicated to our survival, who have not been faithful to our religion, who have sought to minimize our stature among the nations war against those just, who are determined to preserve our ancient heritage, traditions and claims.

These quarrels invariably have meant only one thing: defeats for the Jewish people, and support for our enemies. When Yitzchok Shamir was the operations commander of the Lechi, he is reported to have said that "For a man to go forth to kill another man whom he does not know, must believe in one thing only, that by his act he will change the course of history." He meant an act of terror by Eliyahu Hakim and Eliyahu ben Zouri, who killed Lord Moyne. And the so-called Jewish establishment poured forth its hatred and invective upon these two young people whose testimony in court was a condemnation of Britain for its persecution of Jews and its undisguised assistance to Hitler in the era of the holocaust. True, after Moyne was killed and the boys were executed, admissions were made about Lord Moyne, as the British statesman who responded to the problem of saving Jews with the frigid answer, "What could I do with 2 million Jews?"

Even the fierce Jewish enemy of these young men, David Ben Gurion, as Prime Minister, could say he revered such dedicated patriots who were hanged in Cairo. But who benefited most from this inner warfare? The British enemy who continued to harrow our people. The other day, someone showed me an item on the celebration of the centennial of the birth of Yitzchok Sadeh, the Palmach leader who later as commander coordinated the activities of the Haganah, Irgun and Lechi against the British. What I remember most from my youth was the fierce hatred which existed between Jewish youth in Palestine, where the Hagannah first preached a self control by saying they would defend, but not go out on the offensive against Arabs who were murdering Jews.

And when Shlomo ben Yosef, a Betari, fired a shot at a bus, where no one was hurt, but where it was clear, he was protesting what the Arabs considered cowardice by Jews who would sit in their little cubby holes like mice and not venture forth. For this, however the British put him on trial, and were aided by the fraternal inter-warfare. Who won? Shlomo ben Yosef became the first Jew executed in Zion since the fall of the temple in 70 C.E.. The hatred between Jews only increased and the British were bolstered in their attempts to incite Arabs to murder Jews. We were the losers.

Consider please, a very fine study by David Fromkin, *A Peace to End All Peace: Creating the Modern Middle East between 1914-1922.* Every problem we confront today was in the Middle East created then. Consider that we are reminded by Fromkin of what is called the Arab Israeli conflict today. Two influential Zionist leaders to use his term considered the Arab opposition to Zionism. Ben Gurion, the leftist leader, a socialist, said only our willingness to work confers upon us the right to occupy a country, and as a socialist his policy was to organize the Jews and Arabs employers and landlords. What did this really mean? Oh, I know that Ben Gurion said this would have Jews and Arabs live together and their communities would enjoy autonomy. But actually, these Jews and Arabs have yet to be able to live peacefully together.

Martin Gilbert in his work *Churchill: A Life* believes that Ben Gurion was not entirely frank in his talk about Arab Jewish cooperation. Zev Jabotinsky, on the other hand, the man who founded Allenby's Jewish Legion, saw the situation as it was, intuitively as well as pragmatically, he understood that the Arabs would never stand by peacefully and allow Jews to become a majority in Palestine. He declared we need an "iron wall" of military force to protect the Jewish settlers as they built their community into a majority. He spoke out that the British could not be relied upon and Jews have to form their own army to protect themselves. And the fierce hatred of Ben Gurion against Jabotinsky found certain roots. The leftist parties, socialists, even more radical groups consider themselves the heirs of Ben Gurion, while Herut consider themselves the heirs of Jabotinsky. And Jabotinsky denounced Churchill's decision to remove Transjordan from Palestine, thereby robbing the Jews of 76% of their land and making it a Hitler territory, *Yuden rein, Yuden verboten*, Jews forbidden. And he also demanded the establishment of a Jewish state on both sides of the Jordan. And so the hatred left its scars unto this very day. And who won? Jabotinsky died of a heart attack, shattered by the suffering of our people at the hands of Hitler and by the hatred of fellow Jews. Ben Gurion ended up as an old man rejected by his own people, trying to hold political control over a petty party. And the Jewish people? We were the greatest losers. For that hatred, we have paid in blood today.

You see my Rebbe was forcing me to consider that little verse in the Torah lesson. Yes, there was a conflict between the shepherds of Lot and the shepherds of Abraham; while the Cannanites and Peruzites dwelt in the land. And the great commentator, Rabbi Moshe Alshich said it simply. *"Michamat sheshrarah machlokot uperud bimachane haivrim mipne zeh, Shaltu haknaani vihaperuzi baaretz wenn die yidde hargenen die peruzim balebatium ueb."* "When there are quarrels and division in the camp of the Hebrew's, then the Cannanites and Peruzites rule the country." When Jews fight Jews, the Cannanites and Peruzites live on the Holy soil. And to fight the Cannanites and Peruzites our answer must be *achdut*, unity in our ranks, unity in our support for each other and the uninterrupted faith of *Am Yisrael,* the State of Israel and the People of Israel. The people of Israel must and shall live forever. Because we shall never leave the God of Israel and He shall never abandon us. If we would only remember that teaching, and proceed with dignity, honor and integrity, then peace and justice will be our portion.

THE JEWISH FAMILY

> *"Ve'etnah be'reetee bainee uvainecha vearbeh otecha meod,"*
> **"And I shall give my covenant between me and thee and I shall multiply thee exceedingly." (Gen. 17:2)**

There is a tremendous enemy within our midst, an enemy incidentally which has been called by some, the silent Holocaust, because it literally tears away significant segments of our national and spiritual strength. This silent Holocaust is assimilation and intermarriage, which has menaced us throughout our history and which invariably, resulted in terrible frustration and disappointment to those who embraced it as a solution to their personal or collective needs.

In chapter Fifteen of this Torah portion, we read of the covenant which Abraham made with God, when he symbolically cut in two a calf, sheep, ram, etc. This is known as the *brit habtarim*. This *brit* or covenant is a general obligation that concerns two parties; here it was an agreement between Abraham, the founder of our faith, and God. This idea of a covenant was reaffirmed as it was in another treaty, namely the *brit milah*, circumcision and again at Mt. Sinai through the agency of the Ten commandments. In this manner, in our own eyes, as well as in the eyes of so many throughout the world, we have become known as the people of the covenant. Whether one is traditionally pious or if he adheres to some particular group among our people like the Conservative or Reform, as a secular Hebraist or Yiddishist, no matter that he delineates himself as a member of a Zionist organization or holds membership in a Jewish community organization, one thing is clear, that Jew who seeks to reaffirm his Jewish identity, consciously recognizes or is subconsciously aware that he belongs to a people who made a covenant with God and hence he is obliged to preserve and maintain that people's existence.

Before he was enjoined to arrange this *brit habtarim*, Abraham supplicated God and asked; what will you give me if I walk childless? After all, Abraham was not unique in this situation. Many of us pour forth our affection upon those who may not be the fruit of our bodies but we do not despair of God. What prompted Abraham to voice such profound fears? The patriarch, trembled because he realized that he was inaugurating a new faith which would radically differ from those predominant in his civilization and he wanted to be certain that when he was no longer here in the flesh, that faith would continue. When God assured him that even as he could not count the stars, so would his progeny grow and multi-

ply, he believed in God and that was counted as his righteousness.
But observe that as God continued that divine inspiration and in-
formation and informs him that his people will inherit the land of
Israel, Abraham asks:

"*Bameh eydah key erahshehnah*"
"How shall I know that I shall inherit it." (Gen. 15:8)

And God commands Abraham to arrange for the *habtarim*."
The Imrei Tzaddickim comments that this question by Abraham is
not very comprehensible. After the Torah narrative tells us that he
believed in God, now he questions the Lord? But continues that
commentary, "how shall I know, that I shall inherit it" refers not to
his faith in God, but to the continuation of his faith. How shall I
know that my descendants will have my faith that they will believe in our destiny? That question has always been a pressing
burden upon our conscious. That tradition has received tremendous blows in our times. While it is true that sociologists have
often referred to Hansen's law, namely an observation that later
generations return to cultural values which parents or even grandparents may have spurned and repudiated, it would appear that
this principle does not operate with such alacrity in contemporary
Jewish life. We all know that a past generation has been castigated
criticized and even condemned by its spiritual leaders, because of
laxity in matters of Yiddishkeit and religious observance. This
generation has responded by claiming that those religious leaders
were unable to adjust to current needs, and therefore the
congregants withdrew from supporting religious precepts. But
despite this controversy, such people did remain loyal to the Jewish nation.

We see, for example, that Yiddishists who considered themselves liberated from the *mitzvoth*, that Hebraists who then predicated their entire existence upon a love for the Hebrew language, we witness how Jews who insisted that above all priorities, they embraced only such action which helped them integrate themselves into the mainstream of American life. Nonetheless, all these people, despite their difference in analysis, values and priority, all remain loyal to the Jewish people. But their children, who do not understand this too often, they see parents who have been non-religious parents who have given no indication or evidence of deep attachments or commitment to Jewish aspiration suddenly. These same parents are upset because a son wishes to marry a non-Jewish girl. The same young man also realizes that were he to marry a non-religious Jewish girl, who never attends synagogue, who has no idea of *kashrut*, Jewish dietary law or observing festivals and Holydays. These parents would accept her and never hurl accusations against him that he is marrying outside of his faith. Why is this? Is it because parents see differences in the attitudes entertained by non-Jews and Jews with reference to marriage? Yes, that may play a part.

We should never forget that while Judaism looks upon marriage as a *mitzvah*, and considers it meritorious to marry, Christianity, in spite of its recognition of marriage as a sacrament originally decried the institution of marriage. Jesus did not marry. Paul did not marry. For centuries Christian clergymen did not marry. Even in our day, the present Pope has strenuously rejected any attempts to liberalize or modify that status by permitting priests to marry. But there is another facet of this discussion that must be understood. Although we hear much current publicity and propaganda of the "family that prays together stays together," and the television evangelists shout that the new born Christian alone rallies to protect the family institution in the United States, the fact remains that Christianity is not premised on family. Redemption is promised to the individual who accepts the call of its savior. This savior is someone whom we never understand because the Jew cannot accept the idea of the Lord in carnage, that God somehow became human, so human that in a conflict with the state authority, he could be beaten, tormented, crucified and die, but to be saved from eternal perdition eternal hell. One must accept the call of its savior (who said incidentally that a good follower must be prepared to reject his parents.) One must accept that no Christian is simply born a Christian. Every Christian is the son of a saint, or a sinner is born a pagan and is either baptized by his parents with the portals of their particular church, or as an individual, he becomes converted or born again.

But we as a people differ so radically, theologically speaking, because a Jew is born a Jew since his mother is Jewish. *Af al pi shechata, Yisrael hu*, even though he sins, a Jew remains a Jew. Whether he is religious or not, whether he is *shomer mitzvot*, observes the commandments or selects only a few which appeal to either his ethics or his convictions. He is born a Jew. If a Roman Catholic marries a Protestant, he may be criticized for marrying outside his church, but a Jew is born a Jew because his family is part of that covenant. When he marries outside of a Jewish family, then his marriage is an assault upon his ancestors, an attack upon his family, which is a link in the *shalshelet hadorot*, the chain of Jewish generations.

You see, that is what bothered Abraham.

"Bameh eydah key erahshehnah"
"How shall I know that I shall inherit it." (Gen. 15:8)

that my descendants will understand that I am *Avraham Avinu*, Abraham their father, not just some savior, not just some priest, not just a great political or national leader? But I am the father of a family which is entwined with God, because of the *brit*, the covenant, the agreement between him and us. In confronting our difficult situation today, we might do well to recall the words of the Lubavitcher Rebbe who said on *Shabbat Lech Lecha*, "Assimilation is rife in our times, currently being at the astronomical high figure of 33%, no one needs to be apprised of the catastrophe which is assimilation." The great Rogachover Gaon stated it clearly. "In general, a Jew always remains a Jew no matter how he may have strayed with one exception. When a Jew marries a non-Jewish girl, the result is offspring having no Jewish status: a possible Jewish child has become a non Jew."

Elihu Bergman a sociologist at Harvard University, calculated that in the year 2076 there would be no more than 900,000 American Jews. In short if the death of our present five million members of American Jewry that places upon all of us soul shattering responsibilities, which are challenging and recite demanding when we recite the supplicatory prayers, we say, remember and regard the covenant between the parts. Remember unto us the covenant of our forefathers. And then we say our Father, our King if we have no righteousness and good deeds, remember unto us the covenant of the forefathers and our testimony every day that the Lord is one. Every Jewish parent and grandparent, whether religious or not, subconsciously responds to the fact that he or she has an historical role to play. The mere existence of a Jew makes him a witness to that covenant, a witness against Hitler and all the betrayers of our people, a witness against all the cruel, brutal and bestial acts which mankind has imposed and perpetrated against each other through the long annals of time.

The existence of a Jew also bears witness through the covenant that we say *Avinu Malkeinu*, Our Father, Our King the existence of the Jew bears witness to the majesty of God. *Bameh eydah*, how will I know that my descendants will inherit this vast treasure, the repository of Torah, of love for *Eretz Yisrael*, the Land of Israel and unity with *Am Yisrael*, the Nation of Israel? And God answered through the covenant, or the parts, and that is what we must begin to teach our people again.

> "*Ve'etnah be'reetee bainee uvainecha vearbeh otecha meod,*"
> "**And I shall give my covenant between me and thee and I shall multiply thee exceedingly.**" (Gen. 17:2)

Therein lies the secret of our existence. We shall never disappear, we shall always play the tremendous role for which we have been chosen, if we only remember that a family, our family, the family of Abraham our Father entered a covenant. And that covenant was the assurance given Abraham. And it must serve as the guarantee to all the members of our eternal family, the Jewish family.

LEARN FROM OUR MISTAKES

In this Torah lesson of *Lech Lecha*, we see God speak to Abraham in a vision saying:

> "*Al Tirah Avram, Anochi magen lach, secharecha harbeh meod,*"
> "**Fear not Abram, I am a shield for you; your reward is very great.**" (Gen. 15:1)

The Midrash is concerned as to why Abraham should be afraid. He had apparently just performed a good act, he had learned that his nephew Lot and Lot's neighbors were captured. He had set out after them, defeated the enemy, freed the captives and returned them to the King of Sodom. He had refused any material rewards for his good deed:

"*Im michut viad sroch naal...Lo tomar, ani he'ehsharti et Avram*"
"That I will not take a thread or a shoelace from you, that no one should say I have made Abraham rich."
(Gen. 14:23)

and here we read that God had to assure him not to be afraid?

Some commentary is also surprised that here God spoke to Abraham in a vision, yet this does not appear to have occurred previously. Why? The Rambam explains this by saying that this was a vision that came to him during the day, where as formerly he was receiving divine communication only at night. The Zohar is of the opinion that until he was circumcised, all his prophetic insight was vouchsafed only at night. Whereas the Gemarah (Nedarim 32a) asks, "Why was Abraham punished so that his descendants would have to undergo bondage?" Because he prevented his fellowmen from entering under the wings of the *Schechinah*. Rashi and the Ran explain this as follows: he shouldn't have hastened to return the captives to the King of Sodom, but should have first converted them to the faith of one God and the principles implied in that doctrine, brotherhood of men, equality, humanity, tolerance, kindness, compassion, etc. But because he handed them over to the King, he was punished through the decree his descendants would have 310 years of bondage.

Now it is clear that after this deed, Abraham suddenly realized the erroneous decision he had made. First, he should have realized that he was handing over the people to a system that was essentially tyrannical, antisocial as well as unjust. Had he taught them monotheism, he would have started them off on the right path, kept them close to him, subjected them to good influences and increase the ranks of those who could spread this new doctrine. His entire mission in life was to propagate the doctrine of God, and here there had been placed in his hands these people. He had acquired them and should have first taken tithe from them, that is had them offer some sacrifice, for it was as if he acquired them as it states in the Talmud "Whoever takes vegetables from the market and wishes to return them should not do so until he has taken tithe from them." (Demai chapter 3, Mishna 2)

Since he had now acquired these people, as was the case in those days, he should have first converted them. And since he did not, God was dissatisfied with his action. And so God communicated with him in a lesser manner. Formerly communication was such that it was reserved to him alone, now it would seem that the vision was such that even a blind man could see, that is to say everyone was aware of it. Abraham was downhearted, and regretted his actions and humbly recognized his errors, whereupon God comforted him. If you understand your wrongs, I forgive you. "Do not be afraid," even though your wrongs have resulted in punishments to be visited vis-a-vis your children.

> **"*Al Tirah Avram, Anochi magen lach, secharecha harbeh meod,*"**
> **"Fear not Abram, I am a shield for you; your children will leave Egypt with great riches." (Gen. 15:1)**

What riches? The realization that slavery is bad, that oppression is evil, that minorities should be treated properly as befits children who are the children of God (i.e. Mankind.)

There is a great lesson in this for us. For one, Abraham emerges as do all our ancestors, only human. The Bible does not disguise human errors and is aware of the frailty of the flesh.

Second, a man must learn to be loyal to the principles he professes, and proclaim the Doctrine of God. Perhaps it was superficially better to forget principles. Lot did live in the Sodom area and the defeated King might someday cause trouble for them, be on the good side and return his people, one might have thought.

Third, Abraham wished to show his faith and dependency on God. "I'll take nothing so that you can not say I made Abraham rich." This might have been a proud moment to remind the Sodom King, you will always be indebted to me, the Jewish nation, and our faith in God.

Fourth, the King said:

"*Ten li hanefesh, veharichush kach Lecha,*"
"Give me the people, and you can keep all the loot and booty." (Gen. 14:21)

This should cause us to think about the value of human beings. Our regard of humans must take precedence over material goods. The boss who thinks in terms of produce only forgets that without human beings, there is no one to produce or to produce for.

And last, above all, a man should realize his social obligations. We can not forget that we have responsibilities to each other. Freedom is indivisible, we cannot be children of God, and free and imbued with the truth, but deny it to others. We can not return people to old difficult conditions of bondage instead of helping them onward. If we do that we help create a world which will inevitably harm us. "Abraham, you forgot that you are handing over these human beings to slavery. Very well, you are supporting that pernicious doctrine which will some day reach out at another dynasty and enslave your own people. "Your people will be enslaved." Abraham realized the error of his misdeed. His sorrow was deep. "Very well Abraham, be assured, because you realize your wrongs, your children will leave with the true lesson learned."

May we all take these lessons to heart. Be concerned with and protect all people. See their good, act, live, teach and show that Judaism, Torah, and the Doctrine of one God means brotherhood of all humanity, enduring peace and everlasting justice.

Vayera

— 4 —

וַיַּרְא וְהִנֵּה שְׁלֹשָׁה אֲנָשִׁים נִצָּבִים עָלָיו

"He noticed three men standing before him."
(Genesis 18:2)

WELCOMING VISITORS

The scriptural lesson *Vayera* opens with a little scene of Abraham sitting at the opening of his tent on a very hot day. Suddenly lifting his eyes upwards he notices three men whom he invites into his tent. Later in this very same Torah portion, we find our Forefather engaged in a discussion or better said a bargaining session in an unsuccessful attempt to save Sodom and Gomorrah, two wicked cities from destruction. Earnest analysis will show that these two events are more than simple unrelated incidents, but in reality they represent two contrasting worlds, two conflicting cultures and two ways of life that cannot live in harmony with each other.

The Torah often with its uniqueness narrates a little story, one more interesting than the last. These stories however, when studied within the light of our ancient traditions and commentaries quickly teach us that it is not a legend we read but a unique method of instructing and guiding us in the choices that we are to make for ourselves in our own lives.

Here was Abraham, an elderly sick man, who has just experienced as we have learned from last week's portion the surgery of circumcision. He is recuperating from its effects and the presence of God manifests itself to him as he sits on the plains of Mamre in the glaring merciless heat of the desert, waiting for some passerby upon whom he may lavish his hospitality.

Suddenly he sees three strangers and he rushes forward to greet them. Wasn't that rude asks the commentary? Here is Abraham engaged in communication with God and he leaves the Sacred Presence to welcome mere mortals. Well no, the Sages answer. From this act we learn that welcoming guests as the display of hospitality is greater than welcoming the Divine Presence, especially since Rashi says that Abraham asked God to excuse him and wait until he would welcome these strangers.

An interesting sidelight on this episode is furnished by a discussion that took place between two great Sages, the Noda BeYehuda and the Shpetivka Sage. We learn this from the conduct of Abraham our Father, but how did he know this to be true, that God would not take offense at having Abraham request the Divine Presence to wait while he welcomed these guests?

The Sage answered: The Midrash tells us of an ancient legend that God deliberately set the sun blazing in the sky to make the day hot that people would not venture out on the desert. In this manner, Abraham who was still ill would not be bothered and overtax his strength trying to provide for the comfort of strangers. When God suddenly appeared to him, Abraham naturally was sensitive to, the kindness of the Lord displaying toward him. But when he saw those three strangers approaching he thought if welcoming the presence of God is more important than welcoming mere human beings, God would not have to make this day so unbearably hot, yet at the same time permitted visitors to come by, "Naturally I would be occupied this moment in communication with Providence, but here is God's presence and it is still so hot that one would think passersby would be prevented from bothering me, yet here are visitors in need of attention, so apparently it is a great *mitzvah* to be kind to these humans, than to welcome the spirit of God."

Thus said the Sage: did the Lord inculcate within the heart and mind of Abraham the need for being hospitable, compassionate, understanding, friendly and warmhearted to our fellowman?

Here is Abraham sitting quietly, immersed in deep thought with the sacred Presence, and suddenly there is a change of atmosphere. He rushes forward to meet the people, he hastens to get them into his home, he runs to the cattle for a calf, he runs to his son to prepare a meal and he asks his wife Sarah to do some baking. You note all the details are given, the menu, excitement with which the strangers are welcomed, every detail is noted. Not only the food and welcome, but even accompanying our fellowman is kindness, as the Bible says:

"VeAvraham holaich emom leshalcham,"
"And Abraham walked with them to escort them,"
(Gen. 18:16)

Thus we see now how the Torah has portrayed to us the real character of Abraham our forefather and also has taught us what we, his children should do, and how we should live and how we must act with reference to others.

Rabbi Sholom of Belz points out the different expressions which depict what transpired between Abraham and his guests. Abraham saw three men, *nitzavim alav*, standing over him. (Gen. 18:1) So he ran forward to meet them. However, when the food was prepared and the banquet set before the guests, scripture reminds us *vehoo omaid aleyhem tachat haetz vayochaylu*, and he stood by them under the tree and they did eat. (Gen. 18:8) But *omaid aleyhem* really means not by them, but rather over them. Whereupon Rabbi Sholom observed, when Abraham first saw the visitors, they stood over him. They were angels and he a mere human being. But when he ran forward to greet them, extend his shelter, food, protection and care, he became their equal. But when he began to feed them, and take care of them, he stood over them. Because at that moment, the *basar vedam*, the human being became angelic himself and even towered over these instrumentality's of God. Hence Torah was not given to these ministering angels, because lacking both body and material needs, they were unable to fulfill the *mitzvot* of Torah, those great precepts which make for a proper human being and a decent human society.

But the lesson is not yet finished. The Torah wants us to realize the true sincerity of Abraham, for Torah knows that so many of us display nice manners and cordiality without the depth of Abraham, and so the Torah tells us that two of these angels went to visit Lot, Abraham's nephew in Sodom. Now Lot was a very fine man compared with the scoundrels in whose midst he lived, but he wasn't as great as his uncle. Yet, the Rabbis quickly noted, why is it that the Bible doesn't say that Abraham lifted up his eyes and saw *malachim*, angels, it merely says:

"*Vayar, vehiney shlosha anashim netzavim alav,*"
"He noticed three men standing before him." (Gen. 18:2)

Whereas when they visited Lot, the Bible says specifically:

"*Vayavohoo shney hamalachim Sodomah,*"
And two angels came to Sodom (Gen. 19:1)

Lot was sitting at the gates of Sodom. Why did the angels immediately show their true colors to Lot and yet appear as mere men when visiting Abraham? But herein lies the difference between these two men. Lot was very happy to welcome angels, he was always ready to show his kindness to important people. We all know many people like Lot. As long as they believe others have some important status or superiority over themselves they are always ready to play host, but not so Abraham. Father Abraham showed kindness to all.

O Father Abraham, how magnificent you were, how great a teacher, how proud we your children are of you. May we all look toward him and from him learn how to act toward every human being, then so many fears and sorrows would disappear for peace and happiness would fill our hearts and those who walk the path of life with us.

LIKE THE LIGHT OF THE SUN

"*Kechom hayom,*"
"Like the heat of the day." (Gen. 18:1)

Abraham was sitting at his tent door when he saw three strangers standing over him, says the Bible. I suppose that you and I would first think that Abraham an aged, ill person should not sit at noon when the sun was so hot, and its rays burning. There is something strange about this depiction.

We live in a world that is particularly sensitive to the universe about us. There is so much foolish talk about astronomy. Millions of human beings rush to read their astrological horoscopes. Actually, this is a lot of hokum, because astronomers will tell you that all the astrological tables about positions of the planets and stars are a lot of baloney. They are false, mathematically wrong and of course, morally untrue. Young scientists say, of course it is a lot of baloney. What is true is science conquering the universe.

Without being a scientist, we can all appreciate the sun. We get our warmth and light from the sun. The sun has become a symbol of hope and health to the entire world. Even as we are warned not to burn ourselves too badly, we are encouraged to get enough sunlight to absorb natural vitamin A. The sun gives us strength and energy. Were the sun to change its position, either we would freeze to death or we would all burn up.

There is something about the sun that most of us usually forget to consider. We speak about its axis, its distance in space, the constant radiation of twelve thousand degrees Fahrenheit it exudes, etc. But no one ever speaks about the kindness of the sun. Have you ever heard of the sun refusing to shine upon any particular group of people? Does the sun decide not to warm an individual because he is stupid, violent, or antisocial? Did you ever hear of the sun refusing to shine upon someone because of the color of his skin, the religion he practices, the thoughts in his mind or the actions of his hands? The sun seems to shine upon everyone with equal vigor, regardless of his customs, language or deeds.

Kind Abraham sat in the door of his tent at the heat of day. In Hebrew the words should have been *bechom hayom*, in the heat of the day, rather than what is written:

"*Kechom hayom*,"
" Like the heat of the day." (Gen. 18:1)

The Torah never errs in its use, even of one letter. It should actually be translated and Abraham sat at his tent like the heat of the day, like the rays of the sun, for that is what Abraham was, like the rays of the sun. Rashi comments, "*Shehaim arveyim shemishtachavim leavak raglayhem*," "They were wilderness dwellers who bowed in worship to the dust of their feet." (Rashi to Gen. 18:4) Abraham's hospitality was showered upon everyone even upon heathens. He did not show kindness only to his family and dislike for the rest of the world. The sun's rays shine for everyone. They do not disappear because of a mans skin color, they do not warm only for republicans or democrats, so was Abraham, sweet, kind, generous and overflowing with love for all, like the rays of the sun, his hospitality was ready to receive all.

But you see that is the sadness of looking at the sun. Of enjoying its heat, warmth, light and forgetting to say that sun shines for everyone, and everyone on earth is entitled to justice, freedom, humanity and compassion. But that is what Abraham believed. And so he opened his home and his heart to everyone.

But there is something else I should like to note about this Biblical narrative. The Hebrew expressions are fascinating to analyze, because for example we are told that Abraham lifted his eyes and felt, behold he saw these three strangers standing over him, which is often explained to mean that he saw these three strangers sort of towering over him as they approached. Well as we read further, we learn he invited them to stop, begged them to take part of his hospitality. And he acted in their behalf.

First he said that he would bathe their feet. Anyone who has ever walked on the on a hot summer's day, knows the sand can burn. But that is nothing compared to walking on the desert sands. I speak from personal experience, and want you to know that if you ever have the opportunity to walk in the Negev, wear more than just ordinary sandals, because your feet will suffer. And the greatest thing is to be able to bathe them and draw off the intense discomfort.

But note something else, Abraham says to these people, rest and take a little snack. But he and his wife go ahead and prepare a sumptuous meal. You see many people talk of the great things they will do for you, but usually end up doing nothing. Father Abraham belonged to that group of people who knew how to answer when you say put your money where your mouth is. He promised them little, but he did much. This is in line with the Hebrew teaching

"Emor veat veaseh harbeh,"
"Speak little but do much." (Ethics of the Fathers 1:15)

And so here was Father Abraham feeding these strangers magnificently now.

Of course, our pupils often guess when we read the story to them to yell these strangers must have been angels. And they were. The Midrash tells us: one came to heal Abraham who was recovering from surgery. The second had a mission to tell Abraham that he was going to get his greatest wish, a child would be born who would follow the beautiful teachings and convictions of his parents. And the third angel had a tremendous obligation. He had been ordered above to destroy the cities of Sodom and Gomorrah, because they were full of corruption, iniquity, sins, oppression and immorality.

And that angel told Abraham his mission, because just as Abraham was kind to others especially strangers who were hungry, thirsty, lonely, ill or even lost, these cities of Sodom and Gomorrah were just the opposite. They oppressed the poor and the weak, they took advantage of the stranger, they tortured him and what is more were very critical of his ideas or practices. In fact there is a story about these people that you may have heard. They had a bed reserved for strangers. When people unknowingly visited the city, they assigned them to this bed, but if he was tall, they gave him a smaller bed and then cut his feet off to make him fit. And if he was short, they gave him a big bed and stretched him on the wrack until he fit the bed and of course he would die. Hitler and all dictators would do the same thing. Hitler called this *gleichshathlung,* conformity. Either you do everything my way or you die. And poor Abraham, the symbol of kindness felt bad indeed. But as we read the Bible, after he had bestowed upon these strangers his hospitality, the Bible notes how he served them:

"Vehoo ohmaid aleyhem,"
"And he stood over them" (Gen. 18:8)

Have you noticed when Abraham first saw these strangers they were standing over him. But when he fed them it notes that he stood over them and this Rabbi makes a very astute observation. A man rises even above the stature of angels, when he is engaged in serving humanity, in caring for others, in being sensitive to their needs. That is what we want to learn from this Biblical portion. People are often busy to define religion for us. They tell us about the cathedrals, the temples, and the houses of worship they attend. Sometimes they tell us about eating gefilte fish on Friday nights, chalah on festivals and matzot on Passover. And that is important, because those rituals cement us together in our faith. They remind us of our historical background. But in Judaism is not the first essence of religion when we act hospitably to those who need our help? When we understand that everyone must be free, protected and live undisturbed, then we can show that we are true sons of Abraham. For just as the sun shines on all of us, we must be sensitive to those who are lonely, ill and needy. We must be grateful to those who enrich our lives, whether it is our self-sacrificing parents, our teachers, our neighbors and everyone else in society who helps us achieve progress. When we combine our ritual loyalty in Judaism, when we keep Sabbath and festivals, and combine them with the great teachings of our faith, the instructions of Abraham, then like the sun, we will spread warmth and light to all Gods creatures.

HOSPITALITY TO GOD AND MAN

Those of us who follow the weekly Torah reading carefully, may be aware that the Sabbath in which this Torah portion is read has often been referred to as the *Shabbat* of *Hachnasat Orchim*, the Sabbath of hospitality. That arises from the narrative, wherein we learn that Abraham, an old man who had just sustained the difficulty of undergoing a circumcision, sat at the entrance to his tent, hoping that some travelers might pass to whom he could extend his hospitality. This, at the noon day heat, evoked God's compassion as he dispatched three celestial messengers in the guise of human beings, to pass the Patriarch's tent and thereby satisfy his desires.

In addition, we learn that God visited Abraham, to inquire of his well being, from which we have learned the great *mitzvah* of *Bikur Cholim*, visiting the ill. Obviously, Abraham was stirred by this privilege, and yet the Rabbis looking at the scriptural verse, elucidate another great teaching. Abraham, in the midst of the conversation with the creator, lifted his eyes and when seeing the strangers, ran to meet them, saying "my Lord, if I have found favor in your eyes, do not go away from your servant." In the Talmud (Shabbat 127a), Rabbi Yehuda quotes Rav to imply that unlike most of us who imagine that this plea was made to the apparent leader of the three men, it really was made to God. Thus, we are told, *"Gedolah hachnosat orchim mikabalat pnei hashchinah,"* "Extending hospitality is a greater *mitzvah* than welcoming the presence of God.

But this very statement evokes many questions. One might ask, does this not tend to denigrate or minimize the honor due to the Sacred Presence? The answer however is that this merely falls within the great teachings of our faith, namely, the constant recognition of the two categories of relationships, *beyn adam leMakom,* the relations that man entertains toward God, *ubeyn adam lechavero,* the relations that man entertains towards his fellowman. The latter in terms of hospitality is emphasized in the case of Abraham.

The tractates (Succot 25a and Baba Kama 56b) tell us that when one is engaged in the performance of a *mitzvah*, he is freed from the obligation of performing another *mitzvah*. If this is so, how could Abraham indulge in this conduct? After all, he was already engaged in one *mitzvah*, namely welcoming the Divine Presence. Perhaps it was indicated that the Talmud meant to imply that where one is faced with the opportunity of performing two *mitzvot*, one should fulfill the greater and more significant one. And if such were the case, it would appear that the welcome extended to the passing travelers is regarded as evidence that the latter is the greater deed.

The Talmud discussing this performance of one religious obligation as an act of freeing one from another obligation makes reference to one sitting in his Succah. Commenting upon the verse in the *Shema,* "when thou sittest in thy house, and when thou walkest by the way," that when a man walks for his own purpose, he is bound by the obligation of performing a *mitzvah*, however, if he is engaged upon a religious errand, he is free. The Rashba thereupon asks a logical question, why the need for these verses from the Torah? It is obvious that a Jew who sits in the Succah to fulfill that *mitzvah* can not respond to the request that he fulfill another mitzvah outside the area of the Succah.

It is obvious that one can not fulfill two *mitzvot* simultaneously, if each is set for another direction. What is implied by the quotation is that there is no such thing as smaller or greater *mitzvah*. In this circumstance whether the *mitzvah* one performs is tremendous or simple, one need not abandon one obligation in order to perform another.

Since this is so, why did Abraham depart from one precept, that of exercising hospitality toward the Lord, in order to fulfill another precept, that of exercising hospitality to human beings? The answer is found in the comment of the Shaagat Aryeh.

The Shaagat Aryeh reminds us that we learn in the Book of Numbers that a person who is hired by the day and engaged to watch the red heifer that it not be set to the yoke, he is naturally not paid before the Sabbath, and therefore he is a *shomer chinum*, a bailiff without pay. When one guards a loss which has been found,

Rabbah says that such a person is also a free guardian since he is not paid. Rabbi Joseph however, disagrees and contends that the latter is a paid bailiff. What is the pay he receives, since he receives no financial reward for his service on the Shabbat? Well answers the Sage, he is the recipient of some benefit. Rabbi Joseph contends that since the bailiff is engaged in one *mitzvah*, he is freed from the obligation of performing another *mitzvah*. Should an unfortunate person request bread, he may refuse, being that he is already engaged in another precept.

What is clarified by the Shaagat in his commentary is the following: we must always remember that there are two types of *mitzvot*, those *beyn adam leMakom,* between man and God, and those *beyn adam lechavaro,* between man and his fellow man. Though it is true that the guardian of the heifery is truly not being paid on the Sabbath and that it is a *mitzvah*, it is a *mitzvah* of the category *beyn adam leMakom,* between man and God. But the other man who is guarding the lost and now found object is actually filling a *mitzvah beyn adam lechavaro*, between man and his fellowman. Since he is fulfilling a *mitzvah* between man and his fellowman, he need not perform the same kind of *mitzvah* (in this case one of social significance by feeding another person who passes by requesting bread.) But what happens when a man is engaged in and of a precept between man and God? Does that mean that he is freed from social and moral *mitzvot*?

Abraham was aware of these questions. He knew that he was fulfilling a *mitzvah* by welcoming the Lord's Presence, but that was only one kind of a *mitzvah*. Hence he knew he could turn about and perform the other *mitzvah*, namely that of welcoming the three men. Nowadays, too many of us are confused about the *mitzvot*. Some imagine they are religious enough in their attendance at Synagogue or in their performance of *kashrut*, keeping kosher that they may forget social obligations. Others yell, at heart we are honest, kind and charitable, but they are completely oblivious of God and their duties towards him.

The *Shema* wishes us to perform *mitzvot* with the whole heart. The sages realized that this meant each *mitzvah* in its category must be performed wholeheartedly. One heart, a good heart, must do two *mitzvot*. Father Abraham's piety consisted of both *mitzvot*.

It should be clear that this is an instance of traditional teachings, where we learn that our piety, our religiosity, our respect for and obedience to God is best expressed by our relationships toward each other, especially by the concern we manifest towards our fellow human beings.

Americans have prided themselves on the hospitality the United States has demonstrated at various stages of history. For decades, the country was open to millions of immigrants who came here, escaping religious, political, social discrimination and oppression. So many of our parents and grandparents were enabled to enter this blessed country because of that policy. It is also true that this magnificent hospitality was changed, when immigration laws were passed, which provided quotas for countries from which the immigrants came. These laws sustained a certain subtle form of anti-Semitism, racism, and xenophobia, an ancient Greek term indicating dislike for the stranger. They were racist in their acceptance of Nordic superiority. That is, larger quotas were afforded countries like England, Germany, and the Scandinavians, as opposed to the East Europeans, Italians and other Mediterranean peoples. Later, the United States went a step further by refusing admission of Jewish refugees fleeing from Nazi Germany to its land. It is a shame and a stain upon the United States that cannot be so easily removed.

Today, America demonstrates a better approach of hospitality, by welcoming so many Russian immigrants and a substantial amount of Asiatic, Africans and others who may through their services and capacities, fill a need for a labor supply required by our land.

We Jews particularly cannot help but be undermined by any decisions to limit immigration, because we have been persecuted not only in Nazi Germany, but also elsewhere throughout the world. Jews have been prisoners, and hostages subject to the whim, capriciousness, brutality and cruelty that has been evoked by inhumanity, religious hatred and persecution. To those who are not blinded by irrationalism, wild prejudice and misguided bigotry, *Hachnasot Orchim*, or the precept of extending sympathy, compassion, sensitivity to the stranger, and fellowship which our very being requires, is an ingredient society lacks and needs so badly.

When it comes to hospitality, we must all learn from Father Abraham. A commentary has it that *kemo shekodem shehichnis Avraham et haorchim haelu lebayto,* before he invited the strangers to his home, *badak otam im hem cholkin kavod zeh lezeh,* he first ascertained whether they extended respect one to the other. That is the first basis for hospitality. No threats, no placing others in danger, no looting, plundering, torturing, terrorizing, or intimidating. But extending one to the other respect. We must learn from Father Avraham.

On Yom Kippur, at final judgment, when man stands before the *beth din shel ma'alah*, the heavenly court, what is it that the Heavenly Tribunal first asks of us, "*nesata venetatah be'emunah?*" Have you dealt with other people honorably, faithfully, with integrity and justice? That is the hospitality that the world needs and that is the hospitality that alone can bring peace to us all.

LET NO ONE ABANDON HOPE

If there is one thing that you and I should learn from our heritage and our past, it is never to abandon hope and never to yield to despair. Over the portals of hell, according to the Italian poet, Dante, were inscribed the words, *esciate ogni esperanza voi chyntrata*, abandon all hope you who enter. In our faith, we have been taught to avoid this kind of despair.

> **"*Al titya'aish min haporahnoot*,"**
> **"Never abandon belief in retribution."**
> **(Ethics of the Fathers 1:7)**

Do not imagine that just because evil seems to hold sway at one moment, it will last forever. One of the commentaries refers to the Bertinoro, namely that one should not say, it is ridiculous for me to uphold an ethical standard. Look at the evil man who despite his wickedness is successful in all his endeavors. Don't abandon belief in eventual justice because tomorrow conditions may change very radically for this person.

The same commentary refers to the *Yalkut Shimoni,* the commentary of Rabbi Shimon Ashkenazi Hadarashan of Frankfurt, on Jeremiah (chapter 34.) In this chapter we learn how the advance of Nebuchadnezzar aroused people to the national crisis they faced, and how it also aroused the conscience of the people. And so Jeremiah the prophet appeared before Zedekiah the King of Judah and assured him that he would not be killed or die in battle, but that he would pass away because of natural causes. And Jeremiah inspired the King to call upon the people to free their Jewish slaves. These slaves were Jews who had been ruined by heavy taxation and by wars and to escape starvation they sold themselves and their families into slavery. But when Nebuchadnezzar had to withdraw from his attacks temporarily, because he heard that an Egyptian army was advancing against him, the wealthy Jews and nobles once again forced their countrymen to return to slavery. It was then that Jeremiah warned them that those guilty of the betrayal would be punished and they would be killed by their enemies and would not even merit a decent burial.

The *Yalkut Shimoni* reminds us that there are two types of *Yeush*, despair and abandonment. One emerges during prosperity and the other during adversity. Some who become rich or live very well, think that conditions will never change for them and the poor and downtrodden and suffering believe that conditions will never change for them. So the Sages in telling us that we should not abandon belief in God's justice are reminding us that all conditions are subject to change.

And Baruch Halevi Epstein the brilliant commentator reminds us that in the portion of *Vayetze*:

> ***"Vayachalom vehenai sulam mutzav artzah verosho***
> ***mageah hashamayemah,"***
> **"Jacob our forefather dreams of a ladder arising from**
> **the ground and reaching unto the heavens."**
> **(Gen. 28:12)**

And other Sages remind us that the Hebrew word for ladder, *sulam*, in *gematria* numerology spells out *mammon*, money, *oni*, poverty. So this is a *merumez*, intimate, that both prosperity and adversity are not eternal. But they are *olim veyordim*, they ascend and descend like the ladder, they should never abandon any hope.

The Talmud (Berachot 10a) reminds us that *Cheskiyahu said*: "Even when a sharp sword is lying on a person's neck, one should not abandon prayer." And thus we are also reminded in Jewish Halacha. We have been taught that in sustaining acts of theft and loss, if a person loses hope in ever obtaining the return of his possessions, then they are required to be claimed by the thief who stole them. To this one may raise the question, isn't it enough that his possessions were first stolen, now he is punished by having the thief acquire a claim to his possessions? Why is the victim guilty? The response given is, the victim is punished and penalized because he abandoned all hope. It's forbidden for us to lose all hope with any difficult trouble or injury. This tremendous sense of optimism, or faith or unswerving refusals to withdraw from divine mercy is apparent in this portion of the Torah.

Consider that fascinating narrative which presents us with the deep, reeling heart of Abraham, who stands before God and is told that Providence is disgusted with the evil which predominates the society of Sodom and Gomorrah and therefore God has decided to wipe out the wicked cities. And Abraham as we know, pleads their case before God, hoping to arouse divine mercy by saying that the eternal judge would not punish the righteous together with the bad and evil. And God replied to Abraham's plea. If there were fifty people who were righteous *bitoch ha'ir*, in the midst of the city, (Gen. 18:24) he would save the community. And despite all of Abraham's bargaining and pleading, the Lord sentenced these terrible cities of iniquity to be destroyed.

> ### *"Vayashkaim Avraham baboker el hamakom asher amad sham el penai Hashem,"*
> ### "And Abraham got up early in the morning to the place where he stood before the Lord." (Gen: 19:27)

Consider what the Torah tells us. Most of the time we read this verse to mean that the good hearted Abraham arose early, to look with pain and frustration upon the destruction of the cities. But elsewhere there is another interpretation; although the previous day Abraham pleaded in behalf of Sodom and Gomorrah, he refused in spite of this, tells us the Sforno, to give up hope in saving the communities. He continued to pray in their behalf the entire night. He refused to yield hope even at such a time and only when he arose early in the morning and looked at the communities and he saw the smoke of the land going up as the smoke of a furnace did he concede that God had indeed passed judgement and there was no more hope of changing the situation. Only then did he stop praying.

You see Abraham our Father, who in many ways set the pattern for his seed after him to follow, refused to abandon hope. Now in our day, we often hear expressions like "absolute power corrupts absolutely." And "all politicians are corrupt." Only philosophers who are impractical and theoretical talk about power and politics as some great discipline. But you and I know the truth. No matter who is in power, corruption rules, everybody takes care of himself and the people suffer. But consider the incident with Abraham and God discussing ways to save society. And God says if I would find fifty righteous people *bitoch ha'ir* in the midst of the city, *Tzaddickim* are not those righteous people who sit in Synagogue and pray, or sit in *the Beth Hamidrash* and study Torah. But when people are *bitoch ha'ir*, when they are involved in the midst of the city, working, striving, creating and producing, when they are engaged in the normal give and take relationship with other human beings, engaged in the *inyanei hatzibur*, the issues of the community, then they should be righteous.

If you are concerned with the quality of life, with the future of life, with the freedom and justice of people all over the world, if you will be righteous and if you will be honest, if you will publicly and privately declare that you as citizens are ready to stand up and fight, then there is great hope indeed for the beautiful future of the world. So today let us not *hityaesh min harachamim*, Let no one abandon hope. Because we believe that Providence has promised us a great destiny and magnificent future, because we are the people who have introduced the Messianic ideal to mankind, and because we are a people who have been strengthened by hope to withstand all kinds of pressures and plans. Let us now stand up in that faith and seek to inspire all mankind. Never to yield hope, but to strive and labor, to be honorable and righteous in every facet of our lives, then we may yet achieve the victory of the righteous soon and forevermore.

LONELINESS

Dr. Isaac Asimov was a unique figure, who was erudite in various fields, particularly, in astronomy and other natural sciences. He was also the author of almost four hundred books. Dr. Asimov once declared that he wrote so profusely, because he wanted to be remembered after his demise. I was very impressed by that statement and it compelled me to think about the great masses that are unable to articulate thoughts and opinions in print. "Are we doomed to be forgotten?" That query is conducive to a lengthy discussion, and it is obvious that it represents a complex of anxieties, insecurities, fears about a future in which we would all be very restricted. What do most of us anticipate with fear? Concerns about health, illness that would sap our physical vigor, an ever-increasing lack of value in society, a fear that we would be cast aside, shunted, and totally ignored, a future in which we would be alone. If one were to visit a nursing home or a hospital and observe a patient lying all alone, never being visited, for all practical purposes this person is already buried.

How different from this is the contemporary world. A man works his entire lifetime, struggling to support his wife and children. He sacrifices his very existence for the sake of progeny, denying himself pleasures and even necessities to enable their educational achievements and then, as is so often the case, having attained their own status and personal objectives, parents are dismissed and deeper relationships severed. We remain alone. Isolated like a stone. Alone, alone, that is the word, which best describes the fears and expressions of pessimism, loneliness, isolation, and estrangement, being ignored. That, said one, is the greatest curse of human life. After all, have we not, especially as children, often argued about the appearance of reality or its actuality?

If a tree falls in a forest, and no one is around to hear it , does it make a sound? No, if you are not there to hear it. What is more, what we call sound, is after all the sound waves absorbed by the organic receptacle, that we call the ear. Magnificent, regal, may be the appropriate description of that tree, but if unseen or unheard, what does its existence mean to us? Nothing. What good is a real masterpiece of art, if none ever see it? Why speak about creative impulses if the product will never meet the eye or ear of another human being? Loneliness spells death.

Recall the story of the Rip Van Winkle of the Talmud, Honi Hama'agal. Having fallen into a magical sleep, he returned home, only to find his little girl, grown up and married. Local scholars were quoting his opinions with respect and awe, and everyone regarded him with honor. And yet, when his daughter found him sitting at the curb weeping, and she sought to comfort him, his plaintive words may very well resound in everyone's heart, *chevruta or mettuta* give me companions or give me death.

Even Adam, privileged as no other, to live in paradise, was informed by none other than his creator:

"*Lo tov hehyot ha'adam levado*,"
"It is not good that the human being should be alone."
(Gen. 2:18)

That is true, not only for the sake of procreation, for the ability to rear families, for the need to find physical release in sexual expression but to escape that spiritual shrinkage which results from the isolated existence. How appropriate is the comment, a person who is so lonely is no longer a person.

Some of us remember studies like "The Lonely Crowd," a study of the changing American Character, and who of us, as we get older, has not at one time or another felt lonely in the midst of many people? Numbers by themselves are no guarantee against loneliness. Nor is living in what we consider progressive, advanced societies.

Colin Turnbull a world known anthropologist who studied human cultures of primitive societies on various continents, makes comparisons with our treatment of each other and that of the "backward" groups. We do not emerge with flying colors. In the various stages of human development, they have some natural compassion, delicate understanding and deeper respect for each other than we display. Turnbull discusses our exclusion of the elderly from society. His words penetrate deeply and painfully, as he considers the way in which our moderns pack father and mother off, as easily as they once packed us off to school.

How biting are his words; a weekly visit with some flowers or an occasional phone call is not much of a return for the investment they have made. And why is this so? Because we are unlike those primitive societies that regard the elders as individuals who are still an asset rather than a liability. What is more, all societies and all cultures must manifest the same pattern: we are born, we grow, we mature, we grow old, and one day we shall be called away, but in every stage, the beauty, majesty, inspiration of reaching out and embracing everyone in dignity exists. We live in a world where everyone speaks about the problems of homelessness, the needs of the impoverished, the necessity to combat crime and the drug epidemic, and, of course, everyone engages in disputes, polemics and most earnest desires to solve these terrible problems.

And we demand that more money be set aside for that purpose. It is true that money is required for dignity everyone deserves. The immortal Jewish leader, Ze'ev Jabotinsky, considering the Jewish heritage of the ages, declared that society must provide for everybody the basic "mems," the letter in the Hebrew alphabet that begins the words *ma'achal,* food, *malbush,* clothing, *malon,* shelter, *marpeh,* health care and *michanach*, education. The inner person, the dignity of man, the attempt to evoke his potential ability must never be forgotten. Hence a person cannot be left alone. The Psalm declares:

"Ashrei maskil el dal,"
**"Happy is the person who cares wisely for the sick or
the poor." (Psalms 41:2)**

The verse does not say, blessed is the person who gives to the poor, but rather who deals wisely with an enfeebled person. The frailty may come from illness, or from poverty, but whatever reason, help that person but always strengthen his dignity.

The Talmud recalls how Hillel helped a poor man who had previously enjoyed wealth. The sage performed this *mitzvah* by helping the man live in a life style that did not deprive him of his dignity. *Chaviv ha'adam shenivrah betzelem,* beloved is man who is created in the Divine image. If you belittle one man, you belittle all men and invariably belittle yourself. Perhaps that is what the Rabbis had in mind, when they claimed that *mah shehaba'al habayit noten leani, ha'ani noten leba'al habyit,* what the head of the house gives the poor man, the poor man gives to the head of the house. The poor is given charity and that helps him, but he gives more to the philanthropist who thereby has an opportunity to demonstrate that he is a real person, who is sensitive to the dignity of the other.

Abraham learned this in the Torah lesson of *Vayera.* He learns that God visits the ill to assure him, to encourage him and to help him attain his dignity. Abraham demonstrates that he has learned this lesson. Having sheltered, fed, rested, and added to their comfort:

"*VeAvraham holech emam leshalcham,*"
"Abraham went with them to send them on their way."
(Gen. 18:16)

To which the Rabbis comment, *lemsot lahem livayah,* to provide them with accompaniment.

You see, when we walk with our friends to the door, when we accompany them to the elevator, when we even walk outside for two steps with them, what we are doing is implying a statement, "Look dear friends, I am concerned about you. You mean much to me. You honor me by being my guest." A Jew should not ignore people. No one should be isolated from human concern and care. No one should feel so lonely, so isolated, and so estranged that he loses the perspective, dignity and the insight of a human being. That is what the Torah is telling us when it speaks about the *egla arufah.*

The Bible reminds us that when a stranger was found lying dead on the road and none knew what had happened to him, the distance was measured from that spot to the neighboring communities, and the nearest community must send its judges and leader to swear that they did not shed this man's blood. The Talmud is apparently shocked. What? Does anyone believe that the leaders, the judges would murder this unknown man? The answer is rich in its insight. No, of course not, but they must swear that they did not know that this man was alone that they did not provide him with human escort. That they did not refuse to feed or as court the stranger. Is this strange asks the commentary. A formal escort requires that we take a few steps with a person. We all know today that a very polite host escorts his departing guest to the door. Why then should the leaders of a community have to speak of providing an escort for a stranger who was found dead a long distance from their town or village?

Rabbi Simcha Zissel, the Chassidic leader answered this query by reminding us that when a stranger is not welcomed properly and warmly, he feels inferior. He loses some of his courage when he is attacked by a difficulty whether that difficulty is actually a thief, murderer, some business problem, social concern or any worry which robs him of his peace of mind. His happiness is actually robbed from him. He feels all alone deprived of sympathetic understanding, he hasn't the stamina with which to defend himself, and he succumbs whether from the murderer's bullet or the terrible pressure of life's difficulty. It is not only necessary that we feed a stranger, it is not only a requirement that we welcome our fellow man into our midst, that we help him, but we must also infuse him with faith, courage, and fortitude. We must show him by our respect, the sincerity and the warm heartedness of our welcome that he is not alone.

A person surrounded by friends has immediately a tremendous protection against external dangers. Surrounded by friends we are protected against internal dangers, the pressures of loneliness, of depression, of loss of dignity, of feeling that we are no longer valuable, no longer wanted or needed. Whether they were angels or just ordinary people, Abraham escorted them. Abraham taught us, his children, that we must not ignore each other, but must ever be ready to reach out to each other. May we never forget that lesson.

THE COMPANY ONE KEEPS

"And he dwelt in the plains of Mamre." On this verse we can find a splendid charge for the youth of today. In the Midrash we find that the Rabbis engage in a discussion regarding the word Mamre. Rabbi Yehuda was of the opinion that the word referred to a specific locality, but Rabbi Nechemiah insisted that this was really the name of a person. Mamre procured that name according to other authorities because he spoke firmly unto his friend Abraham. A tradition has it that when God commanded Abraham to circumcise himself, he visited three friends from whom he sought counsel. These friends, the Rabbi deduced from reading the verse carefully were Eshkol, Awner and Mamre.

Awner answered: you are already advanced in age and it does not seem proper that you should undergo a rite that will cause so much pain. Eshkol counseled, your undergoing this ritual will get you bad publicity. Your enemies will know that you are in a weakened condition and will attack you. Mamre however spoke firmly to him: "Your God is He who has rescued you from fire, from the onslaught of kings and from famine and now when He tells you to undergo this ritual will you not obey Him?" When God heard these words He exclaimed: "you have given him the advice to obey me. I swear that I shall appear to him, not in the palaces of Awner or Eshkol, but in your residence," as it is written:

"*Vayara alav Hashem beaylonee Mamre*,"
"And God appeared to him in the terebinths of
Mamre." (Gen. 18:1)

There are many factors that influence our development when we are young, and among the most significant are the home and the school. We often seek to emulate the conduct of our parents and to fulfill in our lives the ideals we have been taught in school. Through the moral goals and standards set at home, and through the knowledge and skill we acquire in school, we set up a reserve of technical abilities and spiritual motivations that carry us throughout life. However, both of these great factors are themselves influenced by another important element, commonly called the street, the social atmosphere outside of home and school, our friends and companions in life. The Talmud reminds us, that he who clings to cleanliness is clean while he attaches himself to the unclean, becomes unclean. Recognize this sentiment in the old adage: "Birds of a feather flock together." Each of us is subject to human frailty of listening to friendly counsel without first examining that counsel thoroughly. My friend means well we may say and hence we should follow his dictates. Those who are prone to criticize you can easily use this to say that either you are unworldly and removed from realities or you just pretend to have religious feelings etc. this interest in your welfare may be honest and sincere but it is not the best etc.

You cannot expect God's spirit to rest upon you, you cannot expect to achieve heights if you hang around Anwer and Eshkol, around those friends who seek to avoid present exertions without realizing that this course will mean future deprivation. On the other hand, present sacrifices that may mean inconvenience and disappointments today often lead to the happiness and rejoicing of tomorrow.

The friends which we must seek, whose influences must count should be those who are like Mamre, those who seek the truth and also seek to make us look at the truth. Sometimes these friends must speak firmly with us. They love us, but do not wish to paint a false picture. They do not seek to advise us to follow the course of least resistance, they appreciate the sacrifices that we must take, but they speak the truth and urge us to follow the truth. Living with such friends means that we shall reach the heights, we can achieve divine inspiration, an attainment impossible if we listen to and live among the Awners and Eshkols.

Acquire a good friend, for they mean much and when we have them, let us appreciate them properly and seek their companionship and company, in that life there lies blessing and happiness. Seek friends who will not lead you away from the ideals of your parents, who will not mock the heritage of Torah, who teach you to be grateful, even if it costs sacrifices. Mamre may hurt but can you refuse God who has been so good to you. The good friend teaches us gratitude. *Kol hamechavair letahor tahor, kol hamechavair letahmay, tahmay*, A man traveling with a clean crowd is clean, however, one can not expect an associate of gangsters to be a law-abiding citizen.

BROTHERHOOD

"*Veharebah et zaracha kichochevai hashamayim
vechachol asher al sefat hayam,*"
**"I will multiply thy seed as the stars of the heaven, and
as the sand which is upon the sea shore." (Gen. 22:17)**

The Torah portion of *Vayera* speaks of the future of the Jewish people. The Midrash makes the following comment: where
Jews are compared to the sand or dust of the earth, we have *zechut*,
merit and shall reap blessing. But where we stand like the stars of
the heavens, we have no *zechut*, and apparently God is displeased
with us.

It is rather an interesting point upon which to dwell. It is a
peculiar comment because the earth is usually regarded as a sign
of *hachnaah*, humility, while stars are associated with heights,
beauty, prominence and being a celebrity. And yet to be told that
this signifies a lack of *zechut* is truly a strange observation.

It can be understood however if we consider the ancient teaching that every *mitzvah* has a counterpart in the human body. You
probably recall the number of *mitzvot asey* and *lo ta'aseh*, commandments that require an action and those that require a forbidden action. One is equivalent to the days of the solar year and the
other to the most important organs of the body or structural design
as was recognized in the anatomy of that times.

Without being physicians we do know that should a person
be deprived the normal use of a particular appendage of the body,
he can still function and be considered a component part of living
in society. He may be handicapped by defective hearing or defective eyesight, or crippled by the loss of an arm or leg. There is one
organ however which removed, irreversibly damaged, or should it

cease to function, results in the death of the individual, namely the heart. True other organs are important, but as handicapped people are still very much alive, without a heart the human dies.

So too is it with *mitzvot*. It is possible that when a *mitzvah* is being despised, ignored or even violated we can say the person involved is a spiritual cripple but still alive. There is one *mitzvah* however, which is the heart of Jewry. Without it, it is like the stopping of the heart. That is the sense of *achdut*, unity. The realization that the Jewish people are one and responsible for one another, *arevim zeh bizeh*, rightly does the tradition say. No utensil brings blessing, as does peace among the nation, the great sign of unity the Rabbis say. Take a large basket and place it full of fruits. If the basket is whole, fine. If there are great gaps and holes in the basket, the fruits will fall through and disappear. The Etz Chayim pointed out, fellow Jews if you do all the *mitzvot,* that is keep the *mitzvot* of *Shabbat, Yom Tov, teffilin, kashruth,* etc., it would be wonderful, but if you have no unity, if you are not for each other, then you die Jewishly.

It is comparable to an accident in the street, a car victim. People run over and look at the fallen man. They examine his hands, his feet, if his body is whole or whether his abdomen is bruised. But what about the heart?

All *mitzvot* are good, but if there is no unity then we are dead, because that is the heart of Torah.

"Veahavata,"
"And you will love." (Levit. 19:18,34)

This is a matter of heart; to love, to be concerned and to help is indication of unity and the feeling of oneness among people. If you have arguments, fighting, bickering and you permit hatred to grow then you have no peace. If there is *machlokes*, argument, the *mitzvot* of *shabbat, kashrut, yom tov, tefillin*, they are all worthless.

The earth consists of dust particles, grains of soil. When watered well, the grains are united, they stick together, the fertility increases, the seeds take root, fruits, cereals, vegetables grow and life is sustained. If the particles are not united, if the earth is parched and dry, there is no unity of particle and nothing grows.

Stars are both beautiful and impressive. They reflect light, which gladdens the eye, and have fascinated us for millennia of centuries. However, they are separated from each other. Between one and the other there are vast distances of darkness. A Zohar makes the observation that there are probably so many stars that their reflected light if amassed together would outshine the sun. But why is it that the sun shines at day and the stars at night? Because the sun is a focused point of heat, it shines and warms, but the stars are scattered over such distances that between one and the other are vast distances of darkness.

Thus too we have homes in which Jewish *mitzvot* are upheld, *Shabbat* and *Yom Tov* are followed, *kashruth*, keeping kosher, *tefillah*, prayer, *mikvah*, ritual bath and *taharat mishpachah*, family cleanliness. But between one home and another there is no love, concern, worry or unity, only vast stretches of darkness. That is what the *midrash* means, stars may prosper but they have no *zechut*. But like the land, like the sand or dust that is watered and unites every particle with every other particle, there is *zechut*. Like the soil, with unity and *zechut*, the people of Israel will produce seed and products that will always be fertile and always produce blessings.

RESPECT EVERY MAN

This Biblical lesson depicts a scene which has been popularized through narrative and art, namely wherein our forefather, the Patriarch Abraham confronts three Angels who visit him while he resides under the shelter of a friend at the oaks of Mamre.

The tale has been subject to much analysis by our commentators. Previously, Abraham had been engaged in an inspired communication with God who had apprised him of the *mitzvah* of circumcision, as well as bolstering his faith by announcing the birth of a son in the future. Now the Sacred came to visit Abraham, as he recuperated from the surgery of the *brit milah*, circumcision from which our sages derived the significant precept of *bikur cholim*, visiting the ill. Despite his obvious discomfort, the aged Patriarch sat in front of his tent, during the intense heat of the day, hoping to be afforded the opportunity to extend his hospitality to a passerby. Suddenly observing the appearance of three travelers he petitions God not to leave him and momentarily disrupts the dialogue between the Creator and himself, to display both enthusiasm and kindness in welcoming the strangers. Here again, we recall that the Rabbis discover an important lesson in interpersonal relations, namely that the welcoming of guests may be of greater moral value that receiving the Sacred Presence.

Whatever we may think about this academic study or clinical observations that are categorized under the disciplines of psychology, we are all cognizant that the influences of Freud, Jung, or Erikson having penetrated many facets of our daily appraisals of our fellow man. Judaism has always been aware of these inferences, and has therefore unlike other religious doctrines refused to define salvation only in terms as belief in God. Although it recognizes that the relationship between *adam leMakom*, between man and God are basic to our *Weltanschauung,* our philosophy of life. That same philosophy insists that we never forget the precept *beyn adam lechavaro*, the relationship which must exist between man and his fellow. This is again emphasized by the inferences of the current Biblical portion.

However, there is another projection of the interpersonal relationship that is implied by the scriptures, which surely merits both our consideration and application. A most attractive feature of this narrative is the manner in which Abraham responds. When the three passersby make their appearance, Abraham did not recognize these visitors. He was totally ignorant of their origins. He was unaware of their birthplace, he did not pay attention to their accent and knew nothing of their social status. He had no inkling of their destination or the business they were pursuing. They were strangers. Ordinary travelers subject to the heat of the day, the fiery sands, the inconveniences and lack of comfort which travelling in that part of the world entailed. There was no way in which he could determine their financial stature, but he rushed forward to greet them with a civility and a courtesy he would have extended to most distinguished guests. There is a complete lack of sophistication in either his words or approach. He does not wish to impress them with his own personal stature, nor does he need or seek their fawning subservience. Without fanfare or flourish, he indicates that he is concerned with their physical relaxation, and offered to provide a light snack, which turned out to be a magnificent meal.

Assuming as we do that Abraham was an outstanding personality, a chief leader who is recognized as such by many of his neighbors, what is it in his personality, in his emotional, spiritual, psychological and intellectual composition that compels him to act with such diplomacy; refined humility and *geschyiaic,* (taste), particularly towards people whom he does not know? Abraham is motivated by his religious convictions and an ethical philosophy which naturally, stems from his belief that there is only one creator and that we have been fashioned in the divine image. Because he is progenitor of our faith Judaism, it is not surprising that he would adhere to the ethical instructions imparted to us:

> *"Al tehee baz lechol adam veal tehee maphlig lechol davar sheain lechah adam sheain low sha'ah, veain lecha davar sheain low makom,"*
> **"Do not despise any man, and do not reject anything, for there is no man who does not have his hour, nor a thing which does not have its place."**
> **(Ethics of the Fathers 4:3)**

This would imply that in the cosmic scheme of all phenomenons, each of us has the potential to demonstrate our capacities at a most appropriate moment in time. Objects of inorganic makeup invariably exist only because somewhere, sometime, somehow, they too, may fulfill a function or respond to a need.

With this in mind, Abraham demonstrates a tremendous sensitivity in the realm of the interpersonal. He invited his visitors to partake of his food and shelter, but refers to himself as their servant. He avoids the guilt of embarrassing them and the responsibility of injuring their self-esteem. He does not desire to be regarded as a squire and host while they are relegated to an inferior status of beggars. Oh no. Abraham is sensitive to the fact that whenever one does extend charity or favors, there is always the possibility that the recipient will sustain some humiliation. What is just as bad is the tendency of the philanthropist to regard his gesture as evidence of a generous, superior personality. With an admirable alacrity, Abraham prevents the accumulation of such sentiments by bluntly telling his unknown guests, I am grateful to you for your graciousness in letting me serve you and attend unto your wants.

That he succeeded is obvious from their response. They too, understood that whatever be his material possessions in life, all these are from the Lord and so they do not flatter him, they do not kowtow to him. We do not read a multitude of platitudes and a *yasher koach* congratulatory, there is no display of *chanifah*, instead they accept his offer and reply as equals, "*Ken taaseh ka'asher dibartah*," "Very well, go ahead and do as you have said." (Gen. 18:5) What a vast difference this is displayed in scriptures between that scene and our own relationships. We are so accustomed to the distorted facial expressions, the artificial smiles, the forced compliments, the hypocritical accolades and the equally distasteful pretence of humility, all of which we pretend to rationalize as the display of good manners and proper breeding.

We may indeed take pride in the dignity and the true generosity of Father Abraham. Yet, there is much that begs our consideration in Abraham's gestures. After all, we do not encourage the picking up of hitchhikers, nor is our social climate conducive to inviting strangers into our home. Daily headlines shriek vulgar and obscene reports of the depravity to which we sink in perpetrating violence and unspeakable pain upon others. These compel us to consider Abraham carefully. He did not bother to ascertain from whence the strangers came, what constituted their *yichus*, ancestry, how stable was their financial status in the community and more, in what manner might they be of use to him. He extended his arms to them only because he understood, "don't despise any human being, for every person has his hour." Here is a stark reminder for even those who cling fanatically to some school of utilitarian thought, whereby everyone is appraised in accordance to what they may give us.

Abraham's Judaism, urges us to extend our hospitality to others and take cognizance of their needs, if for no other reason than everyone has his or her hour. Could we live, could we function, produce and create, were we to be deprived of human companionship? Can we deny that even the anti-social eccentric, the singular unattractive peculiar personality who, invariable ostensibly rubs us the wrong way, that these too may discover their hour and reveal capacities necessary to the humanity about them.

Do you know that there are many schizoid personalities who conduct the business of banking, author books, achieve scientific discoveries and manifest artistic capabilities? Psychiatric analysis indicates that these people regard their activities as the very essence of life, and although they know there are other people in the world they are actively divorced from any real life involvement with others. Yet these schizoids find their hour by running banks, writing books, discovering bacteria and painting pictures. After an analysis of personality classification of those who are prone to failure, it was discovered that crippled personalities redeemed themselves by helping others. All of us can easily recognize that isolated personality who speaks slowly and distinctly, because he fears an unguarded moment may lead to slips of the tongue which will betray the fact that he is not of a certain upper class nor born in a stately manor. Yet even such a person finds his or her hour and becomes a successful person.

Rabbi Joseph Soloveitchik discussing *met mitzvah,* burying of the dead, reminded his audience that the *Cohanim,* Jewish Priests are forbidden to be involved with the dead. But should no less an exalted personality than the High Priest himself on his way to prepare for the awesome and inspiring Yom Kippur obligation come across the corpse of an unknown person lying on highway or in the field, then he must lay aside his plans and occupy himself with the burying of the unknown dead. How can the needs of this unknown person interfere so radically with the significant responsibilities of the High Priest at such a time? The answer given by prominent scholars is simple. Perhaps this corpse belonged to a hobo, a tramp, a ne'er do well, a thoroughly unimportant person in his society. But dare you forget the inherent stature of a human being. Can you forget that this unknown was a mother's son, a child over whom she cooed, wept, prayed and hoped?

The Jewish National leader, Zev Jabotinsky said, *"Hadar, ivri gam beoni who sar, im eved im helech, notsatra ben melech, beketer David ne'etar,"* Remember the inherent dignity that you have, in the midst of poverty feel you are a prince, whether a tramp or servant, you are the descendants of Kings, crowned with the diadem of David. So, too, must we recognize the depth in every human being.

Tradition has it that the cakes that Abraham ordered Sarah to bake immediately for their guests were really unleavened matzoth. You may ask what possible reason would our forebears have to avoid *chametz*, the leavened products at that time? My answer is to quote the Shem Mishmuel who taught: every *chametz* is a symbolic form of falsehood, because the dough that rises is really not more than the original quantity. The yeast has only inflated it and thereby the onlooker may be deceived. He may think that there is more in the loaf though it only seems that way. And the Torah has enjoined us:

"Midevar sheker terchak,"
"Keep you far removed from falsehood." (Exodus 23:7)

There are other actions which the Rabbis considered wrong and urged that we keep far removed from them, but it is the Torah itself which cautions against *chametz* on Passover, because it symbolizes falsehood. Especially that falsehood which Pharaoh sought to impose upon us and the entire world before the Exodus, that people should be enslaved because they may be despised unless they are powerful. But Judaism declares, despise no man. Because every man has his hour and everyone needs everyone else.

What if you are privileged to have many capacities and skills? Would you really paint if there were none to scrutinize and admire your work? Would you really be a gifted writer if there were none to read your creations? Despise no man, because we are all so unique. Only recently have we learned that one of the things that is compelling about the study of the human brain is that its billion of nerve cells are practically all different, even as the fingerprints of every individual differs from those of all others. We are a unique species, always searching for meaning of our existence, and that means despise no man. Keep open the eyes in your head and the sight within your heart. Unfortunately we shut both our eyes and the perceptivity of the heart too. But Abraham looked at the strangers and he saw them in proper light. Look well at each other my friends, and despise no man because we each have our hour.

The Rabbis in ancient days really understood what the *mitzvot* were really all about. They said *"Lo nitnu hamitzvot ela letsaref bahen et habriyot,"* "The basic reason why these commandments were given to us is really for the purpose of refining the human personality." (Gen. Rabbah 44:1) When one fulfills a *mitzvah*, whether dealing with our relations towards God or towards our fellowman, invariably that *mitzvah* has as its purpose, making us better human beings, more sensitive, more compassionate and more understanding. Once we become that, then we see that in a world of misery and ignorance, a world of hostility and prejudice, a world of quarrels and foolish trivial barriers, we have our duty to use our influence to make the world a little bit better and a little more happy. Recognize that which is good in others. Deal with others by being honest, honorable, and dignified. Run after justice, decency, peace and knowledge, and realize that every person has his hour. Respect all men, and all men will respect you.

PERFECTION

We must admit that ours is a New World, new and unprecedented in many ways. Compare what has happened during the past century with the previous hundreds of years. We speak of the world-weary society in times of the Greek-Roman collapse. The 14th century, it is true showed a rapid disintegration throughout Western Europe made catastrophic by the effects of the Black Death. Yet between 1400 and 1900 the years were marked by unequally rapid recovery. The new world was colonized, the forces of nature were mastered, we formulated and developed a new scientific outlook, built methods for controlling natural forces, and if you will, a sheer animal vitality pervaded mankind and we had a tremendous increase in world population. Literature prospered with Shakespeare, Cervantes, and Rabelais: painting with Tintorettom & Breuahel, scientists and philosophers projected themselves in Kepler, Vesalius, Galileo, Spinoza, Kant, and Leibnitz to the giants of the 20th century.

But with all the advances that man has made, what happens if we make mistakes in our basic appraisal of good and evil at the very root of human existence. We may be ignorant of many tremendous mechanical discoveries or inventions yet to come, but the ability to know the difference between right and wrong, to understand that human conduct must be based on reason, habits and customs, must be grounded in morals. And ethics must make us sensitive to our fellowman.

Suddenly in our days, this world, which was supposed to be making progress thanks to the machine, technology and scientific rationalism, was suddenly plunged into darkness. With all our knowledge, skills and talents, we failed in our duty as citizens, workers and human beings to foster life, select higher forms of life, and project further goals for life's development. These in the long run must fit into such larger organic and cosmic purposes as we can discern and interpret. As a species man has a moral obligation to be intelligent, but he also has an intellect and spiritual obligation to further his own moral and esthetic development. Besides his physiological needs, he has emotional spiritual needs that are just as important.

Take the simplest need which all of us can understand, the need for food. This is a common need with all animals. But we all know that the need for food is not restricted to our digestive tract, but it awakens many activities and interests which involve the whole organism. To get food and make it fit for eating, man uses many means of trapping cultivating, preserving and preparing, which no other animal ever used. The original need for eating becomes expanded and transformed into a series of social acts, because when we eat alone, as long as we fill our own bellies, we munch our food and would be satisfied with its nourishment. But what happens when we become aware of the fact that other human beings want to eat, suffer pangs of hunger, must obtain food. If we are concerned with the greedy fact that we must preserve our own lives, we continue to eat the food as we find it. But once we respond to the needs of others, there grows the social characteristic called hospitality. There develops the friendly relationship we call society. There enters the religious ritual in which we thank the Supreme Power we recognize for the food we have and the good we can share with others.

The value of food to man may have arisen in his physiological structure, but it does not remain here, because man is more than body and digestive apparatus. Just as we know today from scientific observation that the offering of food to an infant without friendly interaction or love may cause the infant to reject the food or fail to be nourished properly by it, even though the dieticians will tell us that the diet is adequate.

Life, therefore in not only the physical or physiological impact we see, but the needs, interests, feelings, purposes and goals which transforms us into true human beings.

Baruch Spinoza in his *The Ethics* dismissed the notion of cosmic purpose by saying that "Nature has no fixed end in view and final causes are merely fabrications of men." This may have sounded profound in times when the theologists were trying to deduce all forms of existence from the presumed nature of God. But even those who thought that Darwin theories of revolution and natural election bolstered the idea of no purpose do not realize the immense body of evidence in favor of purpose that had been required by scientists. Even Lawrence T. Henderson, one of the strictest and most meticulous of biochemists has demonstrated that the very number of chemical elements with their specific properties on this planet indicates purpose in terms of eventual life.

In the scheme of purpose, the Jew finds that his greatest goal must not be restricted to the development of the technical to which he has made and is still making a tremendous contribution, but that his specific contribution has been and must continue to be primarily to the development of that social-emotional intellectual response to other human beings.

"Vayara alav Hashem beaylonee Mamre,"
"And God appeared to Abraham in the terebinths of Mamre." (Gen. 18:1)

Wherever, a commentary points out, the tradition refers to an appearance or revelation of God to man, it is to emphasize a specific purpose or objective, to fulfill a command or to perform a function. This is usually followed by the statement and "He spoke," God said. Thus we must ask that, if Divine revelation, the manifestation of God, does not just appear for itself, what then is the purpose of God appearing to Abraham? He appears but says nothing, commands nothing and tells Abraham nothing. Why and what was the purpose for this revelation? The Sages felt this weakness and difficulty and in the classic commentaries tried to interpret it. Rashi for example says, "God appeared to Abraham because he wanted to fulfill the precept of *Bikur Cholim*, visiting the ill." The Rashbam says that the verse does not really mean God appeared, but that his instruments, angels visited Abraham. The Seforno claims that the verse refers to circumcision, since through this practice Abraham made a treaty with God and thereby the sanctity of the presence was manifested.

But observe that these do not quite fit the narrative. Abraham was sitting at his tent door in the heat of the day, and say the Sages, he was waiting for some strangers to whom he could display hospitality. Through this act, says the commentary, was God revealed; that in the heat of the day amidst his discomfort Abraham sat waiting for an opportunity to serve his fellow man. This merited the appearance of the *Shechinah*, God's presence. In a generation following the flood and the dispersion from Babel, in a world of idolatry, violence and hostility, Abraham sought to extend his service to a fellow human being. And Abraham saw three forms in the likeness of men and he rushed to greet them. Because, as we have repeated, it is even more meritorious to extend hospitality and service to a fellowman than to acknowledge the presence of the Lord.

When Abraham became alert to the purpose of life, that its development must be toward the highest goals, that our responsiveness to each other's needs becomes primary, he set for us the pattern of true religiosity. He yearned to serve not merely a fellow convert, but three strangers. It was this deep motivation, which impelled him to seek the rescue of those wicked communities of Sodom and Gomorrah. Josiah Royce in 1913 said the true task of religion is the task of inventing and applying the arts which shall pass over to unity and which shall overcome their original hatefulness by the gracious love, not only of individuals but communities. We have seen humanity imagine that an emperor, dictator and divine personality in human form should solve the darkness which threatens to engulf humanity.

One need not be a Father Abraham in order to do good. When Abraham begged God to save the wicked cities, he said: "if there are a decent number or *tzaddickim*, good men there, won't you save them?" The Rabbis noted that the word *tzaddickim* seemed misspelled in the Torah, a *yud* was missing. To which a Sage commented they were not perfect *tzaddickim* but you don't have to be the most perfect person to help others. When you are surrounded by darkness, unhappiness, problems and you try to help others, even if you are not perfect, you can still be able to save the community. Try to be good and helpful, appreciate how others have helped you and whenever you can, help others. Let each of us emulate Father Abraham and rush toward to serve the other and the world will be better, lighter and happier.

Chayai Sarah

— 5 —

שְׁנֵי חַיֵּי שָׂרָה:

"The years of the life of Sarah." (Gen. 23:1)

BETWEEN MAN AND GOD.....

For the past several Biblical lessons, we have been examining some of the earliest incidents in the lives of the founders of our people and faith, which have an abiding influence and significance for us, their descendants. This scriptural lesson may be analyzed in a similar vain, inasmuch as it starts with a reference to the Matriarch Sarah, the wife of Abraham and the Mother of our people.

This Torah lesson is called *Chayai Sarah*, which means the life of Sarah, but actually it notes her passing at the ripe old age of one hundred and twenty seven. Why funeral arrangements should be called the life of a person recalls the comment of a social observer, namely, that without an obituary notice, we would never know that many people had ever lived. But this is not so in the case of Sarah. The Torah declares that Sarah lived one hundred and twenty seven years, these were:

"*Shney Chayai Sarah*,"
"The years of the life of Sarah." (Gen. 23:1)

Rashi, the greatest of commentators, immediately explains "*Kulan shavin letovah*," "All these years were alike in their goodness." (Rashi to Gen. 23:2) Such a statement might normally bring a cynical smile to our lips. How could all her years be considered happy and good? After all, in her long life, she was subject to many pressures: a husband whom she loved and whom she followed everywhere in his personal odyssey, a search for God which immediately set him apart from his contemporary world. There were also difficult and dangerous experiences in which she had to play deceitful roles in order to save his life from the greed, lusts and immoralities of local politicians and chieftains. She suffered many personal frustrations that were originally evoked by her failure to have a family. She sustained personal insults and humiliations from a regal servant, namely Hagar, who became a rival for her husband's affections because of her own insistence that he add her to the household as a wife. Subsequently, she suffered fears and insecurities when she watched Hagar's son Ishmael, trying to influence her own child Isaac, by his sadistic, primitively passionate ravishment of unsuspecting girls, and an inner brutality by which he hoped to seduce this younger brother to emulate his horror and viciousness against others. Thus, how can Rashi proclaim his analysis of her life as one happy record?

Perhaps, we may discover the answer in considering the fact that *Chayai Sarah* generally occurs on the Sabbath when we recite the blessings for the new month of *Kislev*. A Chassidic leader of another generation directs our attention to the *Yehi Ratzon*, May it be your will, the prayer that introduces the blessings for the month (Berachot 16b), wherein we pray for a *"Chayim sheyesh bahem yirat Shamayim veyirat chate,"* "a life in which we shall have the fear of heaven and the fear of sin." Superficially, both terms mean the same thing and one wonders why tradition bears the repetition.

A European Talmudist whom I knew once explained this practice in the light of a rather famous Talmudic anecdote. When the great Sage, Rabbi Yochanan was facing the end of his life, his many disciples who loved him gathered at his bedside. One pupil begged his master to bless them with an enduring significant teaching, to which he replied, *"halivai sheyiheyeh yirat Shamayim aleychem kimo yirat basar vidam* may you fear heaven as you fear humans." Said the student in amazement," don't you mean just the opposite, that we should respect humans as we do heaven? "No, said the Rabbi, it is as I have said. When you do something wrong, most of the time, you don't worry about God, but you whisper, "I hope no one sees." The prayer really includes no repetition, it actually reminds us that the fear of heaven refers to our relations with God or as we have been taught, the *mitzvoth beyn adam leMakom,* but the fear of sin arouses us to our relations with each other, *mitzvot beyn adam lechavero.*

The other day it suddenly occurred to me that the words of the Bible, *Shney Chayai Sarah,* these are the years of Sarah, may also be read *shney,* which means two. There were two lives for Sarah, an earthly and a heavenly. But at this moment, I find myself interpreting the same words differently. That startling statement by Rashi, that all the years of mother Sarah's life were pervaded by accomplishments of happiness, assume a new significance, when we perceive her existence to have been constantly involved with two features, namely her relations towards God and her responses towards her fellow human beings. One must be an extraordinary personality to entertain this philosophy constantly.

Those of us who are cognizant of our traditions, know that in ancient days a daily sacrifice was offered at the Temple in behalf of all people. This was known as the "*tamid*" and in our prayers we refer to the "*shney tamidim Kisidram,*" the two *tamids* in their order. (*Tamid* here means always, regular.) A great Sage once noted, that since we have no such Temple offerings today, we should choose for ourselves two other *tamids*, and he suggested the scriptural verses, "*Shiviti Hashem lenegdi tamid,*" I keep the Lord before me, always. (Psalms 16:8) The second verse should be "*Vechatatai negdi tamid,*" my sins or wrong doing against others, I remember, always. (Psalms 51:5) You see the tremendous influence that this woman exerted upon our history, our concepts, our ethics, our attitudes towards one another, towards our families and dear ones resulted from this approach.

First, her steadfast faith in God infused her life with meaning and purpose. Do we not see that in our own modern world, we have a plethora of studies, analysis, polemics, explanations, interpretations, all concerned with the frightening pessimism which assaults our generations because purpose and significance in our lives are missing? Political, and social observers, philosophers, psychologists, sociologists, educators, criminologists, and other scholars who are concerned with human behavior and culture bemoan the fact that the drug subculture has infested and infected and polluted our contemporary world because so many have been deprived of finding purpose or meaning in their lives. Is it not a fact, that in recent times, we have been told in no uncertain terms

that the shocking scandalous behavior of youths who terminate
their own lives, do so only because they are confused and do not
see purpose in their very presence here on earth? If one feels that
everything here is just an accidental occurrence, if one cannot
understand the majesty and mystery of life itself, if one is ignorant
of the fact that no two snow flakes are alike even as no two human
beings have the very same fingerprints, if you are unable to appreciate what the scientist Paul Davies has called "The Superforce"
which maintains and keeps the universe together, then you become a lost, wandering soul, suffering in isolation in your own
unhappiness and your own tortured existence. Naturally, that confusion compels you to regard your fellowmen in a disjointed and
alienated manner.

Not so Mother Sarah, having her life always. Always directed by her faith in God she found her happiness and her duty in
her responses to her fellowmen. Of course, she had her moments
of anxiety. Undoubtedly, she wept in the privacy of her tent, and
she certainly sustained all the emotions and sentiments that assail
us in our own lives. But once life is examined from the heights of
"*mitzvot shebeyn adam laMakom,*" from the heights of relations
with God, then invariably the "*mitzvot shebeyn Adam lechavero,*"
our relationships with each other become clarified. The God-fearing person must become aware of the dangers of drugs and crime,
must become sensitive to the cries of the ill and the impoverished,
and cannot withhold his or her comparisons from the helplessness
of the aged or the oppressed. Such a person recognizes everyday
that we are all involved in humanity, that our own peace and well
being depends invariably upon the well being of other human beings.

What is more, the y*irat Shamayim,* the God fearing, that we pray for in that monthly prayer is sensitive to the treasures of the earth which have been entrusted to us and hence ours is the obligation to avoid polluting it too. Protect our natural resources from contamination, from nuclear wastes, from chemical toxins, and above all, not to close our eyes to the needs of our brethren. We must never forget that were those who profess to be God fearing, had they only imbibed the inclinations of Mother Sarah, the poor would not die of starvation, the weak would never have been forced into concentration camps, minorities would never have borne the tragedies, the tortures and the inhuman bestiality which the Holocaust has seared upon the history of all mankind. Yes, it is true that we must pray as our tradition directs, for the y*irat Shamayin* and the *yirat chate*. True fear of God can only mean the true fear of sin.

"*Habitu el Avraham Avichem*,"
"Look unto Abraham your Father, says the Prophet,"
(Isaiah 51:2)

and unto Sarah who bore you. How happy we should be for the privilege of being their children and emulating their principles.

GROWING OLD

The other day, I experienced an interesting expression of thanksgiving which was highly provocative to those among us who invariable associate this holiday with food, family gathering, and various feelings of gratitude which may or may not be engendered at such occasions. This time, a friend told me that he was especially thankful because it was his birthday, and he was celebrating his seventy-ninth year of life. My friends' announcement evoked some serious thinking.

What does an old man feel? What does an old man do? What can he do? *"The Human Cycle"* by the anthropologist Colin Turnbull noted that in every society, we take it for granted old age brings with it an increase in physical deficiency and a decrease in mental powers. We assume that entitled as we are to golden years after a lifetime of productivity, becoming elderly means that we all deserve assistance to retire. To some, this means a state of inactivity comparable to those animals that are tolerated and left free to forge in the pasture rather then being immediately slaughtered. Among our ancestors, this stage meant that we were supposed to receive from our children to whom we have given so much. This implies that they should give rather than continue to take, but everyone seemed to agree that children continue to anticipate uninterrupted help from parents, and when this is not forthcoming, the aged are fortunate if their progeny does not completely ignore them.

Many elders are so. Flustered by American society which is so youth-centered that those who relied upon the optimism of our younger years concerning this relationship, are often frustrated and disappointed, feeling they are resented by many for existing without contributing to society. There is an old Jewish saying, "He who sings before he is really awake, will weep before he lies down to sleep." Was it a touch of pessimism that comes with the advance of years? As children we are very naive, we imagine that our parents are omnipotent and all knowing. And as we continue to grow and see the pressure of time on them, we realize that it is not so. Even as the Midrash indicates, (Ecclesiastes Rabbah 1:3) when we are very young, we are comparable to the pig who wallows in dirt, and then as we grow, we seek to emulate what we consider is the enviable conduct of our elders, it is "monkey does as monkey sees." And the youth that struts about in the presence of girls is, indeed, very much like the prancing horse. But when maturity arrives and with it a family for whose welfare we are so concerned, the years seem to fly so rapidly. Then suddenly, it seems we have increased our burdens not only with anxieties for the children, but now our grandchildren. Then, unanticipatedly, we find there are certain activities we can no longer pursue, and then all of us sing the same refrain, "the old gray mare ain't what she used to be." None of us can remain thirty five forever. Yet what if we could?

Is it not a fact that in Jewish tradition, we define the *zaken*, the elder as *mi shekanah chachmah liatzmo,* he who acquires unto himself wisdom. Yet the old folks always said "What good is the wise head if the feet cannot carry it. On Yom Kippur, at the prayer, *"Al tashlicheynee liet ziknah, kichlot kocheynu al tazveynu,"* "Cast us not aside in our old age, when our strength weakens, do not leave us," (Psalms 71:9) maybe, when one is truly advanced in years, he or she, realizes that they cannot escape this situation. My Father, of blessed memory, had explained this prayer to be a supplication, an appeal to God, *"Al tashlicheynu"* meaning, "Don't hurl us into old age, let us grow old gracefully." *"Kichlot Kocheynu,"* "When our bodily strength no longer permits us every kind of physical exertion," don't desert us but, grant that we continue with the ability to perceive, understand, sympathize, and encourage others.

So impressive to me was this comment from my Father, that I would automatically think of him, whenever I read of Agatha Christie's fascinating Detective, Hercule Poirot, who invariably prided himself that despite the passing of time, "The old gray cells in the brain were working."

Perhaps we obtain such insight when we consider some of our forebears. Jacob the Patriarch is an old man at the closing of the Book of *Bereshit*. When he prepares his children for his departure from the world and seeks to guide them. Such an old man speaks magnificently, with such cadence, with such vitality and sublimity, despite his age. Mother Sarah is also regarded in a similar light, when we consider this Torah lesson.

> **"*Vayihyu chayai Sarah, meah shanah ve'esrim shanah, veshevah shanim, shney chayai Sarah,*"**
> **"And Sarah lived one hundred and twenty, and seven, these are the years of the life of Sarah." (Gen 23:1)**

Throughout centuries, our sages have continued to analyze this statement, and discover in the verse a vast amount of insight for our own choices in life. Rabbi Baruch Kossover, the Chassidic leader, observed that the very first word, *Vayihyu* in gematriah, is thirty seven. This is equal to that of the abbreviation z"*l,* which we traditionally employ when referring to a deceased good person, in line with the teaching, *"Keshemazkirim shmo shel tzaddick,"* "When you mention the name of a righteous person" no longer in our midst, we add the term z"*l. Zecher Tzaddick Levrachah,* may the memory of the saintly be a blessing. Wherein lies that blessed guidance that Mother Sarah projects upon us? Rashi interprets the phraseology of one hundred and twenty and seven as indicating that at twenty, Sarah had the same innocence that we associate with the child of seven, and at one hundred she still possessed the inherent beauty she exhumed at the age of twenty. (Rashi to Gen. 23:1) How can that be, innocent at twenty?

Just listen to some of the street wisdom, the practical. Who among us really believes that the best yeshiva little girl, no matter how we try to shield her, is unaware of the nuances, the double entendre that is literally thrown at us by the TV broadcasts or contemporary literature? And to assert that at one hundred, any woman would be attractive, as the pulsating, vibrant beauty of twenty, seems far fetched indeed. In fact, it runs counter to the wisdom of Solomon we enjoy repeating to our wives at the evening of the Sabbath. Indeed, she may be an *Aishet Chayil*, a Woman of Valor, but *"Sheker hachen vehevel hayofi,"* "Grace is deceitful and beauty is fading." (Prov. 31:30) A vanity which cannot be preserved with the passing of the years.

And yet there it is Rashi's commentary staring us in the face throughout the centuries. And yet there it is, pure innocence, beauty unmarred. The answer lies in the gracefulness with which Sarah advanced in years. *"Kulan shavin letovah"*; every passage in her life, every birthday, every decade continued to match, to be equivalent to the goodness which the previous period evidenced. (Rashi to Gen. 23:1) Because she gave of herself in love to her husband, Abraham the Patriarch. Because she stood by him under all times and under all conditions, because her faith and trust and affections never wavered, she remained pure and beautiful, fascinating to the eye, intriguing to the mind irresistible to the affections. And she was blessed, because she assigned unto her life, purpose. Hers was not an empty life, dependent upon a momentary pleasure or fleeting entertainment; she sought and pursued ideals.

When her husband was imbued with this passionate desire to bring humanity under the wings of the divine presence, then she, too, was found at his side, bringing the women *tachat kanfei hashechinah,* under the wings of the Divine Presence. Teaching, inspiring, guiding influencing them towards this incomparable ideal of the one eternal living God with its unavoidable corollary, one humanity. When she, incredibly, became the Mother of Isaac, then despite her advanced age, she poured forth her love, her instructions and her faith into the very heart and soul of her son. Sarah grew old gracefully, aware that the years would take their toll as they invariably must. Even the announcement of her ability to carry a child within her, evoked hesitancy and doubts, because she recognized her age.

However, over and above all, were those tremendous impulses to make her years count, to infuse her every day with goodness, loyalty, faith and love. No wonder she retained so much beauty in her life. And so let us all be thankful, young and old alike, with the passing of time.

STANDING ON THREE PILLARS

"*Al haTorah, ve'al haavodah, ve'al gemilat chasadim,*"
"Torah, the ability of each to sacrifice, strive and labor
for that world, and acts of loving-kindness."
(Ethics of the Fathers 1:2).

We often forget that in our rich spiritual literature of the past, the capacity for speech is critically studied as an indication of our essential humanity and the potentialities that this characteristic implies. It is through the power of speech that we are able to communicate with each other in a fashion that transcends that of other living creatures. The sermon, after all, basically an attempt by the Rabbi to communicate and share his responses to the issues of life, as a human being, as a member of a community, but above all, as one Jew reaching out to other Jews. And therefore, I feel compelled to share with you some thoughts which are evoked by this Torah lesson, *Chayai Sarah*.

I recall a discussion with several colleagues many years ago at a Rabbinical Board meeting. A number of Rabbis were speaking about marriage and how in an open free society such as the one we enjoy, the family association with marriage had changed. For everybody made fun of the *shadchan*, the matchmaker, who was nicknamed the shotgun. Furthermore, as each of the Rabbis tried to find Biblical illustrations to prove their point, reference was made by a colleague to the picture presented in the Torah lesson, when Abraham wants to assure himself that his son, Isaac, will marry a proper young woman.

Several days ago I was reminded of this earlier Rabbinical discussion by a television advertisement in which it would seem that the *shadchan* is no longer just relegated to Fiddler on the Roof. "Matchmaker, matchmaker, make me a match, find me a catch." The advertisement I had seen spoke of an agency which utilizing computerized data, tries to introduce young men and young women. As both are asked whether they enjoy their isolation, to which they vigorously shook their head in a negative fashion, a voiceover announced the great accomplishments of "Together" a firm engaged in helping people meet each other. The next day I repeated these observations to a neighbor and she replied. "What's so strange about that?" All you have to do is read some of the personal announcements in the Jewish Press or Yiddish newspapers, you would discover that *shadchanut,* arranged marriages are not entirely disappearing. "And it will never disappear," said this neighbor, because without a formal office, there will always be nice people who know what a *mitzvah* it is to help young people meet and fall in love.

I began to think of all the old stories we used to hear, about the young man who was furious with his father because he had arranged a *shidduch,* marriage and wanted to announce the engagement of these young people. When the boy stormed that the he had not been asked, nor given the opportunity to meet the girl the father in righteous indignation said, "if that's the way you are going act, we won't take you to the wedding either." And I can personally vouch for an incident, when in my youth, a Rosh Yeshiva tried to influence me towards a particular girl, and when I said that I knew her, that she was a swell kid but that I didn't love her, he replied, "Who is talking about love? I am talking about marriage." But young people today who want love also want their own sense of independence in choosing their love. Though they still are quite pragmatic and realistic because in my discussions with them, I find that they are aware of the many social, emotional, physical material distractions which, too often disrupt the family relationship.

As a father, I get involved with my children in discussing these contemporary problems and have been moved to hear my sons say. "Look, we don't just want to sing, we want a gal just like the gal who married good old Pa. But I do want a relationship of love, concern, cooperation, harmony and the unity that you and Mom demonstrated to us." Well, what makes for such a marriage relationship?

Consider, please for a moment the Biblical lesson. A narrative of Abraham who does not want his son to marry the idol worshipping girls of their area and hence he sent his trusted steward, Eliezer back to his old neighborhood to the *mishpacha,* family, entrusting him with the mission of finding a proper girl for Isaac. Realizing how serious a responsibility this is, Eliezer works out his strategy. He will approach the young girls drawing water from the community well, and ask for a drink of water. The girl who provides him with that drink and also waters the thirsty camels, that is the woman destined to be Isaac's wife. And we all know the story; Rebecca came forward and offered water to him and his camels. But instead of being overjoyed, Eliezer is still apprehensive, she agrees to accept some gifts from him. What was the problem?

Marriage implies the entrance of two people into a new world. A world, which they themselves must help create and ensure that it is established firmly, so that it may withstand all kinds of pressures, oppositions and even assaults. It is a world wherein responsibility and sharing play a dominant note. It is a world which each of the two partners are summoned to think of the others needs. Even while they do not forget their own individual requirements it is a world in which they want to perform without interference, and yet they both know there is not an isolated world which has no connection with the activities, performances and accomplishments of other people. In short, it is not only a private world, but it becomes an area that reflects to a great extent, the entire world about us. Simeon the Just declared that the world is established and stands firm on three pillars.

"*Al haTorah, ve'al haavodah, ve'al gemilat chasadim,*"
"Torah, the ability of each to sacrifice, strive and labor
for that world, and acts of loving-kindness."
(Ethics of the Fathers 1:2).

As I said, the reading of the Bible would have us see that despite the fact that Rebecca displays an innate charm and goodness, despite the fact that she has literally fulfilled and answered his strategy, Eliezer is still apprehensive. He does proclaim his gratitude that he has found this young girl. The trusted servant of Abraham, however, was satisfied and removed of doubt, when the young girl accepted the gifts he has offered to her. Gifts which are the kinds of jewelry worn at that time and in that part of the globe.

One gift which particularly elevated Eliezer's feelings are two bracelets which she gladly accepts, the Bible reports *hatzemidim al yadehah* bracelets on her hands. (Gen. 24:47) The Midrash observes (Gen. Rabbah 60:4), the bracelets were really a pair, two parts united to each other, *asarah zahav mishkalim* weighing ten shekels of gold. And the Midrash adds its own comment: *shney tzemidim al yahdehah kishney lucho,* the two bracelets on her hands were symbolic of the two tablets, which Moses had brought down from Mt. Sinai. *Asarah zahav mishkalim,* the ten shekels of gold symbolize the ten commandments that were inscribed on those tablets. (Ibid) The Gur Aryeh, a famous spiritual leader, interprets this observation to mean that Eliezer was encouraged by Rebecca's acceptance of his gifts because he just knew that Rebecca would help Isaac build a firmly, uplifting, world. He now watched Rebecca with deeper insight. The good world he intuitively knew depends upon, benevolence, Torah and service to the ideal. Rebecca had demonstrated that she was a benevolent person. She had given Eliezer evidence of her sensitivity, compassion, pity and her ability to understand the stranger by her response to his plea. Please, he asked, give me a drink of water. But she not only gives him a drink, but she says I shall take care of your camels. These poor beasts are also deserving of pity. They too have traveled great distances. They have born the heat of the sun and the harshness walking on hot desert sands. They too have gone without water, surely they deserve a little bit too?

She surely will provide her new world with that element of *Gemilat Chasadim,* benevolence, kindness, delicacy of spirit, which is one of the three pillars on which the world stands. But what about other characteristics? What about Torah? Will she infuse her new home with some of the great traits of our heritage, the

Jewish Heritage? Will she remember that she is Jewish? Will she keep alive our magnificent traditions? Will, she adhere with loyalty to the faith which has kept us alive in spite of all the belligerence and hostility that the world has shown us? Will she remember the ethics of Judaism, the decency, and the desire to live at peace with one another and also, deal justly in all human relationships?

And finally, what about the *Avodah*? The service, which you know, was associated with sacrifice? Will she understand that a wife is just more than another usual acquaintance in life? To become a man's best friend requires not only a harmonious understanding of his needs and outlook, but an ability to sacrifice, to give of ones self for the sake of marriage. This, of course, does not apply only to a woman, it applies to the man as well. We are taught thou shalt love thy neighbor as thyself. This means that we should love ourselves but it is a teaching with which we always abide. Yes it is proper to love oneself. We should not demean ourselves. We should not deny the faculties and capabilities we have. We should not belittle ourselves. Every one must understand that each of us counts in this world and we owe it to ourselves to act properly and satisfy ourselves, but not to the extent of denying the others. Not to the extent of saying: we place ourselves in the first rank of concern. We have to be aware of another. We should be ready to sacrifice some of our own happiness, wants, dreams and aspirations to help the other get ahead, to help our mate and spouse realize their own dreams, to help their own egos and always make the other understand that he or she is but normal. With the acceptance of the gifts Eliezer understood that he had succeeded.

Yes, Rebecca would be interested in Isaac's needs, she would share his experiences with him in a manner of loving kindness, compassion, decency and was ready to give of herself for high ideals. Now Eliezer was satisfied. These two young people would build a better and firmer world for themselves. Their world would stand firm because it would rest on the three pillars of *Torah, Avodah,* and *Gemilat Chasadim.*

That is what we must strive for today. To build a new world in which kindness, understanding, compassion and charity will always predominate. A world which will give evidence of its Jewishness, living with its Jewish ritual and aware of the problems and needs of the Jewish people, never permitting selfishness to ignore one another. A world with love, gentility, understanding and compassion in which all our lives can reflect the joys which pursued Isaac and Rebecca, giving us all, long, happy and productive lives.

JEWISH HISTORY AND THE MACPELAH

The scriptural lesson of *Chayai Sarah* includes several intriguing episodes in the lives of our ancestors and primogenitors, but its traditional name has been introduced by the very first brief announcement of the death of the Matriarch Sarah.

The Bible informs us that Sarah had passed away in Hebron, and that Father Abraham had come to mourn and weep for her.

"*Vayavo Avraham lispod leSarah levkotah,*"
"And Abraham came to mourn and weep for Sarah."
(Gen. 23:2)

The Sages reading this ask, from where did he come? From Mt. Moriah where he had gone with his precious son Isaac to fulfill a divine command, namely the *Akedath Yitzchok*, the binding of Isaac. The *Yalkut Shimoni* tells us that this sensitive loving mother's death was caused by a distorted malicious report that her husband had actually sacrificed their son there.

Almost a century ago, one of the European Rabbis raised a possible question. We have been informed in the previous Torah portion that Abraham returning from that tremendous experience with Isaac traveled to Be'er Sheva. If so, how is it possible that Sarah passed away in Hebron? The response given is that Abraham and Isaac had risen early in the morning, leaving Be'er Sheva and had delayed several days at Mt. Moriah. Sarah in her deep concern became confused and worried and did not know what to think. But Providence wished to privilege the mother of humanity, Eve, by having Sarah interred near her, and that eventually, four couples, Adam and Eve, Abraham and Sarah, Isaac and Rebecca, and Jacob and Leah would be buried in the cave of Machpelah, for reasons only God foresaw. Hence it was a divine impulse that motivated Sarah's decision to leave her dwelling and attempt to meet her husband and son.

Incidentally, the Mishna (Yoma 28a) referring to the *Korban Tamid,* the perpetual sacrifice on every morning of the year, indicates the arrival of dawn for that ritual which Mathia B. Samuel describes with the phrase, *"Hair pney kol hamizrach ad shebeChevron,"* "The whole east is alight even unto Hebron." The *Gemarah* apparently is aware that Hebron was too far removed from Jerusalem and the Temple site, making it impossible for the towers of Hebron to be seen. But the reason the city was referred to resulted from the fact that there was to be found the cave of Machpalah, the sacred shrine wherein are buried the Mothers and Fathers of Israel. It was to this sacred locality that Sarah was apparently attracted.

The Kossover, Reb. Mendel suggests a consideration of the fascinating tale in Tractate of Sukkah (53a) wherein it is reported that there were two Ethiopian scribes who attended King Solomon one day. So runs the legend, Solomon noticed that the Angel of Death appeared to be sad. When questioned he replied that he had been ordered to take the lives of two men. Where upon Solomon who reputedly enjoyed special powers over spirits dispatched these men to Luz, where he felt they would be safe. However, when they reached the gates of Luz, they died. The next day, Solomon observed that the Angel of Death was of merry spirit. Why are you so cheerful? The latter replied, to that place where they were expected to die, you sent them. Solomon considering the mysterious ways of our lives, uttered a saying: "A man's feet is responsible for him, they lead him to the place where he is wanted" so too, are there incidents in human affairs which do not lend themselves to glib explanations. Mother Sarah, was under a decree from heaven, that she find mortal rest at Hebron, and it was to that significant area in Jewish history that she went. There she was subject to the malicious report that shocked her unto death.

And so the Commentary suggests that when Abraham returned to Be'er Sheva and did not find his wife at home, he followed her footsteps to Hebron where he learned that she had passed away. But that incidentally is the reasoning that could explain why Abraham came alone, and not with his son, who would have remained at home, perhaps to await the return of his mother. And so Abraham came to Hebron and lamented and wept over the loss of his faithful beloved guide, his life's companion and friend. And the Rabbis were quick to note that in the word *levkotah*, to weep for her, (Gen. 23:2) the letter *kof*, is smaller than the rest of the letters that comprise the word. And Rashi's comment is well known namely that Abraham did not prolong his weeping, because he realized that she had been blessed with a long life. She had exercised great influence over her household and had fulfilled a historic role in spreading the faith. The Midrash may also indicate another reason, namely, the homilies declare that at the bestowal of the tablets were transmitted *mikaf yado shel Hakadosh baruchho likaf yado shel Moshe,* the commandments were transmitted from the palm of God to that of Moses. And so to in a similar fashion, Sarah handed over her life and soul with her hands to the very palm of God. Abraham realized the love; fidelity and the uninterrupted faith she had sustained in God, regardless of the difficulties which life had often imposed upon her. She always walked with the serenity and security that her faith had granted her. And hence, in the midst of sorrow, Abraham restricted his natural outcry and frustration, knowing that her life was as Rashi explains *"Kulan shavin letovah,"* "all her years were regarded as years being replete with goodness because of that faith." (Rashi to Gen. 23:1)

Abraham at that moment revealed the intensity of faith that his progeny would follow. *Kishem shemivrochim al hatov, mivorchim al harah,* even as we render our blessings and thanks to God in those moments and achievements which we consider good and happy, must we also be ready to repeat similar emotions, when we find ourselves to be the recipients and subjects of incidents which have been unwanted and which must be that of *hashgachah elyonah,* the Providential supervision of our existence. God prodded Sarah to go to Hebron to pass away there, so that Father Abraham would then be compelled and inspired to seek the cave of Machpelah.

Our people have sustained horrible tragedy, pain and agony. We have been threatened with utter extinction so many times and yet we invariably remain, even as our enemies are stronger, mightier and more numerous, they suffer defeat. Even today, when we review in our minds, hearts and very souls those terrible years when humanity rejected the *tzelem Elokim*, the image of God, and sank to a bestiality of the Holocaust, for which it is paying and must still continue to pay. Who can deny that the horrors of the immediate and pulsating before the eyes of the world, was conducive towards having the international community of nations proclaim the State of Israel? And who can stand before the historic facts and not be overcome with awe, when we realize that out of the sinful and vicious attempts by the Arabs to destroy Israel, there emerged a larger Jewish State?

And who of us, recalling the pessimism that first seized the heart of many of our people can not be shaken at the realization that miraculously Israel defeated its enemies in all of its wars. Yes, we must be ready to fulfill the precept, *keshem shemivorchim al hatov mivorchim al harah* that gratitude towards God rooted in our unshakable conviction, that he loves us and will guide us to our destiny with eternity. That is what must inspire us at all times, in hours of laughter and in hours of tears. And not only as a nation, but also as individuals, we have trembled before prejudicial and violence, we have wept at wars, we have sustained *tzar gidul banim*, the problems and pressures entailed in rearing children.

We have been threatened by illness and have suffered despondency, frustration, and fears. We, *basar vedam* are human beings, have had no other course but to bear the pain of watching beloved ones suffer. We have all sustained the loss of precious ones, we have borne burdens during the day and have cried alone amidst the nightmares of the darkness.

"*Habitu el Avraham Avichem*,"
"Look unto Abraham your Father" (Isaiah 51:2)

and unto Sarah our Mother who has borne so much. You, no matter what have been the pressures, the concerns, the sorrows and the problems of life, you have been taught to be:

"*Sameach bechelko*,"
"Happy with your portion," (Ethics of the Fathers 1:1)

thankful for that which you receive. And if life be unfair, unjust, unholy, then we stand up like Abraham against the world for justice, decency and righteousness, that is why we can say every morning, "*Aval anachnu amchah, b'nai britechah b'nai Avraham o'havehchah*, we are thy people, the children of your covenant, the children of Abraham thy beloved. *Lefichah,* therefore it is our duty to thank thee, praise and glorify thee, to bless and sanctify and to offer praise unto thy name. This Parsha often coincides with the weekend of Thanksgiving, and year after year, the presidential proclamation call upon the American people to offer thanks for their blessings and the good we have enjoyed, a noble sentiment indeed. But even as the pilgrim fathers established the first Thanksgiving as an attempt to emulate the holiday of our Torah, so, too must we not only in America but in the entire world learn how to thank God. We thank God for that which we now immediately understand, as well as for the mysteries whose comprehension comes years later. *Ashreinu mah tov chelkeinu*, how happy and how pleasant are we with our lot, and how beautiful our heritage. The heritage which will reveal always:

"*Netzach Yisrael lo yeshaker*,"
"The Eternal One of Israel does not lie."
(Samual I 15:29)

and inspired by Mother Sarah and Father Abraham as they reach out to us from the cave of Machpelah, a link in the chain of our unity with the Land of Israel.

How grateful we must be that through the superficially strange choice of Mother Sarah going to Hebron, she is buried in the cave of Machpelah laying the historic basis of the Jewish presence in that land. The cave of Machpelah, for all times, established the Hebrew presence in the land of our ancient origins and prophetic creativity. How thankful we are for that. When that Mishna in Yoma refers to the time of sacrificial offering, is it not as the Commentary observed, the whole east was illuminated even unto Hebron, *lehazkir zechut avot, key bizchutam korban tamid he korban taharah leYisrael,* to remind us of the merit of our forebears, that in their merit, the perpetual sacrifice was an offering of purity for Israel? The perpetual offering is inherently a reminder that Judaism means a conviction, a philosophy, a faith which embraces not a particular moment only, but one which is constant witness to the security with which we reach out to God. Ever to be thankful to him, always to be aware that even when we can not immediately see the good which may emerge from darkness, that the light of God is never extinguished and we may hope for its beneficial rays to shine eventually upon us.

"*Hodu lashem key tov,*"
"Give thanks unto the Lord"
(Psalms 106:1,107:1, 118:1, 118:29, 136:1),

"*Key liolam chasdo,*"
"For his loving kindness is forever and ever."
(Psalms 106:1, 107:1, 118:1,2,3,4,29, 136:1-26, Ezr. 3:11,
Words 1 16:34,41, Words 2 5:13, 7:3,6, 20:21)

GAM ZU LITOVAH, THIS TOO IS FOR THE GOOD

**"*Vayihyu chayai Sarah meah Shanah, ve'esrim shanah,
veshevah shaneem, shney chayai Sarah*," and
"Sarah lived one hundred years, twenty years and
seven years, these are the years of the life of Sarah."
(Gen 23:1)**

One of the spiritual leaders of another age, the Melechet Machshevet speculates on the formation of the words, why one hundred and twenty and seven years are the years of the life of Sarah? And he makes the observation. Only the first seven years in the life of a person, the years of childhood are the golden years. Only these may properly be called years of life because after that golden idealistic little span in our existence, all the other years which follow, all the various other stages of human life on the face of the earth become heavy with problems, difficulties, troubles, toil and worries.

I believe it was Alfred Whitehead, that great English mathematician and philosopher, who was not only some abstract metaphysical thinker, but also a pragmatic observer of life, when he said: "We should take cognizance of the fact that in life, there are more clouds than sunshine. We need some kind of spiritual baggage, some sources of inner strength which must be developed for us to confront the toil and concerns and pressures of life." The first seven years are significant not only because most of us are protected against the heavier demands of life, during that time, but to many, the feeling has been that within these first seven years, much of our later personality is fashioned so that we may face maturity better. Thus Ralph Waldo Emerson, the American thinker, once claimed: "Give me a child for the first seven years of his life, and then you can try to change him for the rest of his years." Whether we accept the claims that we are so conditioned for a lifetime of emotional responses by the first seven years of our existence, one thing is clear: childhood is displaced by years of toil, problem and anxieties.

How then shall we hear the opinion of Rashi, who looking at the statement, *shney chayai Sarah,* interpreted it to mean "*Kulan shavin letovah,*" "All were years of Good." (Rashi to Gen. 23:1) How so? Since the *pasuk,* verse declares *chayai Sarah,* the life of Sarah and then repeats *shney chayai Sarah,* the years of the life of Sarah. Rashi deducts that "*Kulan shavin letovah.*" All this long life was replete with good years. One does not have to be antagonist to Rashi, one does not have to be regarded as lacking faith to express a reluctance to accept Rashi's explanation. All the years were good. Years of wandering about with a husband who sustained inner conflicts with the entire world, with a man driven by the compulsions of a new perspective on life, years of hunger, starvation, economic recessions, aggravation, subject to the potentials destruction of Pharaoh and Abimelech, waiting until the incredible age of ninety to become pregnant, fighting inner family battles to prevent Isaac from being prey to the viciousness of Ishmael.

And finally, the ordeal of the binding of Isaac, which according to a tradition had a falsely, distorted, malicious report on that event which hastened her death from shock. These are "*Kulan shavin letovah?*" These can be considered good years? But, one of the Chassidic Rebbes, Reb Zusha the Annopoler, expounds the teaching of Rashi by saying: Sarah, a saintly woman, was inspired to confront all her difficulties with faith. No matter what happened she could say, as did a much later sage: *gam zu letovah,* this too is for the good. Our Matriarch, the mother of our faith, that great, Sarah, was the first source of that tradition which teaches a Jew, *kishem Shemivorchin al hatov, mivorchin al hara,* one must be ready to express benedictions and gratitude to our creator for happy experiences in life, as well as for those good, happy, satisfying incidents which form the chain of our lives. And let us not imagine, continued Zusha, that this attitude was restricted only to our Mother.

Abraham our forefather, of him it is written in the scriptural lesson:

> **"*Vehashem berach et Avraham bakol*,"**
> **"And God blessed Abraham with everything."**
> **(Gen. 24:1)**

But did not Abraham share those same experiences with Sarah? Did he not weep in fear that his convictions and philosophies would disappear with his mortal end on this earth? Did he not tremble at the dangers, to which his wife was subjected, even when he pursued actions calculated to save his very life. Does not our tradition refer to the *nisyonot*, the temptations, and the challenges to which Abraham was subject? What permanent man Abraham was, how persistent is his ideal, and how very human he was. A man pursuing an ideal of God, but still, not a God himself, but a very human, sensitive often frightened human being. And yet, he too found blessings in everything. Because like Sarah, having accepted the spiritual objective of existence that his new faith proclaimed, he was immersed in gratitude to God for all his experiences. Were they threatening, frightful, full of angst, yet he too proclaimed, as did the later sage: *kol mah letov avid, rachmah letov avid,* whatever God does, God, the *Rachmanah*, the merciful one, whatever he does is for the good.

Yes, we too were often conditioned in the first seven years of our lives. And after that life was not always a bowl of cherries. We have sustained economic travails; all mankind together has trembled before violence, before prejudice before hatred, before persecution, before torture, before wars. We have sustained *tzar gidul banim*, sorrows entailed in rearing children. We have been threatened by illness. We have suffered desperation, despairs, despondency, frustrations, and fears. We have wept tears at the suffering of beloved ones. None of us because we are, after all, only *Basar vedam*, human beings, we have all sustained the loss of beloved ones and have cried with others, we have cried alone. We have borne burdens all-day and suffered untold horrors and pressures in the night.

But the earliest years of good Jewish conditioning teaches every Jew:

"Al tirah avdi Yaakov,"
"Do not be afraid my servant Jacob." (Isaiah 44:2)

Remember you are the *"Zera Avraham ahuvi,"* "The seed of Abraham, my beloved friend." *"Habitu el,"* "Look at" from where you came. (Isaiah 51:2) Remember Abraham your Father, and Mother Sarah who bore you. Abraham has taught us, no matter what happens, *gam zu letovah*, this too is all for the good. Be a *"Samahch bechelko,"* "A person who is happy with their portion." (Ethics of the Fathers 1:1) Rejoice in the good that God has given you. And even when confronting the pressures, the concerns, the toils, and the worries of life. Be strong in your gratitude, convinced that the Lord God, *koneh shamayim va'aretz* the maker of heaven and earth (Gen. 14:22), he will protect thee and guide and guard thee and even when you do not see this immediately, know in your heart that God is *Rachmah*, the merciful one, and be thankful for the good he has done and that shall be stowed upon us. Reb Avraham Yaakov of Sadigurer explained the verse that we sing in *birchat hamazon*, grace after meals, *vedoershai hashem lo yachshiru kol tov*, those who seek God will not lack all good, which means those who seek God will not be in want. Why? Because *kol tuv*, all is for good. Everything that occurs to us in life, the pleasant and the sad, the accomplishments and the sorrows, are all good. So let us be thankful, thankful that we are still here, thankful that we can still enjoy each other, thankful that we have the privilege of helping each other, thankful for *Eretz Yisrael*, the Land of Israel and thankful that despite all the cruelty of history which have terminated so many nations, we Jews are still here, creating and believing. Thankful that we have an America, where pilgrims established a thanksgiving on which they hoped to emulate the holiday of the Torah. Thankful for all the future potentials and possibilities we still have. Thankful for *olam hazeh and olam habah*, this world and the world to come. *Gam zu litovah*, this too is for the good.

GENERATIONS AFTER

The Torah portion is called *Chayai Sarah*, the life of Sarah, although it opens with a narrative regarding the passing of Mother Sarah and the earnest attempt by her husband, the Patriarch Abraham to inter her not in any ordinary place, but within the realm of a family plot.

The Midrash (Gen. Rabbah 58:3) advises us that Rabbi Akiba was once lecturing and he observed that his congregants were very inattentive. Perhaps they had imbibed a good meal, or each may have been daydreaming, concerned either with pleasant fantasies or even reviewing the multiple pressures to which humanity has always been subject. He regarded them carefully, and noticed they were becoming drowsy. Determined to awake them from lethargy, and arouse them to the positive comments he was projecting towards them, he suddenly remarked. "Why did Esther, that great heroine of Purim, why did this lovely young girl deserve the privilege of ruling over one hundred and twenty seven provinces, an empire which stretched from India unto Ethiopia? The congregation suddenly sat up as he continued, "the reason is this: let Esther, the descendant of Sarah, who lived one hundred and twenty seven years, come and reign as a queen over one hundred and twenty seven provinces." This immediately galvanized the congregation into a mood of analysis, questions, and challenges.

Who of us is not confronted quite frequently with a request to offer some reason or explanation for the brutal destruction by the Nazis of a third of our people? Not only those who by the grace of God have miraculously been spared from annihilation, but even those who were now exposed to the diabolical plans of Satan, are asking themselves earnestly and searchingly, "Why?" It makes no difference whether the question is asked in the harassed spirit of the afflicted Job or in the contemplative mood of an ever faithful Moses. An answer should be given, an answer must be given by the responsible and competent teacher of religion.

The Sage and Martyr, Rabbi Akiba, whose tragic destiny it was to witness the Roman occupation of the Holy Land and the tortures and humiliations to which his brethren were subjected by the alien invaders, was indeed sensitive to the mood of resignation and despondency of his people. He knew the doubt and questions that burdened his generation regarding the national disaster was visited upon them. Therefore, to banish pessimism from their midst and to strengthen a feeble faith, Rabbi Akiba suggested that the reward for a *mitzvah* is reaped generations after its performance. Sarah's compensation for her exemplary God intoxicated life helped Queen Esther, generations later in a moment of need and distress. Someone once suggested that this should be submitted to us as a broad and sweeping outlook on man's interdependency. The actions of one person in a given generation may have decisive repercussion upon the destiny of an entire people centuries later. There is no isolated abrupt experience in human life.

It is true, many were those in the days of Rabbi Akiba who speculated about reward and punishment and the nature of Divine Providence over man. Yet, if one can be guided not to draw final conclusions, however glaring the facts may be, even from the experience of an entire people, the inevitable agony of thousands may be diminished. And this perhaps implied in God's reply to the famous question of Moses when he said, "Show me, I pray Thee, Thy glory." And God answered: I will make all my goodness pass before thee. Not by one experience, however far reaching its results may be, can one draw conclusive generalizations. One must be sensitive to the dynamics of history and view various phenomena in their totality. One cannot speak of the Jewish experience under the Nazis, however gruesome and tragic, without an exhaustive analysis of what preceded it and what has followed. Who can doubt that the strange phenomenon of revival of Judaism as it is beginning to populate American life, witness the Yeshivot, the "born again" Jews in the person of the baal teshuva who fascinates sociologists and other observers because he has swung from one pole of total alienation from Judaism, to the other extreme, of rigid observance and fidelity. Who can deny that all this in no small measure is due to the dramatic events in the Holy Land. It is no wonder, therefore that the keen and wise Rabbi Akiba detected a relationship between Sarah and Esther who were removed from one another by many generations. If that relationship was due to the influence of the Matriarch Sarah, it succeeded because of the nature of that influence.

The Biblical narrative provides us with some insight to this when we review its first lines. "And the life of Sarah was one hundred and twenty and seven. The Rabbis notice the peculiarity, the extended phrase, and so they ask, why should not the Bible have simply said that Mother Sarah lived until the ripe old age of one hundred and twenty seven years. One answer provided is quoted by Rashi, "*Af bat mayah below chate vebat esrim kebat shevah leyofee*," "At the age of one hundred she was as free from sin, as a young a person reaching out into life at age of twenty." (Rashi to Gen. 23:1) And at the age of twenty, she had the beauty of goodness and sincerity that we associate with the innocence of childhood, seven years old. At age seven, at age twenty, and at age one hundred there was something in the personality of Sarah which made her day and life vibrant, interesting and valuable.

A short time ago I read a magnificent sermon that had a rather fascinating comment upon the days of our lives, it suggested that personalities may be compared to various forms of calendars. Some people are like those three hundred sixty five sheet calendars on our desks. When the day is done, the sheet is disposed of, with no traces of it left. That day has been lived but only for the moment and in no way affected its predecessors or successors. It has no relationship to the days that came before or those that follow. There are people who are like the twelve sheet monthly calendars that are destroyed at the end of each month. Some events, birthday, anniversaries and the like are kept in view at least while the sheet is still alive. A chosen few people however, are similar to a single sheet yearly calendar, or better yet, a lifetime calendar. Each and every day is cherished until the very last; each and every moment is treasured because it holds some significance. It represents one rung on the ladder of spiritual ascent?

Sarah's days counted and she in turn helped influence the person who had the greatest sway over her, namely Father Abraham. The result is that when the Bible speaks of Abraham after his loss of his precious wife and beloved companion, the narrative notes:

> *"VaAvraham zaken bah bayamim,"*
> **"Abraham grew old came with his days" (Gen. 24:1)**

This we usually translate as he advanced in age. Standing before the *Kisei Hakavod*, the Divine Throne, each day testified to some worthwhile deed by Abraham, a deed invariably shared by Sarah, another stranger fed, another idolater converted to the belief in the one God, another human being who experienced their charity, their compassion, gentility and goodness. There is an equally enlightening comment by an unknown author who suggests that *bah bayamim* actually refers to *bet yamim*, two days. In this sense, Abraham lived with two days constantly before his eyes, *yom holdo veyom hamavet*, the day of birth and the day of death. The former stimulated research into such perplexing enigmas as why was man born? Why was he divinely endowed with a will to choose freely the type of life he desires to live? The latter provoked thoughts on man's ultimate destiny. How shall man face his Maker? Bearing these two days in mind, Abraham responded with a life of spirit and success.

And as Sarah, Mother of our people and faith set the pattern for Esther and her heroines of our history throughout the ages, we too may speak with pride of how she made her days count and filled each with love of God. May this pattern inspire all of us to emulate her decency and goodness, so that her children and our children may reap the rewards of this goodness for generations to come.

KIRYAT ARBA HE HEBRON

"Vayetain Avraham et kol asher lo leYitzchok,"
"And Abraham gave everything he had to Isaac."
(Gen. 25:5).

In the recent attacks against Zionism, we have recently been treated to an added feature; the insistence by Arabs that they, too, are descendants of Abraham and hence, he has given them inalienable rights to the Holy Land, therefore, their contentions are just and we have no sole juridical rights to Israel. As anyone can see, if he only reads the Bible and traces claims back through ancient literature to which the Torah lesson replies through the lips of the Sages who in Midrash Hagadol comment:

The Talmud (Baba Batra 131a) says, he who distributes his estate during his lifetime as a gift, if he gives to one child more than he does another; or if he balances honors due his *bechor*, first-born with the other children; whatever he does is a fait accompli, and can not be altered or disputed. This is so, however, only with him who has distributed this wealth as a gift. But if he has bequeathed an unequal amount as an inheritance then it cannot be fulfilled; thus did father Abraham act: he divided his estate among his children during his life as gifts.

For a hundred years our father Abraham wandered about various lands in the orient. From the moment God commanded him to leave his home, in Haran and go searching for a land of his own; which He would indicate to Abraham; our patriarch continued to travel. There were lands that he entered that attracted him very little and so he prayed to God:

"I hope that my portion will not be in this territory so that I will not have to remain here always." Other territories however did attract him and he prayed "might my portion be in this land?" But he did not remain long on any specific territory because he did not know where to build his home. He had not yet received the proper sign from God which land would be assigned to him, hence he continued his search.

Our Father Abraham was a very wealthy man when he departed from his father's land to look for a proper home for himself and his children where he might live with spiritual convictions. The various economic enterprises he established in the various lands succeeded and increased his wealth. Even as Eliezer said to Rivkah:

> **"Hashem Bayrach et adonee vayigdol," "Vayetain lo tzone ohvakar vekesef vezahav vaavadim ohshefachot," "And God had blessed my master very much," "And he has grown and given him herds, silver, gold, servants, camels, etc." (Gen. 24:35)**

And because of the great herds he acquired, he purchased large estates of fields and orchards in various areas. Speaking about the conflicts between Lot's shepherds and Abraham's, Rashi says because the shepherds of Lot were wicked and brought their flocks to pasture in strange fields, and the shepherds of Abraham scolded them for robbing these strangers. Abraham did not want to utilize the grazing lands of strangers, and therefore he purchased large estates where he kept his herds in pasture.

Because of the water scarcity in these tropic lands he built wells in every locality where he settled. Although he lived in simple tents, he built all over altars to God. And near the altar he established an *eshel*, a hostel, or hotel, as the *Gemara*, Talmud says: one claims it was a dormitory for those who came to study the new faith; and the other says it served as a shelter for travelers and passerby's. He also maintained business relationships with the countries of the orient, and in neighboring countries he was regarded as a capable businessman and industrialist. The Midrash says all industrial princess magnates of east and west hovers near his door, in order to obtain his counsel for new enterprises. And as we observed Father Abraham did not stay too long in one spot.

Abraham continued to wait for an omen from God where he should settle and make his permanent dwelling. And that omen finally emerged when he and his son Isaac returned from the *akedah* at Beer Sheva. They did not find Mother Sarah at home, but learned that she had gone to Hebron instead to look for them, and there she had died. Abraham now understood through his sadness that God had given him the sign where he was to establish himself.

The land of Canaan where Abraham and his people now settled, and which later became the promised land which God had promised would be handed over to future generations consisted then of little settlements and large deserts stretching from the river of Egypt to the great river the Euphrates. And these boundaries as they are indicated in the Bible stretch from Phenecia to Gaza, and from the Mediterranean Sea to Jordan. It was then occupied by ten peoples who were chiefly of nomadic tribes which wandered from one spot to another.

These nomadic tribes ruled by an elder never attempted to settle the land and develop or cultivate its soil. On the contrary, when they tired or grew bored or disgusted with an area because they had used up its grass, they would assemble their herds and cattle and leave, move away searching for another fertile place which they would ruin. But before they left, they destroyed and exterminated peoples who lived in the vicinity. They destroyed their mud houses and plugged their wells shut.

The American professor Laudermilke, studied the soil of Israel and why the inhabitants of those times let these nomads into their land to destroy it. The inhabitants of the times consisted mainly of nomadic tribes whose main occupation were robbery, murder and fighting one with the other. They also were never interested in cultivating the soil. They had very little love for the land, and when tribes attacked one another, they tried to wreck every source of livelihood that they found, especially plugging up the wells of water, because these wells were necessary for agricultural development in tropical countries. They also uprooted all trees thereby making the land very weak towards resisting tornadoes, or erosion that turned the whole land into a wilderness. Jewish pioneers working the land have found many such wells plugged and made unusable, just to keep the land in a state of destruction and aridity.

But Abraham rose from before his loss and although he first wanted to buy the Cave of Machpelah from Ephron the Hittite, he negotiated not only with him alone. He wanted the agreement of all the peoples in the area, he wanted to establish his national home publicly and judicially. "I came here a stranger (like all nations of earth on colonization and immigration) and today I am a very wealthy landowner. I have decided to make my permanent home here and dedicate all my power, ability and skills to revive this soil and make it productive *imachem*, together with you (Gen. 23:4) we shall build my national home."

It is in a friendly manner and with large sums of money did our Father Abraham possess the land that had been promised to him. And in his advanced years he gave it to Isaac.

"*Vayetain Avraham et kol asher lo le Yitzchok*,"
"And Abraham gave everything he had to Isaac."
(Gen. 25:5).

"*Ohlivnai hapelagshim asher leAvraham natan Avraham matanot*,"
"And the children of his concubines he sent away with other gifts." (Gen. 25:6).

All his estates and lands and wealth in other lands he presented to these other children during his lifetime. And he sent them away so that they would have no claims in *Eretz Yisrael*, the Land of Israel. *Vayishalchaim mayal Yitzchok beno beodehnu chai*, and he sent them away from Isaac while he was still alive (Gen. 25:6). This did Abraham deal legally, basing the rightful claim of Isaac to the land and his children. He left nothing over for an inheritance. For with respect to that law, all children are equal and even the father can not change it. But to divide his wealth during his lifetime, that is his right. And what he did was done, a fait accompli, and no one could change it.

And when the Israeli government refuses to recognize that Hebron belongs to the Jewish People, then the voices of Abraham our Father and Sarah our Mother ring out for all history and for our children's children, for all generations to hear. This land is *Eretz Yisrael*, The Land of Israel, and not *Eretz Yishmael*, the Land of Ishmael. It belongs to the people who always yearned and wept for it. And this land will bloom and prosper only with the children who received it from Abraham. And even as Hebron is the *Kiryat Arba*, the grave of our ancestors, and even as we go there as a people for *kever avot,* to visit the graves of our forefathers, so too is it *kiryat anakim,* the spot of the giants, whose faith and courage will lead us to victory always and forever.

Toldot

— 6 —

וְאֵלֶּה תּוֹלְדֹת יִצְחָק בֶּן־אַבְרָהָם

"And these are the generations of Isaac the son of Abraham." (Genesis 25:19)

FOLLOW THE LEADER

So begins the Biblical lesson of *Toldot*. Every serious student of the Bible is aware of the fact that Isaac did not project the startling charisma, profound insight, startling leadership and the unique exploration of man's relation to the universe into which we have been forced. This was evidenced by the fact that Isaac superficially seems to be squeezed between the tremendous attractive personality of his Father and his own son. Both Abraham and Jacob exude philosophic convictions, aggressive intent and a combination of physical and spiritual determination to endure the stability of their faith and the household from which a nation would develop.

Furthermore, the Torah itself is rather sparse in its biographical data concerning Isaac, even in the tale of the *Akedah*, the story of the binding of Isaac, an incident that has motivated profound religious interpretations from Jew and non-Jew alike. It is Isaac who is portrayed as a passive participant, and it is the faithfulness and the loyalty of Abraham to God that is tested. What may sound strange, is that unlike Abraham's wife, who obviously is a dominant personality in her own right, toiling with her husband in attracting converts to the new faith of one God, and unlike the passionate romantic stirring narrative of Jacob's travels wherein he finds his own eternally beloved Rachel, Isaac may be considered by some as a rather pale and blind personality. Eliezer, his Father's steward, selected his wife for him.

Fortunately, Rebecca his wife turned out to be an intriguing fascinating woman. A wife and mother whose foresights and pragmatic observations, you will, ensured our people's national growth and development. What is more, in his relations with those about him, Isaac was only a carbon copy of his Father, Abraham. And yet this forefather of ours is still regarded with awe, respect, honor and even admiration. Why? Because he was a magnificent follower, a carbon copy, a chip off the old block. This was a man who appreciated the need of being a good follower. In our days, we are accustomed to emphasize the need for leadership. Everyone is encouraged in his youth to be a leader, to take off on new directions, to acquire new possessions, new values new objectives. But our traditions have always been sensitive to the ability of being a good follower or to possess the ability to endure continuity. The Romans used to say "Better to be the head of foxes than a tale among lions." But the Rabbi's used to admonish our people, "Be rather a tail to lions than a head to foxes." You know when students apply to college and university for admission, the candidate is evaluated by the responses that his parents, teachers, or other appropriate people in the community say about him or her. In one case, a father looked at the questionnaire, as it asked, is this candidate a dynamic leader? The father, after hesitation, answered: "I really don't know, but he is a highly cooperative person and an excellent follower." A few days later, the father received a reply from the President of the University. "Dear parent, our current candidates apparently will form the forthcoming new class with about four hundred tremendous leaders. Thank God, that we can congratulate ourselves upon the acceptance of your son. It is good to know that we shall have at least one good follower."

All parents expect their children to do tremendous things, to pursue goals, to reach out to purposes that they may never have sought. Today's generation speaks to us, reminding us that we have to think of the bottom line, that this is the novel channel, this constitutes the new and of course more important aspects of living in contemporary society. But perhaps we ought to tell them that the idea of the bottom line is not new, our grandparents often spoke of the *unterster shurrah*. This was really a hope that we would be good followers, we would marry women as good and as loyal and as earnest and as alert to the realities of life as our mothers. A hope that we would follow our fathers in giving of ourselves unstintingly in love, unity, concern, friendship and companionship. Yes, in emotion and conviction, in sacrifice and uninterrupted devotion.

"*Eleh Toldot Yitzchok*," these are the productions, these are the accomplishments, these are the objectives of Isaac, the son of Abraham. Abraham begat Isaac. This nice, sincere, and unsophisticated personality was the true son of Abraham and he was determined to follow that which was best in his Father's personal life. That is what we fathers still dream about with reference to our children. Isaac materially succeeded in acquiring a hundred fold expansions in material blessings, but basically he followed the positive and constructive example of his father. And that is what we wish for our children. Whatever they have seen of love and devotion, care and fidelity in their background, whatever ethical truths the Jewish past has formulated for us in all generations, that it will continue to be goals for which our children will strive. Hopefully, their lifestyles will be ones, which will cleave of Jewish values, Jewish identity, Jewish hope, and Jewish service. This will not only make them great followers, but also infuse their lives with comfort, delight and pride.

TAKING LIFE ON ITS TERMS

The Biblical portion *Toldot* deals with further incidents in the life of Isaac the Patriarch. Were he an ordinary person, it has been suggested, he would have been very bitter about life, complaining about his unhappiness and bad luck. If you consider his life, you will see how true this is.

As a child an older jealous brother, Ishmael, tormented him. Then, his father took him on a long journey, only to discover that he was intended to be sacrificed. Of course, he was not sacrificed, but can you imagine what a shock it must have been for this young one to learn that he had been intended for such an act? When he returned from this heroic mission, he again received a shock at learning that his very aged mother had passed away. Finally, he married the marvelous and lovely Rebecca with whom he finds happiness. But here again there are problems. They have no children. They both pray very hard to God and are blessed with twin boys. Again, more trouble. The boys don't get along well, because they are so different in characteristics and temperament. Then depression hits the land in the form of a famine, and Isaac who is now getting along in years has to wander in a strange land to find food for his family. Later his eyesight fails him. His two sons contest each other to get his blessings. They outwit one other. But neither is really satisfied with the result. Isaac's whole life is nothing but a series of disappointments and trials.

Yet, we do not find even once that Isaac talks about complaining. He does not utter any words of criticism or dissatisfaction. Why? Is he unaware of what is happening? No. Because this second forefather of our people possesses a rare quality which all great men must possess, courage, the ability to take it. For example, in this Torah lesson, we read how Isaac comes to the land of the Philistines during the famine, becomes a friend of the King, Avimelech, but soon people become envious of his wealth. Rather than complain or incur their displeasure, he peacefully departs and settles in the valley of Gerar. But here, too, he has his problems. His servants dig a well and other people seize it. He digs another well and again they fight over it. The average man would have complained bitterly and quarreled violently. It might even have ended in bloodshed, not so with Isaac. He went away and did not fight, but dug a well elsewhere which he called *Rechovot*, meaning God has made room for both of us and we shall be fruitful.

Now, you must marvel at a person, who goes from one disappointment to another without complaint, until he emerges victorious. Isaac was a man who knew that strength is not only measured by what strength you can extend but also how much you can absorb. Of course, this does not mean that one should run from battle, but that sometimes discretion is the better part of valor as many generals have known and shown. It is suggested that the

Rabbis may have had this in mind when they advised that a person on occasion should be as pliant as reed, and not unbending like the cedar tree. The reeds bend their heads before the wind, and endure, while the proud and arrogant cedar challenges the wind and is snapped. Apparently, experience had shown Isaac that when one studies human life and nature, we see a great deal of validity in the observations of Solomon, who many centuries later declared:

"Mah'aneh rach yashiv chaimah, ud'evar etzev ya'aleh af,"
"A soft answer turneth away wrath, but a grave word sturreth up anger." (Proverbs 15:1)

Even Avimelech, and Phicol, the captain of the army, returned to Abraham pleading, "Let there be peace between thee and us. Let us make a treaty that thou wilt not do us any harm, even as we have not touched thee. And have sent thee away in peace, thou art blessed of the Lord." (Gen. 21:22) They wanted his friendship and good will.

In American history, there was a personality who also had this kind of great courage. He took life on its terms, but continued to strive, toil and keep his eye on his goals. This man was young when he ran for the legislature in Illinois where he was badly beaten. He entered business and failed. For the next seventeen years he paid debts which had been incurred by a worthless partner. He then fell in love with a beautiful young woman to whom he became engaged. But then she died. So he decided to enter politics. He ran for congress and was badly defeated. He tried and failed to get an appointment to the United States land office. He became a candidate for the United States Senate and was badly defeated. In 1856 he became a candidate for Vice President and was again defeated. In 1858 he was defeated by Douglas. But in the face of all this tough luck, all these defeats and failures, he eventually achieved the success attainable in life, by obtaining an undying fame for generations after generations. His name, Abraham Lincoln. Now I'm not suggesting that Lincoln would not battle for his convictions for he did lead this country through the most terrible, frightening chapter of our history, the Civil War.

But what makes this man so great is his ability to accept his fate. Isaac also accepted all circumstances of life calmly and confidently. Why? Because he knew and believed that the Father of all life watched over him carefully and ordained what happened to him. This implicit faith in God and agreement with his plans happens to be typical of great people at one time or another. Jewish children have reveled in Hebrew school at hearing the story of Rabbi Akibah. He once started out on a long journey and rode on a donkey that was his means of transport. He carried with him a rooster to awaken him in the morning, and a candle to dispel the darkness. At the end of the first day, he came to a small community and was turned away at the inn where he wanted to find shelter. Instead of complaining, he shrugged his shoulders and said: "Whatever God does is for the best." At nightfall, he found an empty field, and as he made ready to sleep, his donkey ran away, at night, a little fox came and killed his rooster carrying it away as food. Suddenly an unexpected gust of wind blew out his candle and he could not relight it. Realizing he faced only darkness, no one to wake him up at dawn and no means to travel, he lay down and said whatever God does he does for good. In the morning he was shocked when he walked back to the town and discovered the chaos which greeted his eyes. He discovered that a group of thieves had attacked the community that night. Many had been killed and robbed. After moments thought, he said: "Look how fortunate I have been, I narrowly escaped death. Had I been given shelter, I too might have been attacked. And when the murderers left, the braying of the donkey, or the crowing of the rooster or the light of the candle might have attracted them. And they might have killed me there. Whatever God does is done for the best."

There is a lesson in this for us all. Jewish faith calls upon us to be courageous. Face all problems with calm and courage. You know in football, a tackler is not that good if he can only tackle others, but cannot take being tackled himself. You know a good fighter is not only a person who punches fiercely, but he must be able to stand up against the blows of another and fight to the final round. Men and women, everywhere in life, are struck by unexpected hardships and troubles. They must have the courage to stand erect and continue in whatever work they are engaged. We have to believe as Isaac and Rabbi Akiba did, that all which God does is for the best.

The Story of the Jewish People is a tale of courage. We learned early in our history how to overcome obstacles. Sometimes we had to be passive and meet disappointments. Take the reed that bends before the wind. Waves of persecutions and oppressions came over us. But again we turned up strong and confident. The Jewish Nation is a Nation that has learned to take it on the chin and keep on strengthening its character until a time when it can strike back. We have to have courage not only to stand up against unfair prejudice and unethical practices, but also to have the quiet courage and the duty say the Rabbis, to imitate God.

God is merciful. As God protects the widows and orphans, we must do the same. As God seeks justice and loving kindness, we must do the same. And in the face of disappointment or trial, we must never say we give up, but quietly find the strength and courage to continue despite the obstacles and impediments. This we will find, will bring us success. It will give us an inner bravery and power, which will help us emerge victorious in all conflicts.

DIGNITY AND DOING RIGHT

Ours is a culture from which the Bible cannot be extracted. Our literature, ethics, political, social and economic ideals cannot be dissociated from the Bible, since so many of our most profound observers and philosophers have been nurtured and inspired by Biblical sources. Often as not, our speech manifests unique richness and imagery by resorting to some special semantic that stems from the Bible. Such an expression is the assertion that one has "sold his birthright for a mess of pottage," to indicate the paucity of one's personal priorities and values, in exchanging a treasured possession for a trivial one. Actually, the term, "mess of pottage" does not occur in the Bible, but the thought is still valid. It is derived from an incident recorded in the scriptural lesson that describes a conversation between Jacob and his brother, Esau.

"Vayazed Ya'akov nazid,"
"And Jacob was preparing some pottage." (Gen 25:29)

The Midrash (Gen. Rabbah 63:11) reminds us that Esau asked his Brother, why are you preparing this pottage? Jacob answered, because that grand old man, our Grandfather, Abraham has died. Commentary recalls that Abraham lived one hundred and seventy five years, while his son, Isaac, lived one hundred and eighty. Legend has it that God whittled five years off the life of the first Patriarch, Abraham, because Esau, his Grandson, ran to the fields, not simply to obtain food, but to indulge in many immoral and ugly practices which were countenanced by the idolatry of the times. And God remembered that he had sworn unto Abraham:

"*Veatah tavoh el Avotecha beshalom,*"
"And you shall go unto your Fathers in peace." (Gen. 15:15)

However, it would appear that our forefather was being denied peace in his old age. His grandson, Esau, was attracted to the three features that our faith has always unceasingly criticized, namely, *avodah zarah*, idolatry, *megaleh arayot*, immorality, and *shefichat damim*, the unjustified shedding of blood. Better that he live less and pass away easily, rather than live the extra handful of years by spending them in sorrow, anguish and frustrations.

Now we see that Esau has come home from his usual schedule of unpleasantness and asks why Jacob is suddenly acting like a chef, and he hears that grandfather Abraham has passed away. The attribute of justice has been struck by that great man's passing. Whereupon Esau replied, if so, there is no reward for doing good, and no resurrection and immortality. On this flippancy, the Rabbis apply the words:

"*Al tivcho lemate ve'al tanedo lo, bechoo vacho laholaich,*"
"Weep not for the dead, neither bemoan him, but weep greatly for him that goeth away." (Jeremiah 22:10.)

Weep not for him, say the Sages, applies to Abraham, for in his case, his passing away had a positive aspect, since it prevented him from sustaining deeper hurt at the evil deeds of Esau. But weep greatly for him that goes away, say the Sages, applies to Esau whose wickedness caused his grandfather much pain and injury, and certainly diminished his years on the earth. And so the

Rabbis felt that the greater weeping should be for Esau who surely would at some time be called to account for the grief he had caused the old man and for the bad deeds which led to shortening Abraham's life.

And so the brothers indulge in conversation. Esau says, let me swallow some of this pottage, because I am hungry (tired). Now the Hebrew word which is used for swallow is not found anywhere else in the Bible, because it refers to the voracious swallowing or gulping of food which animals do. And the Midrash explains, the term is likened unto the opening of his mouth by a camel. (Gen. Rabbah 63:16) The camel would have his mouth and stomach filled in this manner to ensure that it would have a reserve, when it had to travel for several days without getting food.

I recall that as a boy, I watched my Mother and some neighbor's literally stuff food down the gullet of ducks and geese. This would fatten them up for some future festive meal. And here in the Torah portion, at this point in the conversation, Jacob replies:

> **"Michrah kayom et bechorahtecha lee,"**
> **"Sell me first your birthright." (Gen. 25:31)**

One commentary apparently feels our first reaction to this report. Why not give your hungry brother some food? The commentary suggests there was some divine intervention at that moment. What after all was the birthright if not so much a promise that Abraham's descendants would be the richest nation in the world, control all the oil reserves, all the metal and precious gem mines of our planet and that they would manage all the finances of the nations? Rather the promises which God had sworn unto Abraham was that to him and his descendants, God would give the

Holy Land of Zion, from which would come forth the Torah and its moral instructions to humanity.

Well, now that Esau has hastened the death of Abraham our Father, by virtue of his immorality and unethical conduct, he certainly does not deserve to inherit the leading role in those sacred blessings. Maimonides, the Rambam, discusses whether in the case of a gluttonous and rebellious son, if the father should move to have his son punished as such, whether the son would still be considered the rightful heir of the father's possessions and property. Rambam answers in the negative, saying would not someone who has been responsible for the death of another be deprived by the authorities of inheriting the possessions of the victim?

Thus, the commentary notes that famous case of the Prophet who stood before King Ahab who had been responsible for the murder of Naboth, whose vineyard he had then seized. The prophets thundered at the King:

> **"*Haratzcheta vegam yarashta*,"**
> **"Have you killed and also inherited?" (Kings I 21:19)**

Now legally, the King had the right to confiscate that land, but from the Prophet's anger, we understand that the murderer should not be permitted to inherit the victim's property. And thus the Prophet makes the King squirm by saying that he had sinned, once through the murder and secondly through inheritance. In the light of this discussion, it certainly would be clear to Jacob, that Esau, having been responsible for Abraham's death, would surely not be entitled to inherit the spiritual blessings of Abraham. It may have been that moral question which motivated the response of Jacob:

"*Michrah kayom et bechorahtecha lee*,"
"Sell me first your birthright." (Gen. 25:31)

This moral question arises, because unlike some non-Jewish commentators who regard this moment as being indicative of Jacob's human greed, the Rabbis differ. They point to teachings in the Jewish tradition against greed, envy, and demanding prices for any commodity, which are far beyond their intrinsic value. Following the latter procedure, the Rabbis feel, would be practically equal to partaking of robbery. It is this attitude which arouses interest in Jacob's insistence for the sale of Esau's birthright.

But it is another aspect of the conversation which is interesting, namely, the expressions used:

"*Halitayne*,"
"Let me swallow that red pottage" (Gen. 25:30)

Esau speaks with a crudeness which is unworthy of a son of Isaac and a grandson of Abraham. Actually, what Esau said to his brother was, "shove the food down my mouth." That may be proper for a donkey, camel or those geese that were fattened for a family meal, but not for a human being. A person who speaks that way lessens his own dignity, manifests a lack of self-respect and self-esteem.

In our Jewish culture, this dignity and self-esteem always has been important. In fact, people who speak improperly, people who eat in the marketplace, which was not exactly, clean or enticing, hygienic or aesthetically pleasing are considered *Pasul May'aydut*, unreliable witnesses. People who walk about in public improperly or indecently attired, those who are engaged in immoral activities or financial pursuits, all these are considered unreliable witnesses, because they lack a sense of shame, sensitivity, and the self-esteem which a person of honor, integrity and high moral standards should embrace. A person who lacks this dignity, who cares nothing for his word, his appearance in dealing with others, really forgets that he is created in the divine image, and as long as this means nothing to him, he does not consider himself as distinct from any animal.

And hence like Esau, such people are flippant and contemptuous of justice and rewards for the righteous. They believe that since we are nothing but animals, there is nothing like resurrection or immortality no matter how one understands the term. In the light of our present discussion of the rabbinical evaluation of human dignity, we may now understand Jacob's response to Esau's wild desire for the pottage. But what is just as significant is Esau's reply. Oh, I am dying, it is the food I want, why should I bother with a birthright? And Esau quickly sells his spiritual inheritance, which only serves to clinch the Rabbinical portrait of Esau as materialistic, the hunter who can easily hold blood and hence more concerned with lusts, appetite, hedonistic pleasures than with spirituality and higher moral standards.

Our analysis is of great importance to adults in our current society, where people must determine what their priorities in life will be. We must all consider these same values. Are we going to become a people who are motivated only by our own appetite? Will we think that life consists only of eating, drinking and having fun? Or will we understand that there are problems in life, that there are those who must be helped, who must be educated and who deserve our concern? Will we be sensitive to the needs of our people? Will we remember that we Jews have been the victims of hatred, unjustified hostility and enmity? That we have suffered as no other people, and will we therefore always display our loyalty to Jews and Judaism and those great ethics of our faith which have played such a significant role in the development of the ideals of democracy, justice and fair play and common decency.

The Bible implies that as Jacob and Esau grew up, each began to show his true mettle. One a selfish, wild, undignified person, the other, a spiritually infused youth with integrity, decency, faith in God, and loyal to the great ideals of his parents and grandparents. May we all follow the best ideals of Abraham, Isaac and Jacob, bringing loyalty to others and honor to our people.

ACCEPTING AND SEARCHING FOR THE BEST IN OTHERS

The Torah lesson of *Toldot*, like so many other scriptural narratives, is chock full of implications and intimations for human relationships in all generations and under a multitude of circumstances.

This Torah lesson opens with a profound personal problem. The desires of Isaac and Rebecca to have a child of their own. To employ modern terminology, they were, as we often say in our own times, trying to start a family. We, who are old timers and supposedly veterans in such matters, often fail to tell younger generations how much alike we are. Often we are insufficiently articulate or we sustain an emotional handicap, and we do not project ourselves properly when we want to tell our children and grandchildren that kids are not simply products of sex, but they are actually the visible fruits of the love we have cherished for our spouses. It would appear that Isaac and Rebecca had a love relationship differing somewhat as compared with ours. But let us leave that aside for a moment.

The Torah inaugurates the chapter of *Toldot* with a reminder that Isaac was forty years old when he took Rebecca, the daughter of Bethuel and the sister of Laban, as his wife. And they were trying hard to start a family, and the Bible simply says:

> *"Vayeter Yitzchok Lashem lenochach ishto,"*
> **"And Isaac begged God in behalf of his wife."**
> **(Gen. 25:21)**

Now, Rabbis throughout all generations were fascinated by the expression, *"Lenochach ishto,"* because the translation that he appealed to God in behalf of his wife is fine, but the Hebrew word *nochach* really means opposite, or against or in front of. Rashi, the great interpreter, explains it to mean that both were really praying at one time, but each in different corners of the same room.

However, another spiritual leader who lived much closer to our times read Rashi in a sense that we might appreciate. He said, poor Rebecca, tense and worried, prayed, "Lord, who am I? What special privileges do I deserve, what tremendous importance does my family have? But Lord, look at this man I love so much, Isaac. He is a righteous man, the son of saintly father, and he deserves to get his wishes granted in life. For his sake, let us have a child."

But Isaac, who was really standing in front of her, facing her, looking at her with eyes of love, prayed quietly. "God, you know how it is when a woman loves her husband, but look at the facts: I have been very lucky, you have been very kind to me and I have learned to be humble because of your goodness. What am I really compared to the greatness, the goodness, the gentility, the decency and the spirituality of my great Father and Mother. But my Rebecca, my beloved, makes such a *tzimmes*, a big deal over the fact that I am God-fearing, but if anyone deserves a break, it is my sweet, precious Rebecca. You know God, she is the daughter of Bethuel, and the sister of Laban, my Brother-in-Law, an S.O.B., a con-man, as crooked as a corkscrew, a fellow who will forget family relations, decency, friendship and his word of honor, everything just for a buck. Yet, think of it, my Rebecca, raised in a home like that, turns out to be a rose among the thorns, God-fearing, loyal, faithful in all her relationships. God, this precious woman deserves to get her wishes granted."

And so Reb. David of Amshinov says, get the picture clear, *lenochach*, he stood facing her, looking at her, reading her eyes and praying for her. What was it in their experience that enabled them to reach this level, especially when you must admit that Isaac wasn't exactly a wild, passionate, youth, pursuing a young girl in hopes of obtaining her submission?

My response was to turn back to a few pages in the previous lesson, in which we learn how these two got married. Father Abraham, like most Jewish fathers wanted to see his son settled, but he was very leery about the young women in his vicinity. Lewd, promiscuous, we know today from scholarly studies how their preferences were conducive to all kinds of diseases and contamination, all due to their idolatrous practices. And so Abraham ordered his trusted steward, Eliezer, to visit his homeland and find a suitable wife for his son. So Eliezer fulfilled that mission by standing at the center of town, near a well because that was the focus of many communal activities. And what did he pray for? "He said, lord, show me a young woman, who will listen to me, a stranger, ask for a drink of water, and of her own accord, will not only provide me with drink, but also volunteer to provide water for my camels." And that is what happened Rebecca came along, heard the request and provided water for him and for his tired weary animals as well.

Now observe, what is it that Eliezer looked for? Did he speak about a pretty woman? Did he want a scintillating gal? Did he search for the sexiest gal possible? An intellectual giant? An academic genius? A woman with a terrific bank account? All these things are attractive features. But he knew what a man needs most in a wife; kindness, gentility, sensitivity toward man and beast, hospitality for those in need; warmth and that inner beauty which embraces us and showers us with an affection and love that encourages us to confront all problems in life, the vicissitudes which all of us must meet at one time or another in life. But this can never be a one way street. A man has to be able to stand, *lenochach ishto*, in front of his wife, as against his wife, as standing opposite her seeing in her all these attributes, even as she, standing opposite and seeing all these same magnificent characteristics in him. Each one sensitive to the magnificence, the goodness and the positive worth of the other.

And that is the implied lesson in the verse that opens this Torah reading. True love means an ability to accept each other and search only for the best of the other. Acceptance is hard, psychological work. Gilbert Keith Chesterton was probably right when he suggested that a humanitarian was a person who loves all mankind, but hates his next door neighbors. Contrast this with the position of Jonathan Swift, who wrote that he hated mankind, but loved the individual.

All these fine words bespeak tolerance, forgiveness, understanding, all necessary to make our lives pleasant, but above all, we need the ability to stand as did Isaac and Rebecca, accepting each other and determined only to see the greatest and the most magnificent which the other may possess.

PLAYING BOTH ENDS

"Shaatnez lo yaaleh alechah,"
"You will not wear linen and wool together."
(Levit. 19:19)

One of the most intriguing aspects of Bible study is the thrill a student experiences when he suddenly discovers that an, incomparable preciseness exists in Biblical writing. Volumes of either psychological intimations or historical facts may be implied in a few sentences. For example, when we read the story of the first fratricide as recorded by the Bible, we naturally, are stirred by the superficial tale of two brothers whose rivalry is such that it culminates in murder. The conclusions that have been elucidated from the narrative of Cain and Abel are many. And each is of course worthy of serious contemplation, conceptions of martyrdom, religious animosities and personal responses of gratitude. However, consider an historic facet of narrative. Cain was a farmer and Abel a shepherd. Now anyone who has devoted some time to the study of history knows that in those simple words are revealed expose of a tremendous historical pulsation. In the study of history, from its earliest times, we know that the original primary basis of what we consider assigned territories, national divisions, feudal holdings, etc. really developed from the mass migrations of people from one part of the world to another. Often these migrations were caused by conflicts between the agricultural and the pastoral (shepherding) elements.

You see, a farmer is a stable element in society, who desires total possession of the land he inhabits, without interference, though that he may be enabled to plow seed, plant and harvest the fruits of the soil. But a shepherd you all understand supervises his flocks, which are by nature Nomadic, since they cannot be restricted to one piece of land. Flocks graze. They nibble and consume all the grass and any vegetation they may find with a result that the soil, too often, becomes bare, deprived of certain chemical ingredients, which enrich the ground. This, invariably arouses conflict between the farmers and the shepherds, and in the past has indeed led to serious bloodshed between these two groups.

Farmers and cattle owners clashed often, with terrible blood shed on both sides. But it is the farmer who feels that he must rise up against the shepherd who is ruining the soil. In Israel, for example, this routine procedure was responsible in great measure for the ruination of the land. The Bedouins simply moved their flock from one spot to the other, leaving behind erosion of soil and the creation of a desert where once there had been areas that were granaries for the ancient world. Well, the Bible in a few chosen words compresses this entire review of world history. And Cain the farmer, killed Abel the shepherd. Now the Bible later presented pictures of a society which had to deal with these problems, not only physically but also ethically. And so we find a law in the Torah known as *shaatnez*. Centuries ago the Torah warned us:

"*Shaatnez lo yaaleh alechah*,"
"You will not wear linen and wool together."
(Levit. 19:19)

When farmers and shepherds were always warring, as they have in modern times too, the Torah denounced deceit, chicanery, hypocrisy and prevarication. If you were a farmer, you wore linen clothing, and if you were a shepherd, you wore wool. But,

"*Shaatnez lo yaaleh alechah*"
"You will not wear mixtures of wool and linen." (Ibid)

There shall be no *shaatnez* over thee. What did this mean practically? One of the immortal Jewish national leaders, Jabotinsky, once analyzed this in a treatment which even those who did not see eye to eye with him, nonetheless consider brilliant. He offered the proposition to us that a man should be honorable in his convictions. And abide by them. Wool, of course, is derived from the shearing of the sheep by the shepherd. Linens were made from Flax that was grown by the farmer.

Shaatnez, it would seem, said to us, What kind of a person are you? If you wear woolens, very well, you demonstrate to the world that you are a shepherd that you adhere to certain convictions and a certain way of life. If you wear the flax linen, you likewise demonstrate to the world that you are a farmer, that you have certain convictions and a certain way of life. But look here, if you are going to wear *shaatnez*, this mixture of wool and linen, what are we supposed to recognize in you? What conviction do you uphold and with whom as do you stand?

"*Vayotrotzazu habanim bekirbah*," ### "The unborn struggled within her." (Gen. 25:22)

The prayers of Mother Rebecca and Father Isaac were answered by our merciful creator. And Rebecca was pregnant and lo and behold, the unborn struggled within her. And Rashi explained the verse: when she passed the school of Shem and Eber, where the holy moral imperative was taught, Jacob feeling the love for Torah bounced around within his poor Mother, and wanted to rush out and join in the study of Torah. On the other hand, when she passed centers of idolatry and paganism, Esau was aroused and sought to escape the womb and join the heathens. This frightened our Mother Rebecca. What kind of a child do I bear? What kind of a man will he be? Whatever be the fad, whatever enjoys popularity, wherever he will be, will he follow the crowd with no convictions?

A person who will have no convictions, no ideals, no sincerity, no courage. A person who will nod his head in agreement when society recognizes God and who will also be ready to join a society which is pagan and idolatrous and sinful and murderous and has no ideas of justice and decency and humanity. Would he go one way and also another?

And so she poured forth her bitter heart before God and in turn she was advised that she had two nations within her. And now of course, she was quieted. This raises the question, why was she calmed? How did the answer given her soothe her anxiety? It was the fear that her child would have no honorable convictions and play both ends against the middle.

"*Vatelech lidrosh et hashem*,"
"And she went to pray to God" (Gen. 25:22)

And so she cried, and asked for comfort. And she received comfort, because she was told, you have two children, each of whom will be the progenitor of a nation. She wasn't naturally elated over the fact that one of her children would be wild, animalistic and physical in his approach to life. But she was satisfied to know that at least each child would have convictions by which they would stand. And one, of course was to be Jacob our forefather, another progenitor or founder of our faith and people. You see no parent really want to see their children grow up into mature adults who will have no ideas or ideals, no convictions, no deep beliefs, just wishy washy, people, lacking courage and sincerity. Grow up into a person of conviction, ideals and objectives to which you will adhere with courage, sincerity, truth and decency. In the course of life, we often are compelled to struggle in behalf of the ideals in which we believe, for which we as Jews have indeed sustained incomparable, unprecedented sorrow humiliations, torture and even death. But we have emerged, despite the entire hostility of the world, because we knew we are on the side of God, moral law, and the truth which spells out both freedom and the redemption, not only of our people but of the entire world.

Esau and Jacob quarreled within the very womb that bore them both. The Rabbis, in their quasi-romantic way say they fought over the stakes. Who would conquer *olam hazeh*, this world, and who would conquer *olam habah*, the world to come? Who would abandon every sense of idealism, every motif of honor and integrity, every impetus of truth for the sake of temporary, material expediency and who would maintain his stance and posture for morality, decency, compassion, honor, justice and truth? That is a struggle that discerned then by Torah continues to plague us to this very day. How many oceans of blood and pain, how many centuries of torture and humiliation has humanity sustained in this war?

Mother Rebecca was really frightened by this playing both sides against the middle. Stop being a hypocrite. You want to follow idolatry, O.K. We know what you are. You want to follow Torah, O.K. we know what you are. But for heaven's sake, you cannot be both a Jew and a gentile simultaneously. You cannot be one who prostitutes religion by being a Jew for Jesus.

Mother Rebecca knew what bothered her and she was soothed when she learned that two different nations were within her. One would follow idolatry, but the other, our Father Jacob would be true to God, Torah, justice and truth. May we, his descendants, be as firm in that faith and that loyalty to God, learning:

"Al tivtichu bendivim, beben adam shehaiyn low teshuvah."
"Do not trust in mortal princes, for in them there is no salvation." (Psalms 146:3)

"Bitchu ba'shem adai ad,"
"Trust in the Lord forever and ever." (Isaiah 26:4)

from him will come our salvation and victory.

THE PURPOSE OF HISTORY

History has been characterized as the account of man's "foibles and follies." To Voltaire, History was "nothing but a picture of crimes and misfortunes"; to the Jew, however, it is a record of past strivings and dreams, an account of past failures and accomplishments which form a pattern for a river of events that inevitably must stream towards those goals which the Creator has set for mankind to attain.

Someone has aptly claimed that in Judaism, yesterday is but a school for tomorrow, for ours is a way of life in which history is integrated with religion, and religion is thoroughly interwoven with history. That is evidenced in our tradition where the highest expression of sanctity is achieved by the prophecy that is predicated on the moral interpretation of history.

This historic prophecy blossoms poetically throughout the Torah where the Scriptural poetry is not restricted in the eyes of the Jew to the dramatic impact, the delicacy or majesty of the word or the picture evoked by skillful description. If you were to understand the Torah vision which embraces history prophetically, then you must plunge into the sacred commentary which reveals the *gedankengang*, direction of our philosophy and the method of appraising life's collective record of man.

Thus do we observe how the Rabbinical mentality is intrigued with the narrative of Mother Rebecca and the fascinating children she brought to the light of day.

"*Vatahar Rivkah ishto,*"
"And Rebecca, his wife conceived." (Gen. 25:21)

"*Vayotrotzazu habanim bekirbah,*"
"And the children struggled together within her."
(Gen. 25:22)

In these simple words did our sainted Sages fathom the great secret of history. Since time immemorial has our people regarded Esau, the progenitor of Edom, as the source of the Greek-Roman elements and their spiritual heirs in our civilization who have constantly sought mastery of the world. Civilization, as we are accustomed to hear it defined; in our times, consists of that Greek-Roman factor plus the Jewish influence. Many are the scholars who believe that Western Civilization, although predominantly adhering to a faith which considers itself a daughter of Judaism, is actually a mixture of these two Jacob Esau elements which they define as Judeo-Christian civilization.

Yet, as we read the Scriptural verse, *Vayotrotzazu habanim bekirbah* (Ibid), and the children struggled together within her, we are conscious that the Torah prophecy does not regard our civilization in such terms, for Torah does not regard civilization as a synthesis of these two philosophies. In nature and in the laboratory, we often see how distinctly recognizable elements become thoroughly mixed to form a new factor, an organic compound.

The most popular example of this is the joining of two elements, hydrogen and oxygen, to form water. The two elements can no longer be distinguished in the water, only the skilled analysis by the chemist can restore the elements in their pristine characteristics to us. Torah, however, is aware that in the laboratory of history, the Jewish and Greek-Roman elements have never been merged. They have merely existed along side each other and are in constant conflict with each other in a struggle that began at the very conception in the womb of time.

Superficially, it would appear that both elements have proclaimed unto themselves the same goal: The establishment of the best human society possible, the attainment of the greatest civilization. With the passage of the centuries, there have been some, who like the elder Pliny believed that "The ages go on incessantly improving" but with the development of complicated cultures, that civilization, another opinion has been expressed that man does not improve with time. Although this feeling is very noticeable today, this does not make it new. Time and again have we heard that the truly perfect society and the perfect man is to be found in a status naturalis, where he cannot be depressed by the evils of modern society. During the French revolution, it was Rousseau who proclaimed the doctrine of the natural man. He believed that the primitive state of man was one of virtue and happiness, but that civilization and the accompanying activities of kings, priests, lords, etc., had corrupted it. Today we hear many sigh for the "good old days" when men were concerned about the automobile as a danger to life and limb and relegated atomic bombs to the realm of science fiction.

Torah is not enamored in the *Ish Sadeh*, the man of the field, the primitive man. It understands that in spite of all the faults history records, history has a purpose; men have to go forward and in their progress there arises the struggle between Esau and Jacob and only when that conflict is finally solved, will man achieve true civilization. Thus we find that Rashi comments upon the struggle by saying, they quarreled and vied with each other concerning the inheritance of two worlds. The Midrash clarifies this thought further by teaching they fought over this world and the world to come.

The natural man, Esau and Edom, it cannot be denied, have been interested in progress, but it is an advance wherein the culture, that is, the instruments to achieve the civilization become the civilization without taking into account the proper goal of civilization. The German historian, Leopold Von Ranke wrote in 1879 "Irresistibly, in many guises, unassailably, armed with weapons and science, the spirit of the Occident subdues the world." That spirit which Ranke had in mind was the spirit of Esau, the man of the field, who places so much emphasis on the military and mechanical aspects of civilization. Esau, the natural man, considers himself the more practical and seeks mastery in this world, the world of immediate concern, whether that is the Greek polis, the Roman empire, or the country of his present rule. He expresses his civilization best when he seeks those tools that will make up for his natural weakness. He contributes to mechanics engineering, physics, chemistry, and of course as a cunning hunter to the military skills and strategies of history. From Esau develops an empire of power, military force, unrestricted, unbridled appetite, impelled by essential desire for material possessions, aggrandizement and the satisfaction or fulfillment of primitive passion.

The younger Jacob is not adverse to these skills. He would participate in these skills. He is a simpler less complicated empire in the technological sense, but a profound power in terms of the spirit and in terms of the search for the fulfillment which alone will enable man to achieve a level for which he and he alone of all living creatures in the world has the potentiality. He strives with his brother Esau, he wants to be part of that world too, but he also understands that the constant physical exertions for these instruments of culture without proper guidance will lead to collapse. Hence, he seeks the birthright, that spiritual authority which will permit him to guide the use of those tools.

True, both facets of human activity come from the same source. Both Esau and Jacob emerge from the same womb, the same mother has born them and the same father has begotten them. This is what all the studies verify. Both are brothers, created by the same God, nurtured and protected by the same mother earth. Both are subject to so many of the same conditions and their children are scattered everywhere throughout the globe.

But Esau cannot see because his attitude towards history is one without purpose; he must go forward to collapse. He himself admits it. Oswald Spengler in his book, *The Decline of the West* speaks of every civilization developing, as does a human being, from birth through adolescence to manhood and eventually to senility and finally collapse. Small wonders that this great prophet of the non-Jews should regard war as the great creative force. All life leads but to extinction, but believes Esau, whether it is a civilization that collapses or a globe that will eventually be unable to sustain life and freeze into extinction.

Even a moral historian like Arnold Toynbee who in his work *A Study of History* divided the record of the past into twenty-six civilizations who too have matured and then collapsed. He seeks to make Western civilization that is, the Christian civilization, the natively best of them all, and casually ignores Judaism because our very existence and certainly the resurrection of the Jewish State and the vindication of our Prophecy, does not fit in with his theories.

Esau is always aware of his struggle with Jacob. He must read our Bible, he repeats our visions for the future which he perverts and even when he seeks to exclude us from the birthright he has abandoned to us, he knows his own bankruptcy. For in the development of history, there surely grows the conviction amongst all peoples that the prophecy of Obadiah must come and come soon.

Of course, Esau produces much, but in the development of history he forgets the purpose of history. Toynbee speaks of saviours who wish to save the world from disintegration. He is aware of "Saviours of the Swords" and their violence. He knows of the "Saviours of the Time Machine" as he calls those who seek forcefully to change the nature of things. He is aware of those saviours who are "The Philosopher masked as a King" the Marcus Aurelius type who seek salvation by detachment from the world through a nirvana-like philosophy. Finally he sees the best saviour in what he calls "God Incarnate in a Man" which refers, of course, to the founder of his faith.

But as we look at history what do we see? The masses inexorably are being forced to climb the Mt. of Zion and judge the Mt. of Esau. For what have those saviours who sit on Esau's mountain accomplished. For the saviours with the sword are always the first failures. Nebuchadnezzar, Alexander, Ceasar, Napoleon, Bismark, the warmongers, the wielders of the sword go down to defeat, generation after generation. And the saviours of all machines are discovering that the robot is running amok and becoming the new master which threatens to eradicate us from the earth as said: in an atomic war, we shall run out of people sooner than ammunition.

And as for the nirvana-like philosophers, the suffering masses of humanity who feel the pain, the terror and the hunger are far too stimulated to be drugged into an opiate detachment. And without seeking to deprecate anyone's faith or religious conviction, what has the God Incarnate in man brought us? But Esau has been able to perform such accomplishments easily because even the record of which he boasts since he accepted the last saviour has not brought true civilization.

And yet, there is a distinct uniqueness to a little member of the human family called Jews or Hebrews. And any attempt to explain that difference in semantics of economics, mode of production, resources, intelligence, psychology, mores and behaviorism or biological sciences in terms of anatomy, physiology, genes or chromosomes, fall flat. Various schools of psychiatry, Adlerian and multiple causation; Freud and emphasis on complexes and sexual motives; Darwin and survival interpretations all are frustrated by the illogic of our history said Carl Weber, the great sociologist.

What is tremendous about this one portion of the Torah, is it lays the foundations of comprehending the isolation of Jewry from the rest of the world. All of humanity has been searching for the deliverance from the evils, the concerns and the pressures which impinge upon us and constantly threaten mankind with defeat, dissolution and perhaps death.

Everyone looks for a *moshia*, saviour, the force that can rescue humanity from our ills, and everyone identifies this saviour. There is the saviour with the sword. Jacob's Brother received the blessing which best fitted this attribute:

"Va'al charbechah tichyeh,"
"You shall live by the sword." (Gen. 27:40)

By the thousands do the volumes on history record those who imagined that by the force of the sword and armaments, they could impose their will up on all people and simultaneously discover redemption for themselves. Whether it was Attila the Hun, Genghis Khan, Alexander the Great or Hitler, regardless of whether the sword was wielded by a savage, a madman or a benevolent despot, the results invariable would be the same, piles of human skulls, millions of human beings murdered, human misery, pain and fear, and always the resultant failure, no redemption, no salvation. The Alexanders die young, the Caesars are betrayed, the Hitlers leave behind a record of revulsion and disgust, while the Stalins are recalled as oppressive madmen and organizers of massacres.

Preaching a doctrine of love and peace is one thing, but living it is another. That messianism has only meant a Hundred Years war between England and France, or a Spanish Catholic war against Netherland Protestants; a St. Bartholomew Massacre in 1572 when in one night ten thousand French Huguenots were slain in Paris and another hundred thousand throughout France, the incredible slaughter of millions by Hitler. This is the slaughter which the western civilized world, Esau's world, wishes to forget.

But Torah comes to us in this portion and recalls that conflict and predicts the elder will serve the younger. Esau may be the stronger; the natural man, the savage, the killer, he may be the elder, the record of history may be an unhappy one, but it is inevitable that the younger will emerge victorious.

For the saviours of all mankinds will go up on Mt. Zion to judge Mt. Esau. The empire of Esau, the empire of power is strong, but only temporarily. Their armies and weapons will crumble. The real saviours will come, and they will go up on Mt. Zion and they will judge.

"*Vehayetah lashem hameluch*," "And the dominion will be God's." (Obadiah 21)

And as the world will see that idolatry, bloodshed, and uncompromising belief in the natural brute of primitive materialistic man has failed and that true civilization will result. And Esau will crumble, because he has set the pattern for his defeat when he said the immoral response "I'm going to die, who needs *bechorah*, the birthright, who needs justice, compassion, decency, understanding, just satisfy my bodily appetites." And Jacob who also prepares the food, because he is human, because he too needs these requirements, but he will not make it his entire life. And he says:

"*Michrah kayom et bechorahtecha lee*," "Sell me your birthright." (Gen. 25:31)

And Esau agrees. Jacob now knows he has the *bechorah*. *Bechorah* problems, pain, suffering, worries and fears. But because he can say, "*Yitgadal*...God's kingdom I wait for" he knows the eventual eternal victory will be his.

For then the kingdom will be the Lord's and all the nations will understand that the great movements of history have had but one purpose. That the rise and fall of empires have but one purpose. That the constant struggle between Esau and Jacob have had but one purpose, the achievement of the true civilization, the realization of God's kingdom here on earth for all men.

JACOB'S STRENGTH

Underlying the Torah portion of *Toldot* and the commentaries it has attracted throughout the centuries lies an incisive psychological study of Jew and the outside world. Every one is quick to observe that the Rabbis were attracted to the fear that within Mother Rebecca she was carrying a split personality who was ready to join either the temples of idolatry or the sanctuaries of God. What continues to disturb so many is the question: was then Esau a split personality, or was he, too, not as set in his specific direction or philosophy as his twin brother, Jacob?

This grave question of harboring multiple, even diametrically opposed philosophies within the single personality reflects itself in great movements and historical trends throughout the annals of time. Jacob and his descendents speak of a monism, to which the Esau's respond: and do we, too, not worship the one God, do we, too, not seek the same center as you? It is this very question which is at the root of so much conflict, and productive of so much hostility and belligerence. Do we not hear Christianity, that great force in the Western Civilization to which we adhere: ask that question: Do we not believe in your ideals, too? Yet consider briefly this sister religion or daughter religion as it so often calls itself. True, it bespeaks the recognition of a single Father God, but then quickly splits into a trinity, a son and a Holy Ghost, or in the form of Catholicism, a divinity manifested by a mother Madonna. A galaxy of personalities, humans who lived and died as is the destiny of all men, are raised to a sanctified position of saints, wherein prayers are addressed to them, as if they, too, were gods.

What is more in their development of the predominant faith, a world of pagan customs and institutions has been retained, true, their proponents explain that this was necessary to wean away the barbarian from his form of idolatry and attract him to the new sancta. But to the Jew, the *ish tam,* the average man who seeks to unify and embrace and make cohesive all phenomena in a universal order emanating from one, how can there be complete cooperation or harmony between the monism and the multiple (many power's)?

Is this not true of the other daughter, brother or sister religion that the historians like to conjure up before us: Islam? True, superficially, Esau in the form of Mohammedism is agreeing with, in acknowledging Allah and the compassionate and merciful. Yet the Monism (superficially) is whittled away almost immediately, with a recognition of Moses and Jesus as similar prophets: the inclusion of ancient pagan notions and customs prevalent in the desert areas all the time, and a philosophy which like the Christian disposition to conversion and missioning becomes conductive to declaring jihad, holy wars or crusades against the non-believers.

And the split becomes apparent in other forms of social expression. For example, Veterans Day, the old Armistice Day, whereas once it was a reminder of the bloodshed which had been halted, it now calls attention to the glorification, even if justified, of the soldier in the fulfillment of the orders imposed upon him by the commanders of war.

Perhaps these days remind us to ask: do we not need this ability of Father Jacob to be an *ish tam,* to be a whole person devoid of the cleavages which make split personalities? The modern man may easily comment: but does not the Torah itself tell us that Esau came forth the first and Jacob later. Has this not been a pattern discernible throughout history, namely that other peoples have emerged first with Jacob trailing all along? But that same history also reveals that the many and the mighty have fallen into oblivion and disappeared from the scene of worlds arena while the little Jacob is still around, a people apart from others, concentrating upon the one idea, the one center, the one redemption and eventually the one humanity. In that lies Jacob's strength and his eventual victory.

Vayetze

— 7 —

עִבְדוּ אֶת־יְהוָֹה בְּשִׂמְחָה

"Worship God in joy." (Psalms 100:2)

PRAYER

As you probably all know, throughout the world, one may observe that various Jewish communities pursue different customs. Scholars have often indicated that the divergences in these customs arise from the various manners in which communities have developed. For example, in addition to the Purim holiday which we celebrate because of the incidents narrated in the Megilat Esther, there have been communities that have their own additional celebration to recall the rescue or salvation of the community when it was threatened by anti-Jewish forces. The prayers we chant have been instituted or ordained as law by a Sanhedrin. Prayer is a practice that apparently is almost inherent within the human personality. The most primitive savages were frightened by certain natural phenomena and regarded all these manifestations as divinities themselves. Every phenomenon was due to a different god, hence they worship the sun, moon, stars, rain, snow, smoke, clouds, hail, lightning, and the very earth itself.

It is a strange habit in which some of us indulge, namely, that of gathering in the Synagogue on the Sabbath to participate in congregational song, to recite age-old prayers, and to declare that we are joining an *Avodat Kodesh*, a sacred service.

This deep need of prayer was first expressed through sacrifice, originally, human sacrifice, and only with the appearance of Abraham our father was mankind introduced to the idea that God does not want human sacrifices. Of course, after the *Akedah*, the binding of Isaac, idolatry did not disappear from the earth, and human beings were sacrificed in various parts of the world. Thus, we know that cultural societies like the Incas, Aztecs, probably the earlier American Indians, and primitive barbarians in many parts of Africa and Asia still continued this horrible practice. Our ancient ancestors were horrified by the terrible manner in which the heathens worshiped Moloch, by offering their own children to this idol. This practice was followed in the land of Canaan in the area of Jerusalem in a valley of Hinnom. Visitors to Jerusalem may still see this ancient spot, as they walk away from the Western Wall. Our people were so horrified at this brutality in the name of religion that the word for hell in Hebrew, namely, *Gehinom* or *Gehenna* is derived from this valley and its ugly form of prayer.

With the rejection of human sacrifice, our faith substituted offerings of another nature, through the *Korbanot*. The word *korban* is derived from the Hebrew root, *karov*, near. The *korban* signified a desire on the part of a human being to draw near to God. After the destruction of the Temple, the Rabbis taught us, "God desires the heart," and the offering of the heart became *tefilah*, prayer. In our own modern times, many have spoken about the isolation, the alien, and the sense of loneliness that pervades our lives so often.

Psychology tells us that when a person is subject to these emotions, he often cannot determine his own identity as an individual, he looks upon the entire world as some kind of machine which is totally impersonal and completely unsympathetic. He therefore regards himself as isolated and often he must focus only on himself. He seeks only those objectives that may satisfy his immediate needs or desires. Judaism saw in prayer an opportunity for man to elevate himself from this sorry situation. He may avoid despair and despondency, by reaching out to God he is no longer alone. He looks out at the universe and declares,

"*Mah rabu ma'asehcha Hashem.*"
"How abundant are your works God." (Psalms 104:24)

In wisdom you have created them all. In times of trouble, he may cry out to Hashem, "*Shma koleinu chus verachem aleinu*," "God, listen to our prayer and have mercy over us." And if his conscience bothers him because he has committed an act that he evaluates as wrong, he may pray: *Shlach lanu Avinu*, forgive us our Father. And when we are grateful to God for his blessings, we recite *modim anachnu lach*, we thank you God. All these are beautiful, good and valuable in their guidance to us in life but down deep within us, we probably pray because it is some type of a spiritual imperative within the human heart to pray. The Rabbis, you know put it beautifully, they recognize that Torah is the expression of God talking to us, and in prayer, we talk to him.

Let us consider the counsel of the chapter, where *Shammai* tells us:

"*Asey Torahtechah kevah,*"
"Make your Torah fixed," (Ethics of the Fathers 1:15)

which may mean, set apart a fixed time to study Torah regularly, or fix it in your mind so that it may not be forgotten. We understand that because Torah study is a sacred duty. But how shall we understand another sacred duty, namely prayer, when another verse declares:

"*Al taas teflatecha kevah,*"
"Do not make your prayer fixed."
(Ethics of our Fathers 2:18)

Why this apparent difference between one sacred duty and the other? That is because in Torah, God speaks to man. Reverence, obedience and awe impels us to fix Torah study, not to make changes to suit our convenience or comfort. But prayer is the channel, whereby we speak to God and this should not be just a repetition of words to be recited mechanically.

Prayer takes on many forms and hues. Many of us can recall the Chassidic narrative of the *ba'al agalah*, wagon owner who was tending his wagon, and whose hands were covered with grease, but who also was reciting his prayers. People passing by were shocked: look at the stupidity of this man, who is so coarse, so removed from any aesthetic appreciation that he recites the prayers when his hands are filthy and covered with grease. But when the famous Berditchver passed, the tender hearted spiritual leader, whose life was spent defending his fellow correligonists, Reb. Levi Yitzchock lifted his hands and eyes heavenward in ecstasy. *Ribono shel olam*, look at this magnificent Jew, in the midst of his menial labors, in the midst of this unpleasant chore of greasing the wheels of his wagon, he still continues to adore and praise your eternally holy name.

In contemporary times we occasionally hear a criticism or complaint that at religious services, we must formally recite the same prayers, that is true, because the formality constantly prods us to remember our need and duty to pray. But it does not mean that your individuality is completely restricted. For example we have a *Minhag*, tradition in our family that I follow carefully. In the midst of the silent *Shemonah Esray* prayer, at the paragraph of *Refueyna,* I always insert a special paragraph in which I pray for the health and healing of people who I know are ill. At the *Shma Kolienu* I insert personal prayers for those who are close to my heart or for purposes that I believe are important. *Yiddishkeit* is not entirely formal. Who cannot remember a mother or grandmother who prayed so deeply and personally when she lit *Shabbat* candles on Friday night?

And what about the famous story of the Jewish boy who was attending services on Yom Kippur, but he could not read the Hebrew since he had not been taught. He wanted so much to emulate all the Jews about him who were praying with *kavanah*, intent, and with enthusiasm and zeal. He could not daven but he too wanted to indicate and express his love for God, he pulled out his whistle and began to blow it with all his might, hoping that God would understand that he whistled to please his creator. And when the congregants were excited and wanted to scold and rebuke this untutored boy, the Rabbi silenced them by saying, that stronger than the *Shofar* sounds were these blasts from the whistle, which God immediately accepted.

My wife z'l had a grand Uncle Rabbi Abraham Steinmetz. A great scholar who, at the age of 96, recognizing that his life on earth was drawing to a close, asked his students who had filled his home to join him in reciting the *Shema*, which he continued to repeat over and over. At the end, realizing that his strength was ebbing, he instructed them to continue praying until he closed his eyes. When his nephew, my Father in law, z'l Rabbi Samuel Rosenberg recalled that event to the family; I could not help but think one thing. "A man is dying, he can no longer even hold a Prayer Book in his hand, he no longer can respond to the words, the tears, the weeping of beloved children and grandchildren at his bedside, but there is one act he can still perform. His lips keep on moving in prayer. We hear no sounds but his soul returns to the source from which it came." Like the prayer from the primitive tribesman in Africa who greet the morning sun with, *Ruwa*, "protect me and mine," to the Ana tribe who greet the day at their shrine with, "good morning Father," to the Bretagne fisherman who prays, "God, your ocean is so wide and deep, and my boat is so small and weak, protect me, dear God," we all feel the need to talk to our creator.

When I was very young, one morning, I ran out of the house and bumped into my Father. I explained that I had a tremendous amount of work to do and could not even speak to him. "I understand," he said, "of course, you must do your work, but first say good morning to the boss." What is our work, ambitions, visions, schemes, plans and hopes without him?

Of course, decorum, aesthetics, beauty and dignity of religious services call for a specific structure or pattern, but prayer, our conversation to the creator should come from our hearts and not be restricted to formal declarations of words. There is an enduring emotion within man that propels him to seek his creator especially when trying circumstances arouse fears and anxieties for his very existence or that of his beloved ones.

For Jewish prayer, the Chassid emphasized:

"*Ivdu et Hashem besimcha*,"
"Worship God in joy." (Psalms 100:2)

Ashkenazim start the morning prayer with *Mizmor* and then *baruch sheamar*, and later the *hodu*. Chassidim recite the *hodu* earlier. My father in looking at these differences quoted Rashi who harmonized these differences by saying, no matter how and where they start *Shacharit*, they arrive together at the same prayer of *Yehi Kahvod*, let the glory of God endure forever and let the Lord rejoice in his works.

What prompted this chain of thought on prayer is the result of this Torah portion. True, the Rabbis ordained Jewish law and practice that we hold communal, formal services three times a day, specifically at *Shacharit*, *Mincha* and *Maariv*, but the *Chazal* actually declared that *Avraham tikun tefilat Shacharit*, Abraham instituted the morning prayers.

How profound were our Sages in formulating that Morning Prayer, "*Leolam yehay adam yiray Shamayim, beseter obagalui*" "At all times let a man revere God in private and in public." Let him recognize the truth. That life is fragile, temporary and we are all subject to accidents of the flesh and the onslaughts of time, rich and poor, famous and unknown, scholar and ignoramus. *Nos habet humus*, as in the Latin academic song, the earth possesses us. Man and beast are alike in this respect, but ours is the privilege of true *avodat kodesh*, the real sacred service of carrying the divine moral law to humanity. Thus, we assemble on the Sabbath, to hear God speak to us through the Torah, and we turn to him through our prayer.

Scholars often quote Daniel (6:11) to demonstrate how old are our *Shacharit, Minchah* and *Maariv* prayers. For we learn that "he kneeled upon his knees three times a day and prayed." But Rabbinical sources consider this tradition as instituted by our fore-fathers. Abraham ordained the morning service, Isaac established the afternoon service and Jacob arranged the evening service. Rabbi Shmuel bar Nachman taught, "*Shlosh tefilot keneged shloshah peameem shehayom mishtaneh*," "One prays to meet the changes by which the day develops." The evening prayer included *a yehi ratzon* supplication, may it be your will my God, "*Shehiotziani mayafaylah leorah*," "To lead me out of darkness to light." In the morning he should pray, "*Modeh ani lefanechah*," "I thank thee O Lord that thou hast led me out of darkness into light." And in the afternoon, *Minchah* service, he would pray, "*Shehkishem shezichatani lirot chamah bizrichatah*," "As you have permitted me to see the sun shining, so permit me to witness its setting."

One commentator explains that each of our Patriarchs insti-tuted a service, motivated by the circumstances of his own life.

Abraham was saved from the darkness and shown light. He was saved from the fiery furnace of Nimrod, rescued from Pha-raoh and the war with the four Kings, and finally after withstand-ing many challenges, he became famous, wealthy and highly respected and hence his prayer was one of *hodah*, with thanksgiv-ing to God.

Isaac was born in better circumstances, with the sun shining upon him, but he feared that the sun might set for him before his allotted time. In the Torah portion of Chayai Sarah we learn:

"*Vayetze Yitzchok lasuach basadeh lifnot erev*," "Isaac went out in the field to meditate before evening." (Gen. 24:63)

And the Rabbis and the Targum interpret this to mean prayer. The Talmud, (Berachot 26b) explains, and Isaac went out into the field to meditate at evening and meditation means prayer. And we derive it from a phrase in the Psalms, a prayer of the afflicted when he fainteth before God poureth forth his mediation. The famous Baruch Halevi Epstein, the Baal Torah Temimah, expounds it in this manner. The Chazal derived the word *lisuach* from the expression of speaking and meditating. For example the Psalms say "*Bepekoodecha ahsecha, ve'ahbeetah orchoteecha*," "I shall meditate in thy precepts, meditate upon his wonders." (Psalms 119:15) And that is because the meaning of the root *sehcha*, indicates only talking and meditation, but do we not find any place in the Bible where that word means walking or promenading? And therefore the Sages interpret it in the depth of simplicity. Tosefoth in Pesachim researches and labors much to explain this term as meaning the *Minchah* service. Hence his prayer at *Minchah*, indicating humility and decline, supplicated the privilege to see the entire day through to sunset.

And so the *Mincha*, a lowering of the day, when the day begins to reduce itself, when the sun begins to descend, from that term we have derived the word for the service, *mincha*. The *Keli Yakar* says that the term mincha was used for the service *linot erev*, towards evening, when the sun descends.

Father Jacob, on the other hand, sustained a difficult life, household conflicts, the hatred of his twin brother, his harsh experiences at the hands of Laban, the loss of his beloved Rachel, the agony of Joseph's disappearance in his older years, etc. Surrounded by such darkness, he prayed that God would permit him to witness the light. When we consider this interpretation, we realize that prayer was not only a channel in which the Jew could appeal to God for his needs, but it also becomes a vehicle for self-analysis and self-understanding.

When a Jew says, *"Ani mitpallel,"* I pray, we should understand that the word comes from *pillel*, to judge, evaluate. Prayer is a way of judging yourself, of analyzing yourself, of trying to perceive what you are, given a slogan, *"Sheviti Hashem lenegdi tamid"* "I have set God before me always." (Psalms 16:8) Morning, noon, and evening, always the Jew must seek a communion, conversation with God.

"Karov Hashem lechol korav, lechol asher yekrauhu be'emet"
"God is near to those who call upon him in truth."
(Psalms 145:18)

The gates of prayer are never closed, Jacob changed his brother's hatred through prayer. Joseph rose from the prisons of Egypt to rule the empire, through prayer. Hezekiah beat back the mighty foe, through prayer. Samson, shattered and blind, through prayer rallied the strength to smash the Philistines in their own temple. And Elijah through prayer, resisted the King and the Queen and the priests of Baal, so that now, we may shout at the end of Yom Kippur:

"Hashem Hu haElokeem,"
"The Lord he is God," (Kings I 18:39).

Prayer must be personal, prayer must come from the soul, prayer must mean thanksgiving, whatever we desire to perform, accomplish, envision, whatever be the goal which summons us to labor and toil, to sweat and suffer, must first be accompanied by prayer. Prayer is synonymous with *emunah* and *bitachon,* trust and faith that infuse our hearts with joy. And such joy makes for a healthy body. Prayer also keeps us alive by arousing our senses to the wonder and mystery of life and the very cosmos. Do you know that by computer assisted plotting, we know today that there are at least one billion galaxies in the universe? That superclusters of thousands of galaxies resemble a giant many-pedaled flower that our solar system has traveled around the Milky Way four and one-half billion miles? A great scientist recently declared that even evolution appears to be more than the mere product of chance. The earth is shifting underneath our very feet. There are changes in the Atlantic and Pacific oceans.

Did you read of the *Kabalist* who claims that looking at the map of the world carefully presents an impression of a human face? Lewis Thomas noted sometime ago that when one looks down at the earth from the moon, one gets the impression of a well organized, live creature. The symmetry of nature, from the way in which the heart is on the left side of the body to the manner in which one can study the movement of atoms within a small mass, or the comparison of the rose window, which depicts the story of Genesis at the Washington Cathedral with the computerized picture of an axial view of a DNA molecule. They both present a similar artistic design, all pointing to "Everyday we learn how the universe and our world is constantly being created," this is the wonder and the mystery of life and that is why *"Dah lifneh mi atah omed,"* "Know before whom you stand." (Berachot 28b)

The Jew, who at least recognizes the wonder and mystery, knows that gratitude must be everlasting. He knows that it is a privilege to assemble in the Synagogue, to pray, with soul, heart,

mind and that through our speech to God, we may enjoy his benevolence and exult forever in his mercy and infinite grandeur.

MAN MAKES THE OFFICE

Centuries ago, our ancestors were debating the theme,
"*Ha'adam michabed et hamakom, O hamakom michabed et
ha'adam*," "Does a person honor his position, or is it the position
that honors the man?" The impulse of this inquiry found its expression in another philosophic polemic: namely, does history make
the man or does man make history?

Thomas Carlyle, the Historian and Philosopher was of the
opinion that man makes history, that the determining factor in this
discussion was the personality of man. It is a theme that continues
to attract many contemporary minds.

Let me first share with you an anecdote about the Vilna Gaon,
the Vilna Sage which has an association with this theme. For the
benefit of those who are not acquainted with this personality, let
me tell you that Elijah of Vilna was a tremendous mind who delved
into the natural sciences, mathematics, sociology, philosophy, ethics, history, whatever you name, the discipline fascinated him. In
addition to that, he was a child prodigy in matters of our faith and
scholarship. At a very tender age he started school. Two or three
centuries ago, Jews were still the object of shock among other
peoples. They could not understand how Jewish parents who were
always known for their fierce love for children, for their self-sac-
rifices for their children, had the heart to awaken a small child
early in the morning to send him out into the bitter cold of Europe,
so that he could attend school. And these little children sharpened
their minds and their intellect, and emerged in mature years as
knowledgeable Jews, who knew and hence were proud of their

heritage and were also often inspired, to study and absorb the knowledge and contributions to humanity made by other scholars.

Now, it is related that when Elijah of Vilna, who became known in history as the Vilna Gaon, when he was a little boy, he already was studying the Bible in Hebrew, amid pupils who were older than he. And one day, a classmate, startled and stumped the teacher. They were studying the story of Jethro, the father-in-law of Moses, who came visiting the Camp of Israel, after they had been freed from Egyptian slavery. Obviously, Moses respected his wife's father and so the Torah tells:

"*Vayetze Moshe likrat chotno*,"
"And Moses went out to greet his father-in-law."
(Exodus 18:7)

Whereupon *Kavod gadol nitchabed Yitro beotah sha'ah*, At that moment, Jethro was highly honored in that Moses went out to greet him, as did Aaron, the brother of Moses, and often his spokesman. (Rashi to Exodus 18:7.)

Now, this youngster asked, how did Rashi know that Aaron joined Moses? It doesn't say that in the Bible. The teacher was really startled. He looked into the Bible, he'd turn one page after another, and he couldn't find the answer. But suddenly little Elijah jumped up and said, I figured it out. You see it says *"Vayetze Moshe,"* and "Moses went out," it doesn't say *Vayelech*. He went to any special location. For Example, Aaron was once told, *"Lech lekrat Moshe,"* "Go and meet Moses." (Exodus 4:27) We have to understand this in the light of the Biblical lesson, we happen to read today.

In this Torah portion the commentary looks at the words that begin the lesson:

"*Vayetze Ya'akov miBe'er Sheva vayelech Charanah*,"
"Jacob left Beer Sheva and went to Haran."
(Gen. 28:10)

Rashi himself is influenced by others to ask: If he went to Haran, why does the Bible have to say he left Beer Sheva? Who cares where I'm leaving? Ah, answer the Rabbis, it was very important to note that, because when Jacob left, he took the pride, glory and honor out of the community. Now, continued, little Elijah, since Moses and Aaron were both so important to the entire camp, when Moses left, the word *Vayetze* implies, he took all the glory of the community with him. However, had Aaron remained in the camp, and we have been told that

"*Moshe ve'Aharon shakulim echad*,"
"That both Moses and his Brother Aaron occupied a similar status of honor." (Rashi to Ex. 6:26)

it follows that there would still have been glory and pride in the community. And if the words imply that all the glory and pride were taken out of the camp, to greet Jethro, it is clear that Aaron, obviously, followed his brother.

What makes a place great? If I were going to ask you what made New York great, the answers would be many. You might remind us that the Yankees play in the Bronx, that Brooklyn has the Botanical Gardens and the Academy of Music. Others may point out the art galleries, the Museums of Natural History and Modern Art, Ellis Island, the Metropolitan Opera Company, and the Philharmonic Orchestra. Yes, these are known throughout the world. But if these are so great, why does there continue to be crime, mugging, and drug plagues? Why are innocent bystanders, little children shot, in their very cars or homes? Because while all these agencies and institutions are of such tremendous significance, they don't guarantee New York City's greatness. You and I and all the people are what guarantee greatness. That is the Torah teaching that fascinated the young Vilna Gaon.

Vayetze Ya'akov, and Jacob left the community of Beer Sheva. Why is that event so important? Because Jacob was a decent, honorable, trustworthy compassionate human being, and "*Kesheyetze tzaddick min hamakom, az panah panahzivah, panah hadarah,*" "When a righteous man leaves a community, he takes with him its pride, its glory, its honor, its illumination and its attractiveness." (Rashi to Gen. 28:10) It is the human personality that makes for status, for good community, for the security of neighborhoods, for the strength of a city and for the repute of a country. Yes, it is the decent human being that makes the place, the position and the status of an office great.

The seat of the Presidency is great in American history because George Washington declared that the United States would give to bigotry no sanction. It is great because the spirit of Jefferson proclaimed the inalienable rights of all human beings; it is great because the Presidency refused to tolerate the ugliness of the Barabry Pirates. It is great, because from there an Abraham Lincoln gave his life to preserve the Union and abolish slavery. It is great because a Woodrow Wilson could sustain a vision of international justice. Yes, it is great because the charismatic personality of a John F. Kennedy projected a Camelot for all Americans to lift themselves up to the search for a higher America.

The pride, glory and honor of a position is not its formal trappings. The pride, the glory, the honor, the greatness of a community lies not simply in its industrial potentials, in its real estate or even its banking. No, the pride, glory and honor lies in the hands of its decent people.

Years ago, there was a little undersized man in India called Ghandi who had inner strength, will power and certain determinations and compelled the British to yield to some of his demands. The immortal Jewish leader, Vladamir Jabotinsky, who was a short, quiet, studious, cultured gentleman, in addition to being one of most eloquent orators of all times, he also created the Irgun, an underground and inspired Jewish boys and girls to fight the British oppressor in Palestine by forcing Britain out, according to Churchill and playing an enormous role in the creation of Israel, the Jewish state.

The Bible tells us that Jacob was left alone and he had to wrestle with a stranger the entire night until the day broke. Superficially, that is surprising, because the Bible tells us something about Jacob and his twin brother Esau. Esau became a hunter when he grew up, the Rabbis say that when he was Bar Mitzvah he was a man of the field, while Jacob was a studious boy, dwelling in tents (that is he liked school). From this we usually think of Esau as a macho guy, and Jacob as an undernourished small boy. But it was Jacob who was really strong and Esau cowardly. Esau was athletically well built, but what did he do with his strength? He trapped innocent but defenseless animals, and morally he was weak. He sold his greatest possession, his birthright for a pot of beans.

Jacob on the other hand was different. When his cousin Rachel brought her sheep to the well for water and waited for all the men shepherds to gather and remove the stone cover, Jacob stepped forward and removed it by himself. But Jacob was also strong morally, because he was studious, cultured, and modest and though a full-grown man, he was kind, considerate and self controlled. The Rabbis have truly said, "Who is strong? The man who has control over himself." (Ethics of the Fathers 4:1) You see one can be strong physically, but if you lose your temper easily, afraid to risk any danger, can not control your appetite and eat or drink too much, then you are really weak, maybe you can not tear a telephone directory in half, but if you do not lose your head, stand up bravely for your friends and the truth, and when tempted to do wrong, will not do that thing, then you are really strong.

A concern with the homeless, a sensitivity to the aged, empathy for those who are ill, a determination to provide good education for our progeny, an insistence to hold the criminal, the rapist, the murderer, the terrorist and the scoundrel who robs the life savings of our fellow citizens. The desire to maintain law, order, decency, kindness, gentility and generosity. This is what makes a community great. This is what we must demand from ourselves and this is the ideal that we must impart to our children. Because *"Shebizman shehatzaddick bair hoo hodah hoo zeevah,"* "When the righteous person is in the city he is its magnificence, he is its splendor." *"Yatzah meesham panah hodah peenah zeevah,"* "And when the good person leaves the city, the city loses its magnificence and splendor." (Rashi to Gen. 28:10)

Live with decency, goodness, compassion, sensitivity, and justice. And within this decency and goodness, and desire to help those less fortunate than ourselves, we can guarantee the greatness of the community in which we live.

THERE'S NO PLACE LIKE HOME

"*Vayetze Ya'akov miBe'er Sheva, vayelech Charanah,*"
"And Jacob left Beer Sheva and went to Haran." (Gen.
28:10)

"Vayifga bamakom vayalen sham ki vah hashemesh,
Vayikach maiavnai hamakom, vayasem meraashatav,
Vayishkav bamakom hahu,"
"And he encountered upon a place, and stayed there
because the sun had set, and he took one of the stones
of that place and he put it under his head, and he lay
down there." (Gen. 28:11)

"Vayachalom,"
"And he dreamt." (Gen. 28:12)

And our spiritual leaders considered these words, and asked, "Why did he lay down upon this stone?" Did he not have anything with him, a pillow, a cushion? *Amar Ya'akov*, but Jacob said, *"Chavivah alai ehven ahchat shel Eretz Yisrael, mikarim uhkistote shel chutz laaretz,"* "A stone of the Land of Israel is more precious to me than the pillows and cushions of other lands." (Otzair Chaim)

How do we see the personality of Jacob emerging in the Torah portion? He is alone and isolated. A poor wanderer who has lost everything. He possesses nothing. Not the wealth he had inherited from his grandfather Abraham, nor from the wealth of one hundred-fold from his Father Isaac, nothing had remained. He is a refuge in fear of death. In need and poverty the first Jewish refugee. He is left with nothing except one thing, a dream. What sober minded person will not dismiss that possession? That is all that the Jewish Patriarch possesses? A dream? What is a dream? What is it worth? What reality does it include?

Let us not laugh at dreamers though, nor mock them. Dreamers often have more reality than those you consider realists, more essence than reality. Consider if you will Jacob's dream, a ladder whose foundation was on the ground, but whose top reached the

heavens. Let us learn from Jacob's dream, according to the interpretations of that brilliant contemporary scholar, Nechama
Leibowitz, consider the dream, and God standing over it.

Only superficially is it Jacobs's dream, actually it is the dream
of the Jewish people. The Seforno notes that when the verse refers
to *olim*, reference is made to the nations, the empires that in their
mad search for power imagine that they can easily disperse the
Jewish people and abolish them from the world. But they go up
only to come down because God stands over Jacob and will not
abandon his people.

The poet Nachman Yitzchok Fischmann once proclaimed that
the song of a dream, once it looms in the soul, is never forgotten.
Our people envisioned a society of security, liberty, justice and
peace. This was the dream that our Prophets foresaw. It was a
dream in which our wandering people would return to the land
from which they had been driven by force.

This dream of Jacob says Nechama Leibowitz is really a reflection of human history. Referring as it does to the ascendancy
and descendancy of people which were throughout the world wres-
tling for existence among giant powers, driven from land to land,
and yet watched empires fall, e.g. Babel, Persia, Greece, Rome,
etc. And the Sages who lived at the height of power foresaw the
fall of the grandchildren of these powers.

Today we are permitted to raise a generation of Jews who
really know nothing of what it meant for us to be without a State
and a Land of Israel. A generation that reads of the Holocaust but
apparently cannot totally feel the anguish that other generations
sustained at the sight of our people, humiliated, persecuted, assaulted by violence, terrorized, tortured and murdered with incredible bestiality.

Who of us has not felt that we are not in complete accord with every movement in Zion? But those of us, regardless of such opinions, know that above all, we must remain a people, united by our national history, by our faith of millennia, by our determination not to succumb to either treachery or attack. Yes, we who must be grateful that they live in comparative safety, that many of them do not suffer the economic, political and social deprivation that led to the murder of a third of our people. That we, above all, should understand that the only great heroes are those who follow Jacob. Those who facing the rocks and stones cast at them by the enemy, nonetheless, *vayachalom*, continue to dream.

Those who continue to envision a growing Land of Israel, a whole Israel, the entire land which Jacob heard the Divine say:

> **"*Lechah etnenah ulizarechah*,"**
> **"This land I shall give to thee, and to thy seed."**
> **(Gen. 28:13)**

This land, this rocky soil which you must revive by sweat and toil and struggle and dream. For only then, will the peoples of the world, toiling for their own national resurrection, respect and understand the renaissance of Israel, the children of Jacob who shall return to the land which is theirs forever. For those who prefer the rocks of Israel to the cushions of the Diaspora, for them the dream will persist and remain forever.

APPRECIATING GOD'S GREATNESS

We often hear the quotation "out of the mouths of babes" to indicate the possible sources of wisdom which may emanate from the speech of the very young, which is conducive to earnest thinking. The other day I was telling some children the narrative of the Torah portion of *Vayetze*, the experience of Jacob's dreams and how these affected him. One of the children responded by saying he could not quite understand these stories because since Jacob was surrounded by miracles which embraced him, how is it he asked God for bread to eat and clothing to wear? I began to consider this comment and its implications.

That this Torah portion includes the report of a miracle isn't that so an intriguing tale, the story of a dream, a ladder, angels and the Divine Inspiration. God who told Jacob that the land would be his and his children's after him. God who said:

"Vehenaye anochi emach ushemartecha bechol asher taylaich,"
"Behold I am with thee and will keep (watch) you wherever you go." (Gen. 28:15)

And Jacob now made his petition that God be with him and watch over him and give him bread and clothing. And Jacob indicates his thanks to God by promising that in return for God's goodness, he pledges a tithe, ten percent of his material prosperity to the service of God. And yet someone, even someone as young as a child, feels that there is something else in the response to the miracle of Gods presence.

What constitutes a miracle? Our first response to that is rather commonplace, a miracle usually refers to events which transcend the natural. Many current movies, literature, fiction and even non fiction include so much about the occult, mysterious unknowable, the inscrutable, the incomprehensible events and incidents which go far beyond our normal experiences.

And yet, what really is a miracle? Paul Davies, a very prominent British Physicist, in his work *God and the New Physics*, decries this concept of miracle, whereby God intervenes by violating the laws of nature. You know science denies this by declaring that the desire for magic is a primeval element that is deeply rooted in us, and when religion declines, these feelings come up again and again. We use modern jargon about mysterious force fields, mind over matter and combining primitive superstition with space age physics. The scientific mind, we have been told sees no miracle, and if something occurs which cannot be explained now, perhaps in the future when our knowledge of such phenomenon increases, we too shall find the correct answer. But still, what really are miracles? There is a strange, but fascinating verse in the *perek,* chapter wherein it is stated, ten things were created on the eve of Sabbath, the twilight, i.e., the abyss which swallowed Korach and his cohorts, the well of Miriam, the strange phenomenon of a donkey communicating with Balam, the rainbow, the manna, etc. Rabbi Singer commented, all phenomena that seemed to partake at once of the natural and the supernatural were conceived as having had their origin in the interval between the close of the work of creation and commencement of the Sabbath. The Chief Rabbi of the British Empire, the late Dr. J. H. Hertz also includes this and comments by Israel Zangwill in his Bible commentary, namely, that the Sages were not fantastic fools, but subtle philosophers who regarded these miracles as part of the natural order of the world, specifically created for a special moment, and not as interruptions in the laws of nature.

In this light there are miracles in the very fabric of the universe and of the cosmos. For what shall we make of contemporary physics as it recognizes a form and order in the universe? The spectrum of colors is concealed in a beam of sunlight. Isn't the form and arrangement of a rainbow miraculous? What of the fascinating forms of crystals, the design of snowflakes, the nautilus shell or the forms that plant life takes? What is it that gives all organisms the power to maintain themselves or to regenerate their form when it has been disturbed? It has been asserted that life first appeared on earth three and one-half billion years ago. Also, despite the interruption of a few ice ages, the temperature range of the earth has not changed appreciable since life first appeared. Research physicists and other allied scholars try to explain these strange incidents by declaring that these and other strange phenomena could have occurred by chance and have been sustained by a series of coincidences. On the other hand, we have been told through mathematical demonstrations that chance could not play so great a role in the formation of life. When rejected the contention that the universe is a machine but operates like a mind, there were hesitancies.

Physicist Gerald Feinberg and biochemist Robert Shapiro, in their work, *Life Beyond Earth: The Intelligent Earthling's Guide to Extraterrestrial Life*, argue for life beyond the earth, for the organization of nature which makes possible imagining, a supermind existing since creation directing and controlling and pervading the cosmos by operating the laws of nature for some specific purpose? With all due respect to the criticisms, the acceptances and the analysis of such proposals, is this not miraculous per se that such insight of the human mind should develop? Perhaps therein lies the depth of Judaism that Torah did not encourage specific attempts to explain God. The Jew does not begin his appearance by saying to the world "I believe in God." He knows that God is and hence he does not regard science with hostility and antagonism. *"Chotmo shel hakadosh baruchu hu emet,"* "The signature of God is truth." (Shabbat 55a) When science learns new, when the new physics discovers the composition of the cosmos and universe, we are ready to listen and accept the truth from whatever sources it comes, but to the Jewish mind, it is the *mitzvah*, the moral imperative that counts. True, to the primitive man, science is probably correct, must progress and advance his earlier conceptions of the universe. But that person is man, not only because he can contemplate the universe, but also because he can respond with compassion, empathy, beauty, symmetry and with a driving desire to help other human beings. That is perhaps the greatest miracle of all. Yes, in addition to the allegorical meaning that miraculous tales may possess there is also the deep recognition that the commonplace may be miraculous and hence should not be disdained.

A contemporary commentary tries to understand Jacob's reaction at Beth-el. Had not God already told Jacob in that inspirational dream:

"Ushemartichah,"
"I shall guard thee wherever thou goest." (Gen. 28:15)

To suggest that Jacob was upset by the miraculous, the Gemarah in Shabbat speaks of a man whose wife unfortunately had died. Left behind with a suckling infant and not being able to afford to retain a wet nurse for the infant, a miracle happened, his chest went through changes and he developed breasts as a woman so that he could suckle his child. Reb. Joseph then exclaimed, how great this man must have been for such a miracle to occur in his behalf. On the contrary, said Reb. Abayai, how low this man was that the natural order of things should have been interrupted because of him. Rashi is of the opinion that this man's lowliness was now due to the fact that he could not earn a livelihood normally.

The Maharshah, another commentary remarks, this was a miracle. Certainly a very rare occurrence of this sort is recorded, but it also means that any merit he may have had was reduced, because elsewhere the Talmud observes, where miracles are performed for one, his merits are reduced.

We may then see this discussion as an attempt to face those infrequent, peculiar or queer strange occurrences that apparently do not conform to the normal order of things. And in this light they are reduced in significance because they deprive a person of the normal status he would enjoy in nature. One commentary observes: Jacob heard the assurance that God would guard over him wherever he went and he considered the possibility that he was being assured of divine intervention along miraculous lines that he would lose status as a normal being. And so he asked God to guard him *bederech hazeh,* in this manner, the normal manner in which man exists, bread to eat and clothing to wear not more. For did he not later declare:

"Yesh le kol,"
"I have everything." (Gen. 33:11)

Rashi explains this is to indicate that he lacks no favor. Let me just be well and healthy, to eat my bread and wear my garb in a normal manner. I do not seek thee God, in superficial interruptions of nature, no God. I do not need miracles to recognize thee. I see thee in the tremendous operation of the cosmos and nature that you have established. I see thee in sunrise and sunset, in the rains which help frutify the earth, in the Suns rays, the light that combines with the carbon dioxide to make starch through photosynthesis. I see thee in all knowledge, and I witness God in the tremendous vastness of space where light must travel millions of years from one galaxy to another.

When the scientist tells us that he sees the universe as having come from disorder and chaos, we remember how our Sages taught *veha'aretz hayeta tohu vavohu,* the earth was unformed and void (Gen. 1:2). When the Jew calls out the world hangs on nothingness, he is only accepting the power of gravity over compositions in space. But he need not deny the researchers of sciences towards discovering constant facts about the universe. But he knows beyond this speculation is the serious labor of living for oneself, and in relationships to others. God, give me health so that I may obtain and live naturally, health to eat the bread I obtain, and strength to wear the clothing I may procure. And then, let we never forget how different I really am that even when clever men, scholarly men and profound minds continue to penetrate the mysteries of the cosmos, let me not forget that they too will crumble like everyone else. That with all our advances notwithstanding, there are no inherent guarantees that men will live properly. Wernher Von Braun was willing to serve the Nazis, physicists who developed the soviet space programs supported an oppressive government and system, Nazi physicians tortured and experimented upon human beings, but let me live normally, for in the natural order of life I see thy presence and let the spirit of gratitude arise in me. Gratitude which may exist no where else save in humans. And let me if not repay these at least, show my gratitude by returning a tithe to thee for thy service. And thy service means the support of all who search for truth, all who stand up for humanity, and for all avocations which should do good to thy creatures.

KNOW FROM WHERE YOU CAME AND WHERE YOU ARE GOING

Consider the narrative of the Torah lesson *Vayetze*. Jacob leaves home, where he has been encouraged to high standards of decency, goodness, faith and self-sacrifice. Home, where he has

been a "*Yoshev Oholim*," "A simple person," a person sitting quietly, engaged in Torah study. Now he is sojourning with Laban.
And throughout all these years, he is subject to a constant inner
war with himself and his ideals. The clash between the heritage of
his Father stressing spiritual and ethical imperatives, as compared
to the amoral and crafty experiences of Laban. This gave him no
peace. There were times when the gravitational pull of Isaac and
Rebecca were stronger, willing upon him to be a decent human
being. Other times, the push of Laban's avarice was paramount.
After all, when one sees an amoral person getting rich and getting
away with improper actions, it is natural for one to wonder, maybe
I should follow his way of life?

As a matter of fact, Jacob in his stay with Laban is mirror of
the polarities of life that magnetizes so many of us. This Torah
portion of *Vayetze* heightens the problems besetting us as we sin-
cerely and even heroically grapple with titanic issues.

In his response to the pressures of life about him, Jacob begins to change because he keeps his eye on other goals. His dream
marks the height of his involvement in the mundane affairs forced
upon him by Laban's intrigue. You will recall that he came to Laban
not only fresh from his Father's tent, but also from the academic
tranquility of the schools of Shem and Eber. Now he finds that he
has to throw himself into the hurly burly conditions of business.
He becomes a shepherd par excellence, earns more rewards than
Laban had ever bargained for,

> **"*Vayifrotz haish meod meod, vayehi lo tzon rabot*
> *ushefachot va'avadim ugemalim vachamorim*,"**
> **"And the man increased exceedingly, he had large
> flocks, maid servants, man servants, camels and
> donkeys." (Gen. 30:43)**

Jacob began to play Laban's game with relish and concentration. He could imitate Laban and vanquish him at his own game. So, the man of God becomes a versatile breeder of sheep. With his ingrained enthusiasm and acumen, he now amassed a fortune. But what happens to his dreams? When he first started out, he had the tremendous dream of the ladder extending from the earth to the heaven, but now he dreams of sheep. His visions are of becoming rich and powerful.

> **"*Vayehi Beait yachaim hatzon vaesaw ainie va'areh***
> **bachalom vehenai ha'atoodim haohlim al hatzon***
> **ahkudim nekudim ube'rudim,"***
> **"And it came to pass, at the time that the flock**
> **conceived, that I lifted up mine eyes and saw in a**
> **dream, and behold the goats which leaped upon the**
> **flock were streaked and speckled and grizzled."**
> **(Gen. 31:10)**

Suddenly, his career of imitating Laban and becoming increasingly rich is interrupted. In fact, it comes to an abrupt end, because he now sustains a new dream. In this dream he hears: I am the God of Beth El, where you originally set up a *matzevah*, monument where you vowed unto me, now arise, get yourself out of this and go back to the land of your birth.

This vision becomes a turning point in Jacob's life. It cautions him to involve himself no more in material things. Jacob! Stop imitating Laban. Laban's involvement is related to things; sheep, donkeys, servants, money and wealth. This involvement refers only to external objects and not to the inner self. Involvement is a necessary phase of man's striving for economic health. But involvement is never fixed on one subject. Life becomes a kaleidoscope of various colors, streaked, speckled and grizzled. They claim our temporary allegiance, but once they hold us enslaved in their grip, we lose our soul. One of the Rabbis pointed out that Jacob understood that he should be thankful for what was happening. If this vision had not interrupted him, he might have become another copy of Laban, rich, powerful and apparently important, but also a liar, betrayer, slanderer, contemptible and vile person. Instead, in this critical juncture of his life, the almighty appears to him and reminds Jacob of the commitment that he made at Beth El. He anointed a *matzevah*, monument to God. God sharply reminds him not to lose himself in trivial pursuits. He asks him to return to his native land, resume his spiritual commitment, and know that the most important thing in life is to be a *mensch*, a man of manners and dignity.

We are all ordinary flesh and blood. We become engrossed in our involvement on business matters or social obligations. We want to be important. We want to hit out at people and things because they do not follow the pattern of our desires. But in such a moment, we are in danger of losing our ideals and calling. We are sensitive to the voice calling us to make provisions for our spiritual commitment and development. We are called up to leave the lowlands of pettiness and attempt to climb the mountains of decency and *menschlichkeit*. At one time or another, every one of us like Jacob has made a vow. We have intended to be a decent and proper human being and we have to remind ourselves that we should use that vow as our guide in life and be thankful that there have been moments in life when we are called to remember those vows, and stop emulating and imitating others who are no longer *mencshen*, men of manners and dignity

Vayishlach

— 8 —

וַיִּשְׁלַח יַעֲקֹב מַלְאָכִים לְפָנָיו אֶל־עֵשָׂו אָחִיו

**"And Jacob sent angels before him to Esau his
brother." (Genesis 32:4)**

ROME AND JERUSALEM

There was a time when those who called themselves Zionists tried very hard to discover their own personal identities by studying ideology, history, comparative political, social and economic influences which exerted pressures throughout the world. Often this intellectual pursuit distinguished itself from the broad, traditional, love of Zion resurrected, which permeated our religious philosophy and the tremendous spiritual and cultural heritage which the passing of centuries neither diminished nor obliterated from the hearts of the Jewish people.

It is strange to observe that the more Zionism formalized its organizational structure, the greater its advances and progress were transformed into the area of pragmatics and practicality. The broader study of Zionist affinities became weaker. True, controversies could still engender acrimonious polemics, but historical names like Frederick Reines and Moses Hess chiefly evoke ignorance.

Consider Moses Hess, whose "*Rome and Jerusalem,*" became a Zionist classic. Most people assume that he was concerned with the Vatican, but they do not realize that Hess was one of the great theoreticians of contemporary socialism. He was not only a pioneer on the level of Marx and Engels, but he actually towered over them in spirituality. What is more, unlike Marx who was pollute with a self hatred which bristled with anger and spite against the Jewish religion and its traditions, Hess, on the other hand, matured into a personality who recognized the positive powers of nationalism. He was stirred by the concept of the Holy Land and the eternal city, Jerusalem, as inseparable from the inheritance of our ancestors.

Interestingly, he perceived of history as resulting from racial and class struggles and regarded modern society as being fashioned by two racial forces, the Aryan and Semitic. The Aryan was supposed to interpret life aesthetically, while the Semites would hallow life by moral power. This gentle philosopher believed that races were neither superior nor inferior and hence there should be no racial oppression. He also declared that our religion was the best way to preserve the Jewish people and until we had achieved our independence and national freedom in *Eretz Yisrael,* the Land of Israel, when we might introduce the Sanhedrin again into our lives, we should cling to Judaism with loyalty. So, this pioneer thinker, who in his younger years believed that we should assimilate, returned to his people with pride, spirituality and a call for faith, as he considered Rome and Jerusalem the poles of humanity in its eventual destiny.

While we must acknowledge Hess for his insight and perceptions of nationalism as a powerful historical force, *Rome and Jerusalem* implies more of a religious struggle, an ideological, spiritual combat and moral clash, upon whose outcome the future of all humanity depends and its ancient roots are implied in the Biblical lesson:

> **"Vayishlach Ya'akov malachim lefanav, el Esav achiv, artzah Seir seday Edom,"**
> **"And Jacob sent messengers to his brother Esau, to the land of Seir, the field of Edom. (Gen. 32:4)"**

Now, Esau and Edom are names that symbolize the world alien or hostile to Jews and Judaism. The Rabbis have employed Edom, very often, as the veiled name for the oppressive, tyrannical power of Rome, and later it was a reference to the persecuting church. It was in this same work, that the term "Rome and Jerusalem" developed into the symbol of antagonistic conflict that was too often characterized by bestiality and brutality that demeaned the essence of man.

Rome, the church proclaimed itself as the successor of Israeli. Rome claimed it represented the Jewish Messiah awaited by Israel for centuries. Rome declared that despite the insistence of the Nazarene that he had not come to change the law, the church rejected Torah by its philosophy and its ritual. Rome sponsored the doctrine, *ex ecclesia nullus salus*, there is no salvation outside of the church.

As for Esau, he entered this world as Jacob's brother, even as Ishmael had expected special consideration as the son of Abraham. And yet did not Malachi the prophet preach

> **"Hahlo ach Esav leYa'akov,"**
> **"Was not Esau Jacob's brother?" (Malchai 1:2)**

Yet God declared:

"*Vaohev et Ya'akov,*"
"Yet I loved Jacob." (Ibid)

While Ishmael was *metzachek*, he displayed before his young brother Isaac, acts of bloodshed, cruelty, rape, and idolatry. Now Jacob was aware of this reality. And so he proceeded with caution in his diplomatic efforts towards Esau. The *Al HaTorah* expresses it very succinctly. And Jacob sent messengers to Esau his brother, *lo histapek Ya'akov*. Jacob was not satisfied with sending his agents to Esau, but he also dispatched his emissaries to the land of Seir. For Jacob thought, "*Me yodea haloh zeh, sheva toevot belibo.*" This diplomat, this statesman Esau, is thoroughly corrupt, immersed in deception and treachery, "*Eyn peh velibo shaveem*" "His tongue and heart differ." Perhaps in his councils in Seir, he plots hostilities as he pretends to meet me with affection and regard. And so Jacob dispatched emissaries to Seir and they reported, "Things are quiet, but remember he may attempt to harm you, if not through his direct efforts, but through attacks launched by other allies," for example *malchai Arav viAram*, through Arab and Aramian rulers. Hence Jacob also dispatched his representatives to the field of Aram, to ensure that he would not be the target of the latter. But could he be certain and secure in his encounters and negotiations? Could he be certain that Esau had removed all the previous evil he entertained in his heart?

Jacob is the voice of Jerusalem that rejects the proclamations of Rome that only the church possesses salvation. Jacob is the voice of Jerusalem which today confronts Esau and Ishmael and those who designate all others as infidels denied equality, doomed to live with no rights, over whom the rule of the sword, the rule of violence, terror and murder is justified. Jacob is the voice of Jerusalem that meets the hypocrisy of Edom, who confronts those who shut their eyes against the murder of innocent people. Jacob is the voice of Jerusalem that preaches *halo kikushiyim atem li,* are you not as precious to God as the black children of Ethiopia who preach peace unto the world? *"Mipney sheayn licha keli avoor berachot kishalom,"* "Because no vessel can contain blessings as does peace." (Num. Rabbah 11:7)

> **"Vayivater Ya'akov levado vayaavek ish imo ad alot hashachar,"**
> **"And Jacob was left alone, and a man wrestled with him until the breaking of the day." (Gen. 32:25)**

The Chatam Sofer notes that in the opinion of Rashi, Ramban and many other commentators of the Bible, the word *vayavek,* and he wrestled, is derived from two possible words.

One is the word *"avak"* which would mean they raised dust in their combat, and the other is *"Vayichabek."* And he embraced, that is the opponent embraced Jacob with his arms. These two terms intimate the manner in which Esau, our enemy seeks to undermine Jacob, either through attempts to defeat Jacob in physical battle, or by pretending to be his friend, by making empty, shallow, false, hypocritical deceitful displays of affection and friendship. Like those who denounce anti-Semitism and who weep at the suffering of all innocent people, but manage to bolster their attacks upon Jews. Those from without and those from within. Yes, we do have those cowardly members of our people who hurry to bow before prominent world leaders; who rush to kowtow to the enemy, who pretend they seek our benefit but instead want to give us a *mitat nishikah,* the kiss of death. But now, as ever, we should recall the words of Moses Hess, the socialist, the humanitarian, the friend of Marx and Engels who realized the truth. That we must be free, and that *Eretz Yisrael* is ours and that only the traditions of Torah can preserve us, ensure our survival and our inevitable victory over Ishmael, Esau and Edom. Until the hour when "*alot hashachar*," the dawn will break, and humanity will confess its errors, and all government will truly destroy the evil within their hearts and all shall proclaim the words of the holy one.

"*Al tirah avdi Ya'akov*,"
"Do not be afraid my servant Jacob"
(Isaiah 44:2, Jer. 30:10, 46:27,28)

for Esau may be thy brother but because of thy truths and justice, God prefers thee.

FLATTERY AND DIPLOMACY

It is quite appropriate that the Torah *Sidrah* of *Vayishlach* often occurs in close proximity to the Holiday of Chanukah. It behooves us to consider as component parts of Jewish history not only the military ventures associated with the heroics of those days, but also the definitions of dignity, pride, and stature vis-a-vis other peoples, which is also a heritage of the festival of lights. How shall we comport ourselves in the proximity of other cultures, philosophies and world viewpoints, as occurred in the Hasmonean era? With characteristic regularity, we turn to the portion of the Torah, hoping to discover some guidance from its verses to answer this question.

Superficially, the scriptural narrative is an account of a family quarrel. Two brothers, at odds with each other, now meet, after many years of separation. That there are personal suggestions in the Torah portion cannot be denied. Too many brothers and sisters

have been estranged from each other because of misunderstand-
ings. Many families have been rent asunder, with terrible pain and
anguish visited upon suffering parents, because of siblings who
magnified dissensions that were really trivial. Sometimes, brothers have suddenly realized that the years have passed, wasted with
envy. Peace is initiated only when they understand that the years
can never be recalled. Often as not, it is only a repetition of the
tale involving Jacob and Esau.

Proper relationships are not really established, but the Brothers tacitly agree not to fight with each other and to stay away from
each other. In addition to the personal insight afforded by Torah,
there are instructions of a broader nature for the Jewish people.
How shall Jacob face Esau in the invariable confrontations that
arise?

One thing, we should have learned already, is that we cannot
guarantee the responses of Esau. We may arrange brotherhood
meetings. We may speak of good will and mutual respect for all.
Certain institutions in western civilization may even admit that
their great ethics are derived from Judaism, but having said all
that, we cannot guarantee how Esau will react to us. Experience
has demonstrated that Esau strove for the growth of the church.
Today, we have lovely melodies proclaiming, noel, noel, born is
the King of Israel, and peace on earth and good will to man. The
church however, feels ill at ease when the subjects like that of the
inquisition or its behavior during the Holocaust are raised. Though
steadfastly denying punishing heretics saying that it only interro-
gated them, however it did turn them over to the state, and it was
the state that implemented *auto da fe*, the wrack, confiscation of
wealth, kidnapping, and decreeing exile. The state was responsible for horrors. But this pattern of logic is essential to the de-

fense of Esau's descendants, particularly, his most famous progeny, Adolf Hitler.

Sometime ago, George Steiner wrote a parasitic fantasy that
perturbed many theatre goers. Because he had Hitler on stage shout
"the Jews have claimed to be a chosen people, chosen to be the
conscience of mankind." OK, but continued Hitler, "the Jews have
been the bad conscience of man, while we are the good conscience
of mankind." The anti-Semite sought a rationale by saying, do not
the Jews say they are *am echad*, one nation, and is that not what
we have said *a ein volk, bin rasse, bin furhe?* Esau always seeks a
rationale by distorting truth. Centuries ago, he hated Jacob for
stealing his birthright. Of course, he did not admit that he disdained this treasure and sold it for a bowl of porridge.

Today, the distortion is a denial of the Holocaust. When Hans
Jurgen Syberberg made his monumental film, *Hitler, ein film aus
Deutschland*, it became apparent that the murder of the Jews was
not vital to this western German director, but rather the disappointments that the Fuhrer caused the Germans. He has them say
to the dictator "You took away our sunsets, you took away our
enjoyments, you occupied and corrupted everything." But the disgusting, nausea's, vicious, bestial horror, the murder of the Jews,
that is not so important. And the legacy of Esau, the heritage of
dealing with every dissenting idea through might and violence is
still operative, whether in Eastern Europe or in Islam. Nicholas
Sombart, writing in the *Allgemeine*, said it bluntly, "Yes, William
Shakespeare, the evil which men do lives after all."

Jacob meeting Esau understands this. He mulls over his experiences with Esau and perceives that wherever he goes, he must
live with Esau. He will never be free from his brother's hatred and
perhaps his brother's own insecurity. Oh, Esau is insecure. Think

of the manner in which a commentary regards this meeting. "Accept my gifts, brother,"

"Yesh li kol,"
"I have everything" (Gen. 33:11)

says Jacob."

But says the Yalkut, one who is not overwhelmingly wealthy may utter these words, because whoever is satisfied with his portion in life, may very well proclaim, *"Yesh li kol."* But for one who is not secure, who is not content with his role in the scheme of things, who feels that his own distortions and untruths may find him out, he may have all the material wealth of the globe, but he cannot say, *"Yesh li kol."* True, the Talmud notes: he who has one hundred dollars wants two hundred, and no one dies with even half of his desires fulfilled and hopes attained. Esau looks at Jacob's gift and says:

"Yesh li rav,"
"I have a great deal." (Gen. 33:9)

Perhaps he wishes to imply, "whatever I take from you is really not that significant." True, "I accept your Bible, I take your ethics, I even speak your words, God, love, justice, but I really don't need them because I really don't want them." The idolatries of his civilization, his lusts for power and subjugation, his fragmented emotional and spiritual energies really leave no room for those seized treasures. How true Esau spoke then. Judaism wanted the world to recognize and accept only one, eternal God, and in that faith it proclaimed, *Yesh li kol.* I have everything. And it preached no doctrines of oppressing, suppressing, torturing, nor killing everyone who did not see eye to eye with it. How the Rabbis sigh over the well meaning but misguided zeal of Hyrcanus in pushing conversion upon gentiles. Had Hyrcanus spared the Edomites alone, we might have been spared an Antipater and thereby not have to suffer his monstrous son, Herod, and rejoiced that:

"*Kol Yisrael yesh lahem chelek leolam habah*,"
"All Israel have a portion in the world to come."
(Sanhedrein 90a)

Rabbis were not reticent to include the righteous of all nations. But Esau really had no room for such concepts. The Church has taught, *ex ecclesia nullus salus*, there is no salvation beyond the Church, and Islam, too, divided the world between the blessed adherents of Mohammed, and the remainder who could easily be put to the sword.

But of Jacob it is written, "I was frightened and grieved" frightened that he might kill his brother in warfare, and grieved that he himself might be killed. The commentary includes the monologue: "If he prevails over me, then he will kill me, and if I prevail over him, then I may murder him." (Rashi to Gen. 32:8)

Esau sets out with passion, vengeance, and anger escorted by four hundred armed men, but Jacob is assailed by conscience. He thinks, perhaps Esau has certain moral justifications. He has lived in Israel all these years while I have been away. Is he not strengthened by the Holy Land? All these years in which I have been away, he has lived near our parents and could fulfill the tremendous commandment of "*Kavaid et Avechah ve'et Emechah*," "Honor thy father and mother. (Exodus 20:12) And so he is very frightened and not very grieved. How come he is very frightened and not very grieved asks the Commentary? Since it notes the word "*Miod*," "Very" (Gen. 32:8) which occurs only in association with fright and not grief. The explanation again reveals Jacob. He greatly feared that he might kill his brother and grieved that he might be killed. The wholesome personality is more frightened that he impose violence or injury upon others, than that they might impose such harm upon him.

And so Jacob embarks upon his objectives with diplomacy. Pay gifts, render bribes to Esau, flatter him and address him as Lord. Some defend the act and let that be our guide. Subordinate yourself to the tremendous power of Esau. Flatter him if it brings peace, move with the current and not against it. And yet, do we not hear other sentiments emanating from the Rabbis? If Esau attacks the sanctity of God, if he profanes our faith, then raise the banner of revolt as did the Macabees, but when the physical countenance of Israel sustains injuries, be diplomatic. Yet this same Torah lesson narrates the challenge of Dina and the anger of her two brothers, Reuben and Shimon. Unlike their Father's flattery, and concessions to the people of the City of Shechem, they seek and obtain revenge. They are not deceived by the empty assertions of newly found brotherhood with the men of Shechem, whose calculations include Jacob's women and taking his wealth.

Of course, there have been differences of opinions amongst us. Let us not arouse those who are against us, but swallow whatever they cast at us. Let us avoid their anger, their envy, and their violence through flattery and bribery. To which the immortal leader Vladimir Jabotinsky responded, "Are we to live like mice, holed up in the little crevices of the wall? Golda Meir tried to ascribe dignity to that attitude, when she said "we may forgive the Arabs for killing our children, but we shall never forgive them for forcing us to kill their sons."

Father Jacob, we understand your fear of killing. And we acclaim it. But still. We do not want to forgive anyone for killing our children. We understand those brothers who were ready to battle for the welfare, the dignity and the security of their family. Looters, murderers, animals who kill Jews must be hunted down and wiped out. There is no flattery here. For are we not taught that God himself was displeased by the *chanif*, the flattery. When Jacob declared, and I have sent to tell my Lord and find favor in your eyes. God retorts. You humble yourself before your brother and call him lord. I shall raise Kings from among his descendants eight times before I support your royalty. It is not proper, not dignified for him who serves God, to call this servant Lord.

"Vayerah Ya'akov miod, vayatzer lo, vayachatz et haam,"
"And Jacob was frightened and he divided his people."
(Gen. 32: 8)

Perhaps Esau will come and smite one camp and others will be saved. Or Jacob, Jacob, you should be frightened. Frightened and grieved because the camp of Israel is divided. Let this be one camp. Without weakening in the energies and splitting there is only one camp in the confrontation with Esau, and then Jacob need neither worry, nor be afraid or grieved from either Esau or Ishmael. Let the lessons of the Torah loom large in our minds and lives, so that we struggle to live and work with dignity, pride, and honor.

FEW AND MANY WORDS

The Hebrew Bible, we all know is a creation that has left a most tremendous impress upon the mind of western man. It has influenced his linguistic attempts at communication in a multitude of ways. To the Rabbis of old who perceived a significance attached to every word, the very letters and the subtle manner were a way in which the Hebrew language sought to impart profound truths to our people. Simple translation of *Lashon Hakodesh,* the holy language into the many languages that we employ today did not cover the finer innuendoes that the record of our historic trials has presented to civilization.

Sometimes the Hebrew narrative is full, and records not only portray an incident but details. Thus it is not enough for the Torah to tell us that our ancestors prayed through *korbanot,* sacrifices, but these are explained in great detail, so that we know there were *zevachim,* sacrifices of various natures, *shlamim,* offering *chatat, kapara,* atonement etc. Other times, we cannot help but intuitively feel that the Torah is purposely avoiding great detail, giving us just enough words to stimulate our own thoughts and search for the truth.

This is similar to the ability to speak, the characteristic that delineates human beings and makes them distinguished from the rest of life here on earth. Some people are able to be communicative by finding many words by which they can define, portray, develop, clarify their thoughts, and make us understand and share them. Others have another gift, the rare ability to find the correct word immediately and thereby not only express themselves, but have us comprehend their ideas as well. This process of human thought varies according to the individual involved.

Thus we find that the thoughts of the HaGra, the Vilna Gaon were like a constantly flowing fountain. But it was only the slightest part of these thoughts that he committed to writing. His style was profound, precise and abbreviated. This was also observed among other spiritual thinkers. For example this was true of one of the great brilliant minds of Chassiduth, Reb Menachem Mendel, known as the Kotsker. He was accustomed to speak in very precise, sharp, penetrating and exact phrase.

One day, it is reported, that one of the Kotsker's close associates looked at this Torah portion and asked what was so notable about Rashi's statement (Rashi to Gen. 32:4): "What do we gain in placing the letter *hay* after the end of a word rather than the letter *lamed* before?" *le'eretz Seir, artzah Sahir?* Displacing at best one letter means saving a second of your breath, surely nothing else. And he stood quietly, expecting a long profound perceptive, but the Kotsker answered him briefly. "If you can limit yourself for one moment and get rid of an extra letter, that is also good." It would seem that the Torah often follows that sentiment with a momentary observation which upon analysis, turns out to be rich indeed in its truth.

If we consider how Jacob prepared for the unavoidable encounter with Esau, we may learn some insight for our own encounters within the world today. It is strange how many historians and social observers try to understand the Jewish People's survival, and to what they attribute it.

Many volumes have been written in which authors display erudition, quote extensively, recall many historical events and list impressive observations, but all rotate around their belief that Jews survived because they had to fight anti-Semitism. And because of that, the Jews were compelled to sharpen their intellect, learn the vulnerability of their enemies, and through that method were able to carry on and escape total extermination.

In line with this thinking there is another collary, namely that Jews learned to cringe and fawn upon their would be oppressors; and by licking the boots of their enemies, by being amiable and yielding, this strategy of appeasement kept them alive. Actually, our faith did not believe in appeasement. If you think of the story of Jacob's returning to his homeland, his fear in meeting his brother Esau, the twin who hated him and who once vowed to kill him when their father died, superficially, it would seem that Jacob was too, a person who was afraid of facing the enemy. A person whose policy was to avoid confrontation at all costs and who pursued this policy by instructing his representatives to bring gifts to Esau:

"*Limtzah chen be'eynechah,*"
"To find favor in your eyes. (Gen. 32:6)

However, the Sages warn us in the Talmud (Masechet Sotah 41b) "Whoever tries to flatter and appease his neighbor (the wicked,) ends up by falling into his hand." And so we see that the Sages did not agree with such a policy. It is strange that Jacob should be thought of as representing that attitude. Furthermore, when the messengers return to him their report, it is a distressing one indeed. "We came to your brother Esau, and he is going to meet you, but there are four hundred armed men with him." And the Bible now says, that Jacob was very frightened and he was upset. Again, the Rabbis apparently are confused with such descriptions of Father Jacob.

We find in this stirring picture of Jacob, our forefather immersed in his own thoughts, perturbed by considerations of his past and concerned over his possible guilt. This may have evoked some valid grievance from his brother and the realistic apprehension that a meeting with that brother, Esau, may be not only unpleasant but also physically threatening. Thus, shaken by all these thoughts, his prayers are both moving and, he implores God's help.

"*Hatzileyne nah miyad achi, miyad Esau*"
"Deliver me from the power of my brother, Esau."
(Gen. 32:12)

Once again, the Hebrew mind perusing those words was prompted to inquire; if he prayed for rescue from the hand of Esau that is understandable, why the need to remind God that his brother was Esau? The Sefat Emet, anticipating, perhaps, some of our own contemporary problems interpreted the verse to mean that Jacob appealed to God for assistance because his proximity and association with Esau might impel the latter to declare himself as a brother. Ah, he prayed, "God deliver me from Esau's hatred, hostility and from his brotherhood that may be just as dangerous for my existence as is his enmity. We too may very well appreciate that cautionary approach.

When the Pope visited the Rome Synagogue, he referred to our faith as that of an "elder brother." For centuries, western culture heard Christianity and Islam described as "daughter religions," an admission that their ethics and humanness were lifted from Judaism. The Pope however, now embarks upon a new strategy, we are no longer parents, but an elder brother.

"Hatzileyne nah miyad achi miyad Esau,"
"Deliver me from the power of my brother, Esau."
(Ibid)

One commentary suggested a comparison with the Midrashic tale regarding the creation of iron. (Gen. Rabbah 5:9) When trees became aware of the propensities of this metal, they began to weep and tremble, "Woe is us, they cried, the iron will smash against us, assault our bark, chop off our limbs, destroy our leaves and fruits. Woe is us." Whereupon an old wise tree reassured them, "why are you trembling? There will be no axe unless you trees provide the wood for the handle of the axe? Without that handle, iron may form blades but they will not be employed against you." How true a tale this is. When the Toldot Ya'akov Yoseph interpreted it, it is one thing to pray "Deliver me from the power of Esau," but too often the hand of Esau is attached to the hand of our own brother. How often have we suffered from the fact that the enemy's plots and schemes have been aided by some that comes from our own midst?

Our generation has been privileged to witness many things. We have sustained the most horrible experiences of the Holocaust. Even though we have witnessed the emergence of *Medinat Yisrael,* the State of Israel, we have suffered even in that country constant attacks, murderous onslaughts and massacres directed against innocent men and women riding buses to work, children learning in the school classroom and cowardly attempts to murder our children from ambush. We have also seen the gallantry, bravery, courage and determination displayed by our brethren in Israel to fight against these terrorists and murderers. But what is the picture that is most frightening in the framework of these developments? Is it the fear that our enemies will drive us into the sea? No, these dangers which must be combated, will not succeed in dislodging Jews from Israel. So what is our enemy then? It is the same weakness that has plagued us too often, the dissension within the ranks. Even when the Romans besieged the walls of Jerusalem, they would fall back before the united onslaught of our people. But the moment they did so, disunity again prevailed among our brethren.

In the Talmud (Masehchet Berachot 4a), they discuss,

"*Vayirah Ya'akov,*"
"And Jacob was afraid." (Gen. 32:8)

How is this possible? Jacob is the "*Yoshev Oholim,*" the dweller of tents, the man who studies Torah and is imbued with great spirituality. Is it proper that such a *tzaddick*, a righteous person should be afraid of a human being, an ordinary mortal? In the *Shaar Hayirah*, reference is made to a Chasid who used to flee into the forests. When he was asked, aren't you afraid of thieves and wild animals? He answered; I would be ashamed before God to fear anything besides him. If that is so, how could a righteous God-fearing person who had been inspired by the Divine assurance, "Behold I am with you and shall guard you everywhere that you go," this Jacob who sent messengers to Esau, which tradition says were *malacahim mamash*, real angels, a Jacob who admits to God:

> **"*Key bemakli avarti et hayarden hazeh, Veatah hayiti lishney machanot*"**
> **"I crossed this Jordan river with only a staff in my hand, and today I have become two camps."**
> **(Gen. 32:11)**

How could such a person should be afraid of Esau and seek to fawn, flatter and cringe before such a *rasha*, evil person?

But it is these very words

> **"*Hatzileyne nah miyad achi Esau,*"**
> **"Rescue me from the power of my brother Esau,"**
> **(Gen. 32:12)**

that are few in number and do not run on to become a volume that we find tremendous observations about Jewish history, Jewish survival and the Jewish future.

Yes, dear Lord, save us from Esau and from ourselves. Be sure to help us when our own brethren hasten to support tyranny and hatred.

Let us learn from Jacob, that in dealing with the world, we need not cringe and fawn. True we should try to be diplomatic, Jacob sent gifts, but first he cleansed himself in prayer and faith, and finally he was ready to stand his ground and fight for his rights. May we learn this and above all learn to keep ourselves united, with love for our people, our heritage and our ideals. For this unity will bring us victory.

KATONTI MEKOL HACHASADIM, I AM NOT WORTHY OF ALL YOUR MERCIES

"Katonti mekol hachasadim,"
"I am not worthy of all the mercies " (Genesis 32:11)

In the Torah portion *Vayishlach*, the Bible presents us with a stirring picture of Jacob who returns home to Canaan, after an absence of twenty years. He is concerned with the report brought to him by his scouts. (We need not, at this time, concern ourselves with the debate whether the scouts were Jacob's servants or literally angels, as is the view of Rashi.) Namely, that his brother Esau, who had sworn to slay him years ago and whose wild oath was really the primary cause which impelled his parents to send him away, was now coming forward to meet him and he was accompanied by an entourage of four hundred men.

We can easily see in our mind's eye the scene that is produced by this report. *Vayishlach*, presents us with a dramatic moment in Jacob's life when he quivers with insecurities, fears and anxieties for the welfare of his family, that his brother, Esau, still continues with his passionate, irrational, desire for vendetta and revenge against him and his household. The strategy Jacob employs is first to divide his own entire entourage into two separate camps. Probably, there is excitement, concern and many are the schemes proposed to safeguard the camp and family. Later in a moment of isolation, alone with his conscience, his fears border-

ing upon panic, he resolves to pursue a policy of appeasing his
brother through gifts. Determined that if this should fail, he de-
cides that he will resist with force, hoping that at least one of the
camps will escape if the other is defeated.

What attracts us at this moment is the figure of Jacob. Hearing the report, we learn that he was afraid and distressed. This is a
phrase that requires more than momentary consideration. After
all, Jacob was a man of profound faith. Surely he felt as did
Jeremiah the prophet:

> **"*Baruch hagever asher yivtach ba'Hashem, vehayah
> Hashem mivtacho*,"**
> **"Blessed is the man who trusts in the Lord and the
> Lord shall be his trust." (Psalms 17:7)**

Certainly a God fearing man would rely upon the Lord's assurance to him, and abide safely in Divine protection?

As we discussed, the Rabbis give us a clue to Jacob's concerns when they say he was afraid that he might be killed and he
was distressed lest he kill others in the conflict which might erupt
between him and his brother, Esau. (Rashi to Gen. 32:8)

We know that Jacob was a God fearing man who put his
trust in the Lord, he could not possibly be motivated by the primary idea that he would be killed. God's assurance to be with him
must have comforted him in all his trials. I choose to think that
what frightened him was actually the worry that Esau's desire to
kill him was due in some measure to his own failing. He probably
thought, why should Esau still be full of fury after all these years?
Esau was powerful and prosperous. He should no longer feel that
he would be affected materially due to the loss of the blessing.
Jacob probably wondered "did I act improperly, even in the pursuit of my mother's instructions? Or did I show a lack of tact in

failing to keep in touch with him, even occasionally, and help him realize that I have taken nothing away from him? Perhaps I failed to display sufficient foresight and so the result is that he still hates me for which I am responsible. Alas to think, that after all these years, in which I have benefited from God's goodness, I have failed to show my gratitude by placating my brother and cementing peaceful bonds between us." In brief, Jacob thought, "if I am killed, or even if I escape personally, but suffer because of harm which is inflicted upon my family and this would be tantamount to suffering these blows on my own person. I shall be responsible for this evil."

He was distressed, say these Sages, because he also feared that in an open conflict he might kill another. Of course, we might try to wave away this kind of bloodshed by saying it would have happened purely in self-defense. We need not deny that, but to kill others, even in self-defense meant a violation of the fundamental principles to which Jacob clung, namely the peaceful, just and righteous life. Here was Jacob the *ish tam*, simple man, the dweller of tents, the man immersed in the sacred principles of sanctity, a man who dreamt of peace, harmony and proper social relations, and yet this man would be compelled to kill, in self-defense it is true, but in a conflict which he feared might have been prevented.

It is this realization of possible failures on his part that evoke the real humility of Jacob. He still is immersed in his faith and pours forth his heart in prayer. And what does he say? We find him crying out in pathos, and stirring humbleness:

> *"Katonti mekol hachasadim umekol haemet asher ahseeta et avdecha, ki bemakli avarti et hayarden hazeh, veatah hayeeti lishnay machanot,"*

**"I am not worthy of all the mercies and of all the truth
which thou hast shown thy servant; for with my staff I
passed over this Jordan; and now, I am two camps."
(Gen. 32:11)**

It is a moving scene that is depicted; Jacob had fled years
ago from the anger and hatred of this same brother. Then carrying
no wealth, attired only with the clothing upon his back, armed
only with the staff of a shepherd, he fled, passing over the Jordan
River. He has suffered much, he has been exploited, dishonorably
abused by his own relatives, manipulated into a position where he
literally was enslaved, toiling for fourteen years in order to marry
the young woman whom he loved so deeply. Life had treated him
neither kindly nor gently. And yet he can say "*Katonti*," "I have
become small, I am unworthy." He repudiates any arrogance. He
does not assert and he does not believe that the wealth he has
acquired, the magnificent family he has sired, the herds of cattle
and other wealth which is his, all represented by his ability to
divide all his possessions into two camps, is due to his ability,
talents, skills or clever plans. I am grown small, "*Katonti,*" "I am
humble," and unworthy of all the goodness thou hast shown me.
Katonti, I am humbled, because I am grateful to thee, God.

**"*Katonti mekol hachasadim uhmekol haemet asher
ahseeta et avdehcha,*"**
**"I am not worthy of all the mercies and of all the truth
that thou hast shown unto thy servant." (Ibid)**

Compare this attitude towards life, the humble being as compared with the arrogant and the proud. In modern psychology we
often hear much about the arrogance which expresses itself in superiority complexes. It is true that these are often nothing but patho-
logical attempts to substitute a mode of conduct exactly opposite

to the real feelings of inferiority, inadequacy or insecurity that one may feel. Psychology recognizes that this superiority may develop from inferiority, and it is also cognizant that this complex of superiority may lead to socially destructive tendencies.

Characteristic of this type of pride is poverty, spiritual poverty, like a nut rattling in its shell. If Nazis and Neo-Nazis demean Jews, blacks, and gays, and prattle about racial superiority, behind their facade of superiority are feelings of inferiority and inadequacy, the refusal to face self-failure.

"*Katoni,*" I have become smaller. Yes, I can recall all my problems and pressures and am grateful to thee for all thy good. Father Jacob reminds us that we must always be sensitive and express our gratitude to kindness shown to us. In the midst of our prosperity, surrounded by what we may consider our accomplishments in life, we must always be ready to remember, even when faced with many difficulties, we must be thankful for the good and the blessings that have been manifested to us. The inheritance of Jacob is, of course, the heritage we all share. That is why throughout the day, at every regular service, three times daily, do we declare "*Modim anachnu lach,*" we thank thee God.

Did not Father Abraham include the emotion of *hoda,* thankfulness in his inauguration of the *Schacharit,* the morning prayer, because he was grateful that he had been rescued from overwhelming darkness? And so it has been unto this very day: the observant Jew starts his day with reciting benedictions of gratitude for the very necessities of life that have been bestowed upon him.

Every time we partake of food and drink, whenever we acquire new clothing, dedicate a new home, win the heavenly blessings of obtaining a spouse, we rejoice and utter benedictions of thanksgiving to our creator.

Not so Father Jacob. "*Katonti*, I have become smaller," Jacob says. I realize that everyone is good and important, whether a printer, tailor, cobbler, builder, nurse or teacher. Let us all be humble like Father Jacob. Let us look for our own failures instead of scape-goats. Look for our own failures instead of attacking others. Let us wrestle with ourselves. Jacob wrestled with himself, and he emerged a greater personality, *Yisrael*, Israel. "*Katonti*, I have be-come smaller, I am humble." Let us wrestle with ourselves so that we may emerge greater. A greater spirit who over comes, a greater spirit who grapples successfully with the challenges of man and God.

In our faith, we are of the opinion that a person who is not a *makir tovah*, who does not take cognizance of the good that is shown him, ends up by being a *kofer bikur*, a person who ends up denying God. So obviously, gratitude is a sentiment associated with deep spirituality even as we have heard that *mikol melamdai hiskalti*, a direct implication that one learns from his pupils, so too may he be influenced in our gratitude towards all kinds of human beings. Oh yes, we have much to be thankful for.

OLAM CHESED YIBANEH, THE WORLD IS BUILT WITH BENEVOLENCE

The American people, as we all know, find their origins among the nations of the world. To a certain extent, that is true of all people, since the world was not created along political lines, but along geographical and natural demographics. The French who regarded themselves as hereditary enemies of the Germans appar-ently forgot that the Goths and Franks were of the same tribe. The history of the world is really the record of colonization, not only that of the imperial, exploitative type, but simple colonization due to the migratory movements of people to and from across the globe. National cultures have differed because of varied experiences; these have sharpened with the passing of time.

Now, America is actually a very young state and people, and to a large measure, we find that we often emulate others. But there is one great national holiday that appeals to all of us and that is Thanksgiving. Southerners may think that Lincoln was not quite so great. Others may try to reduce the image and accomplishments of a George Washington, even the founding fathers have been accused of being motivated only by economic factors in their struggle for American independence. So we can understand why the celebration of one great American hero finds more popularity in one section of the United States than another section. But there is one holiday in which we all participate, in which we all thrill, and despite all the various differing analysis of historians, we all continue to see great meaning in that national holiday. This particular weekend is always set aside by religious leaders as a Thanksgiving Sabbath. In the Synagogues and Churches of the country, Priests, Ministers and Rabbis preach on Thanksgiving, which is the nearest thing we have to a religious national holiday. This attracts all of us.

The Talmud (Masehchet Berachot 35b) tells us in the name of Rabbi Hanina bar Papa, "whoever enjoys anything in this world without making a blessing is like one who robs God and the community of Israel." Because it is written: "Who robs his father or mother and says it is no transgression, the same is the companion of the destroyer." Who is the father if not God, for the Torah teaches us, is thy father who has gotten thee? And who is the mother? Isn't the community of Israel, as it is written, hear my son, the instruction of your father and don't forsake the teaching of thy mother, what is the meaning of the companion of the destroyer? This refers, answered Rabbi Hanina bar Papa, to a companion of Jereboam, son of Nebat, who wanted to destroy Israel's faith in the Father in heaven. Some careful thinking must be prescribed to understand that one who eats or drinks without a *Brachah,* thanksgiving is compared to Jereboam, who sinned and caused others to sin and hence is considered as one of the greatest sinners in Israel.

Everything has its form and inner substance. This is true of Torah and *Mitzvot,* and their substance is that the *Bracha* acknowledges and thanks God for his loving kindness. Its form is deep too, namely to understand the general kindness of God. For *olam chesed yibaneh,* the world is built by Torah that deals with *Mitzvot* between man and his fellowman, but also that great category known as *Mitzvot* between man and God. Unfortunately, we often err by imaging that the main component of *Chesed,* benevolence is our giving food and drink to others, but that is a form of *Chesed,* benevolence whose superior substance consists of the sentiments of our heart and the comprehension of our minds.

Abraham for example, was a loving kind person whose influence upon others led to their conversion to the true and only God. Likewise when God sought to ease his discomfort after circumcision and increased the heat of the day to prevent people from disturbing him, Abraham still hoped to show *Chesed* to others because it is imperative to recognize all goodness, not only between man and his fellow. True, *derech eretz kaydmah letorah* and gratitude to people is so important. But we should recognize the very essence of goodness itself, and the basic quality of gratitude.

The Midrash reminds us when God summoned Moses at the burning bush to go to Pharaoh in the struggle for Jewish national liberation, Moses first replied "I cannot go immediately, you know that Jethro was kind to me, a stranger, he opened his home and his heart. How shall I just leave him without first obtaining his agreement?" Right now we all understand how important it was to Moses to fulfill the will of God and to emancipate our people from slavery, yet the demand of gratitude set aside the first response to these great emotions. And God agreed that he go to Jethro.

Thus we can understand why the Talmud makes such a bold statement, that enjoying the productivity of the world and life without thanking God and reciting a *Brachah* is tantamount to robbing God and the community of Israel. Because *olam chesed yibaneh*. The world is established by *chesed* and rejecting that recognition and gratitude means repudiating God and his word. It is that awareness of the inner fabric of the world that prompts Rabeynu Yonah in his Gates of Repentance, Gate Three, to say we know that in observing the inhabitants of Sodom, we see a city of iniquity, sin and revolt against God. A community which corrupted justice, which vaunted its immorality and yet, is it not surprising that Ezekiel the prophet is critical of Sodom by declaring, "This was the iniquity of Sodom your sister, pride, fullness of bread, and a careless ease was in her and her daughters." Neither did they strengthen the hand of the poor and the needy. What doesn't Ezekiel see, the viciousness in killing guests and strangers? Their cruelty in passing legislation which imposed the death penalty upon anyone who fed guests in secret? A community which imposed torture, agony, and various forms of disgusting cruelty and death upon its poor victims? The prophet complains that they did not show *Chesed,* loving kindness, they did not help the poor and needy. But the truth is their response of cruelty was because they ignored *Chesed.* Sodom did not realize that loving kindness and the compassion it exerts constitute the factor without which the world cannot exist. *Olam Chesed*. If there is no *Chesed* then the world cannot be established. It is unable to stand firm and stable.

That is what the Proverbs implies:

"*Orech chayim lemaehlah lemaskeel, lema'an soar mishole matah*,"
"The path of life goes upward for the wise, that he may depart from the lower world beneath."
(Proverbs. 15:24)

Every person has to strive to ascend in order to escape deteriorating, collapsing and into lowering unworthy undignified standards. The Jew who does not aspire to emulate father Abraham and constantly increase his sensitivity to *chesed* in the world begins to deteriorate and corrode into the realm of the inhabitants of Sodom. The Vilna Gaon stresses that the path to take is that of Torah. This is the Torah attitude and philosophy on enjoying life's blessings by reciting a *Berachah* of Thanksgiving. He who is no longer sensitive to *hakarata tovah*, no longer recognizes goodness and is without gratitude, he becomes like Jereboam, who sinned and caused others to err because he too lacked this quality of *chesed* which is a foundation the world is built on.

We see the importance of gratitude as recognized by Rashi, as indicated in the Book of Exodus. When the Bible tells us that the plagues of blood and frogs were produced after Aaron, not Moses, had smitten the waters and the dust of the earth, God himself reminds Moses, "You were saved by the waters of the Nile that might have drowned you in the basket made by your mother to keep you alive, have you no gratitude to the water? Have you no gratitude to the dust of the earth in which you concealed the Egyptian oppressor whom you killed? Had that dust not covered him, you would have been caught immediately and executed by pharaoh. Show your gratitude to inanimate things like water and dust. You should not be the one who transforms the water into blood and the dust into frogs, though this is a plague sent by Providence." (Rashi to Exodus. 7:19)

Chesed olam yibaneh. The world can be built and become stable only through this element of sensitivity between one and the other and the spirit of gratitude and thanksgiving. *Olam chesed yibaneh.* The world can be built, established, stabilized, and be secured only through *chesed*, this quality of sensitivity to others, the readiness to display gratitude for the good which has been demonstrated towards us. Small wonder that Jacob can cry out, "*Katonti mikol hachasidim*," "I have become humble" (Gen. 32:11) when I consider all the mercies, kindness and compassion you have shown me God, throughout my life of problems, frustrations and fears.

Thanksgiving which is upon us, is a great holiday indeed, one which summons us to be thankful. The *chesed* for which gratitude can arouse the salvation of the world. So for America, so for all our progress and advances, for all the miracles which have been vouchsafed to our people, here, in Europe, Israel and elsewhere. Let us be thankful. Thankful to each other for the decency we may show one another, thankful above all to God whose *chesed* makes possible our lives, our existence and our future, always be thankful and grateful to him.

Vayeshev

— 9 —

וַיִּתְמַהְמָהּ

"And he lingered" (Genesis 19:16)

SHALSHELET: THE BATTLE WITH TEMPTATION

Our forefathers lived in a simple world. They did not know of the industrial revolution. They were not subject to the temptations of radio, television, movies or the attractions of a culture and civilizations such as we are today. It was perhaps easier for them to respond to the call of faith. In our day, we are subject to different pressures, which is why many say it is hard to arouse religious sentiments in the human heart today. We live in such a confused world, where there are so many conflicts in our hearts.

Is it true however that our fathers before us were not subject to temptations such as we and that is why they responded warmly to the call of faith?

I should like you to note three particular incidents in the recent Torah readings and see how this assertion falls to the ground.

If you will note, the Torah readings carry certain cantillations commonly called *trup*. It is true that these cantillations in recent times
are being completely ignored. In some countries years ago, Jews
utilized them essentially not for melodies as much as a gauge or
punctuation. Even in some European countries, the Torah portion
was not read with much emphasis upon the cantillation and it is an
art that many feel is disappearing. However, certain cantillations
managed to remain associated with certain patterns. For example
the *shalshelet* represented a quivering series of notes, arising in
high frequency until it ended abruptly. Now in three cases you
will find this note on certain words as if they seek to emphasize a
particular event to which I refer.

The first is found in the chapter of Torah that tells us of the
incident between Lot and the angels who came to visit him in
Sodom.

The second is found over a word in the story wherein Abraham tells his servant Eliezer to procure a wife for his son Isaac.
And the third appears in when the Torah portion speaks of the
incident between Joseph and the wife of Potifar. You may ask,
"what possible connection are there between such three widely
separated tales?"

Let us consider them in order, Lot because of economic advantage, after his difference of opinion with Abraham chose to
live in the plains of Sodom, a rich community, but a community
full of sin, iniquity, cruelty and horrors. A totalitarian community
that had its dictatorship crush anyone who did not want to conform with their religious requirements of inhumanity. And so God
decided to wipe out Sodom and he sent his angels to warn Lot, and
to order him to leave the city, so that he and his household might
be saved. And so Lot went to his married daughters and told them

they must leave, but his sons-in-law said, "what are you talking about, you must be fools to leave a city as this." And when the morning came and the angels said you must leave, the Torah says:

"Vayitmahmah,"
"And he lingered" (Gen. 19:16)

with a *shalshelet*."

He had a tremendous conflict within him. Shall I really leave this community? I know this is not a good community for decency, honor or morality. But still I am making a great deal of money here; my sons-in-law don't want to leave. How can you uproot yourself because of some threatened catastrophe that may come because of immorality? This scene is repeated millions of times in history and in our lives.

The German Jews, Polish Jews and others who could have saved themselves often lingered, because they asked the same questions. How does one uproot himself and throw away the possibility of living well and making money and enjoying the material comforts and luxuries of life? The Torah then says the angels laid hold upon Lot's hand. The commentator Ibn Ezra says that in his fright he grew weary and couldn't move. Ramban says it means they forced him outward. But are we so wrong to see that in reality they placed their hands upon his hand to encourage him so that he might make his decision to leave in accordance with God's wish?

In *Chayai Sarah* we are faced with the story of Eliezer, the servant of Abraham who went forth to find a wife for Isaac. The Midrash tells us that Eliezer himself had a daughter and would have loved to arrange a marriage between Isaac and his daughter. (Gen. Rabbah 59:12) After all, Eliezer was the steward of Abraham's household, a most trusted adviser. He probably looked at all the wealth of Abraham and figured, with a proper marriage, this would all come to me. In those days a father had great influences over his daughter. If he came back and said to Abraham that he could not find a wife for Isaac or that the girl he decided upon refused to accompany him. Now Abraham depended upon Eliezer and so did Isaac take his advice seriously. Abraham made him swear that he would not take for Isaac a wife from one of the idol worshipers who would take his son away from the land. Eliezer could have said, "I couldn't find a wife for Isaac, but my daughter is available. After all you know she is not an idol worshipper. She will not lead your son astray. I shall continue to be not only your trusted advisor but also a real in-law." It will be a perfectly natural arrangement, and he thought of this, "*Vayomar*," "And he said to God" (Gen. 24:12), and one word is the *shalshelet*, Eliezer was faced with this temptation. Who of us doesn't understand it? A father's desire to ensure his daughter's future. A man's ambition is to make himself more than a trusted advisor, but a real chief of the clan, not only a good manager, but also a real boss. Yet as he fought within himself he realized how wrong it was and he forced himself to throw away that idea and pray for guidance instead, so that he might really fulfill the desires of Abraham.

In the Torah portion *Vayeshev*, we note a similar occurrence. Here is Joseph, a nice young boy, an attractive physical specimen, brilliant, with a fascinating personality. He had entered Egypt naked and is today a manager of his master's household. He is becoming recognized for his ability and attracts much comment and opinion.

Rashi says he became important. He became vain. He realized that he was handsome, he ate and drank and curled his hair. (Rashi to Gen. 39:6) And God said, "Change. Your Father mourns for you and you are dandy. You will see that this will lead to difficulties." And his master's wife fell in love with him and asked him to lead an intimate life with her. And the Torah says, *Vayema'aine*, And he refused (Gen. 39:8) and over the word is a *shalshelet*. You see he did not refuse so easily. Be realistic. Here was Joseph, a slave, an important slave, but still a slave, and by agreeing to this woman's scheme, his entire life would become one of tremendous ease and comfort. He was a young boy and he was certainly intrigued by the proposal. He said to himself, what if I accept her proposition? After all, who knows me here I'm just a slave, I'm not suppose to have any moral standards and after all I'm not to blame. I didn't bother with her. She is starting up with me. And why should I care about the people, after all they purchased me like they purchase any slave. What do they care about the human personality? I am nothing; life is nothing, they care after all for their selfish ease. But then he asked himself other questions. This man, this husband and this master, he is so decent to me, he likes me, and he treats me properly, with respect and courtesy. I may be a slave legally, but he treats me well. And what if something were to happen, would I like my children to come forth from this woman? And how would I feel if this were to happen to me as a married man, how would I feel, if my wife were to carry on with other men? And then he thought what of the things I have been taught at home? And he decided that he would refuse. You see Joseph was a righteous man, but also a human man facing the problems we all face, but he emerged victorious because he wrestled with temptation within him.

That is what the Torah tells us here and that is what Chanukah tells us. There were many Jews who were attracted by the Hellenic culture. They wanted the easy life, the fun, and the enjoyment, the feeling of belonging to the majority. But after the *shalshelet*, after they went through the inner conflict they responded to the call of God. So let us not say that our forefathers responded because they had no temptation, but because they wrestled with temptation. They came forth victorious. May their spirit of strength and courage and bravery inspire us to follow their example now and forever.

ENVY

From my earliest childhood, I recall my father reminding my brothers and myself that each and every child was precious to him. My brothers and I were careful indeed, never to upset him with prolonged bickering and petty quarrels among us. However, poor Father Jacob was not as fortunate. Despite the fact that his children who were destined to be the forefathers of our nation, and hence are often referred to as the *Shevatim*, the Tribes, despite their basic decencies and attractive characters, hostility towards their younger brother erupted.

The words that open our current Biblical lesson are certainly familiar enough to all of us.

> **"*Vayeshev Ya'akov be'eretz megurai Aviv*,"**
> **"And Jacob dwelt in the land of his Father's**
> **sojourning." (Gen. 37:1)**

Here was Father Jacob, whose past had been so harsh and who had now achieved old age. Every student of the Jewish homily recalls the sharp comment by Rashi, "*Bikesh Ya'akov leshev beshalvah*," "Jacob requested to sit in peace." (Rashi to Gen. 37:2) All he wanted was to live tranquilly, at ease, at peace, the normal desire to take it easy as we get older. But instead, he must confront the sad scenes of belligerency and anger erupting among his children.

Consider, however the Midrash (Gen. Rabbah 84:3) from which the opinion was drawn. Rabbi Acha says when the saintly are at ease and wish to continue that ease, the adversary comes and criticizes them; isn't it enough that the future world has been ordained for them, they want to have it easy in this world, too? That is what happened with Father Jacob, because he wanted to live at ease in this world the problems of Joseph fell upon him.

The *Yalkut Yehuda,* that so often brims over with magnificent insights, once again proves stimulating, trying to understand why the adversary should arise in such situations and why Rashi should comment that because of this, the anger of Joseph's plight befell our forefather. This commentator observes, it is not proper that a righteous man should want to dwell at complete ease when the situation of so many about him indicate that their problems are so much more than his labors amid happiness. The Yalkut says, only a select minority witnesses blessings and tranquility in their lives, and these people always arouse the envy of the rest of us. This is so, because most feel their own difficulties sharply when they observe the apparent ease of other lives. Therefore, a wholesome personality ought to be satisfied with his portion, even if he is not overflowing with blessings, he should be cognizant of the situation of most who lack rest and ease. Hence when the Hashem observed that Jacob wanted to take life easy without considering how humans should avoid arousing the envy of their contemporaries, he suffered the tragic situation with Joseph so that he might better understand how evil befell his family and home due to the envy which Joseph evoked from his brothers. If you find this a provocative thought as I do, please take a moment to consider another commentary.

The *Yalkut Shimoni* offers another insight. When Joseph disappeared, Jacob wept, "Woe to me that I married two sisters." The Midrash obviously wonders about this statement, because it is of a later vintage than the *sidrah* itself. In Jewish law, one cannot simultaneously marry two sisters, therefore; it would appear that Jacob was guilty of a transgression. Well, we are all human and make many mistakes. But the observation of one scholar is, that he was not guilty in marrying two sisters. The Mahrasha notes that when Jacob came to Paddan Pram, to be with Laban, he new that both girls were the product of an environment which was not immersed in Jewish faith and ideals, so he converted both Leah and Rachel. The *halachah* also indicates that conversion to the Jewish faith transforms one into a new personality, and hence, there no longer existed the previous relationship between Leah and Rachel. Hence they were not forbidden to Jacob in marriage.

Now, if Jacob knew this and recognized that he was not guilty of any error, why did he utter that complaint? The suggested answer is that he examined his act in the light of future influences. He foresaw that from this choice would emerge the character of Jereboam with the historical consequence that befell the Jewish people. And so his judgment was not restricted to the present situation, but rather an evaluation of the future, and so he groaned: "Woe is to me that I married these sisters."

Poor Father Jacob bemoaned his marriage to the sisters because he prophetically envisioned the arrival of Jereboam. The man who led the split in Jewish unity after the era of Solomon, the split which led to the Kingdom of Israel as opposed to the Kingdom of Judah. Jereboam was also responsible for setting up golden calves as a religious symbolism in his Kingdom and thereby committing a grievous sin against the monotheistic ideal of our faith. Father Jacob realized that his actions would in great measure be responsible for the emergence of Jereboam and hence he wept at his error.

Two differing Midrashim, each superficially far removed from the other, one deals with the sad but undeniable realities of the human condition. Each of us is subject to many basic, intuitive and animal instincts. Primitive desires for whose release we try to achieve in one way or another. Some try to control these desires by subjecting them to the convictions to which we have been taught. Others try to adjust into our lives under the comparative influences of the society and times in which we live. Sometimes we are successful and emerge in what sociologists call normal functioning which does not clash with either the sentiments or philosophies of our fellow human beings. On other occasions in our pursuit of happiness, escape from tensions, temperamental incompatibilities, cashes with others in habits, manners, memories, sentiments and basic values, we find that we have failed to achieve the accommodations we sought, and we suffer the pains of defeat. But always it appears that we must face the responses of others, whether these are reactions of nature, communities, individual, national or international. The emotion that the Midrash considers, *kinah*, envy is indeed a very deep emotion. We see it demonstrated among children in their relationship to other siblings.

Here was Joseph, the younger, apparently baiting the elder brothers with dreams whose symbolism could be read without the assistance of a trained psychiatrist. Obviously, the lad believes that he is superior to his brothers. Perhaps, what was most galling was their uneasy belief that there was some truth in his assertions.

His father, watching the family, could not help but realize that the child had an intuitive regality, a simple nobility, a manner in his relations with others, which was evidence of his perceptions, insight and skilled capacities. The alert father should not reveal preferences for one child over another. This should have been especially evident in the life of Jacob. Did he not sustain grief and pain, enmity and threats of violence in his younger years because he had been involved in domestic strife, all because his mother favored him over Esau, the rascal who managed to ingratiate himself with the aged Father, Isaac, by sweet tasting morsels of food? Yet, Father Jacob was only human. This Joseph lad was the son of his beloved Rachel who was no longer alive and so, perhaps to encourage this son, or to counterbalance the growing conflict between him and his other sons, he bought for him, a coat of many colors, and the conflict grew stronger.

Rabbi Yosef Dov Bar Soloweszcik in his classical *Beth Halevi* commentary offers us this analysis. Joseph tells his brothers about his dream:

> "*Vayosifu od snoh oto,*"
> "**And they increased their hatred of him.**"
> **(Gen. 37:5, 37:8)**

But, when the Bible records the conversation of a second dream, it also notes:

> "*Vayikanu bo echav,*"
> "**And his brothers envied him.**" **(Gen. 37:11)**

Why should they hate him for one dream, but envy him for another? Well, in the first dream, he saw the sheaves of his brothers bowing down to his sheave, which easily meant, that he would be wealthier than they, that they might have to turn to him, for financial help, and so they disliked him because of that possibility. But his second dream was really bizarre; the sun and the moon and eleven stars were bowing down to him, this was very upsetting. After all, it is possible for one brother to become wealthier than another is. We'll chalk this up to luck, or a break in circumstances. However, to speak about them bowing to him, this was just too much, because this was not a matter of good fortune, this was an assertion about the quality, attributes and character of everyone involved. Joseph was now saying to them, "not only shall I be more fortunate than you, but I am better than you." This aroused their jealousy and when jealousy is combined with hatred, then violence, grief, pain and tragedy invariably results.

Consider the results of these scenes. Envy and hatred impel the brothers to imprison Joseph, first in a pit and then, in a moment of anger, hatred and envy, they sell him into slavery, little realizing what this will do to their future. Because of a coat of many colors, because this brother walks around boasting of his dreams, the family is shattered. The aged father continues to grieve and lament, while his sons and daughters fail to comfort him. The brothers suffer the pangs of a guilty conscience as they fabricate stories about a wild beast having probably killed their brother. Developing from these turn of events is the spectacular rise of Joseph to prominence, while the brethren must turn toward Egypt, eventually, all Israel is enslaved and the nation must sustain bitter experiences, the exodus, and the redemption which must lead to Mount Sinai.

This envy and hatred has, unfortunately, plagued our people in its long and fascinating history. The prophet Isaiah warned that our detractors, our enemies would come from within. Centuries ago, the Syrian Hellenists were determined to rob us of our freedom, because when one is deprived of his right to worship in the sacred traditions of his people, when a person is subject to harassment, state sanctioned punishment all because he wishes to uphold his traditions, that person is denied freedom to think, freedom to worship, freedom to express himself and freedom to create. Unfortunately, there were Jews then, as there are Jews now, who are quick to abandon the teachings, the values and priorities of our people for what they hope will be their salvation.

There were those who were ready and eager to betray their own, hoping thereby to be accepted by the dominant culture. That holds true today. Because today there are still powerful voices who are little concerned with truth. Voices who try to please rulers whose sole positive attribute rests in their ownership of oil resources. Voices whose owners have still not learned the lessons of the Hitler period and the incredible Holocaust, who still are ready to pursue policies of appeasement to totalitarian heads. Alas, there are fellow Jews who would join such nefarious policy, some because they feel it would attract for them, the approbation of others, some because they feel it would be a weapon against fellow Jews who are highly critical of their severance from Jewish traditions.

Yes, our hopes for tranquility, uninterrupted ease and peace can be interfered with by present actions. Each of us becomes aware of our mistakes in our personal lives when we look back upon faulty calculations and misguided actions, even though our intentions were originally good ones. If that is true of our individual lives, is it not also true about our national destiny? Today, every one of us can pose as a *chacham*, a wise person by looking backward and criticizing one leader or another. "You Jewish leaders should have fought the British deception with more courage;

you should have demanded a better response from America when Hitler was murdering our people."

Long ago, I heard an inspiring Jewish leader warn against the enemy within. Jacob's descendants have always managed to escape extermination from the fierce enemies who have persecuted them, and despite the long and bloody battle of centuries, our people have never lost their courage or their faith. But some of their most tragic losses have resulted from the envy and hatred that have been projected by some Jews against their own brethren. Once, it was the *Yevsektzia*, the so-called Jewish division of the communists who were the worst persecutors of Jews in Soviet Russia. All the talk, the denials, the explanations and the defenses cannot alter the simple truth. Even in those terrible horror days and nights when our people were subject to a brutality and a torture and a murder that nauseates every decent human being in the world. Even in those never to be forgotten and never to be forgiven nightmares, we know of the establishment across the world, those who were against those who were militant, aggressive and desirous of placing their knowledge, protest and their demands for a greater rescue effort to save European Jewry. Yes that envy and hatred unwittingly helped the fiendish enemy in his plot against us.

Today, we must continue to struggle for our existence and rights against an immoral world. A world whose cultures and civilization are as drugged by idolatries which threatened us as in the days of the Maccabees, as our moral stature is menaced by the plague of narcotics that have penetrated into every facet of our society. We dare not permit any Jewish group, infected with envy and hatred to contaminate Jewish life, to exacerbate violence or menace against the destiny of our people because of the fierce desire for power. All Israeli leaders must work to avoid the cry of Jacob: "Woe is me because an act in my lifetime now will cause pain in the future of our people." (Yalkut Shimoni) This should be a time for an awakening to the terrible threats we may be to ourselves. I should compel each and everyone of us to seek the other in the same spirit that Joseph speaks in the Biblical lesson.

When he is approached by an outsider and asked what he desires. His answer must be the response of every Jew, in every generation, in every place of the world:

> ### *"Et achai, ani mevakesh"*
> ### "I seek my brothers." (Gen. 37:17)

Not power, fame, wealth, envy, hatred, or the approval of the world, only my brethren. They do I seek, today, tomorrow, forever.

UNITY

Like so many other Jews I am aware that the brothers of Joseph, The fathers of the twelve tribes were themselves called, the *shevatim*, tribes because they are the fathers of our people, though they were basically good people, righteous men, though we have seen that they were very human, in their indignation and in their anger, even as Reuben and Shimon proved in their violence. And yet, from our very childhood, many have often been confused and perturbed with this Bible lesson and have asked the question;

How could the brothers, the *Shevatim,* act as they did, towards Joseph? We can start our exploration of this question with an analysis of the first words of this *Parshah*. The Midrash (Gen. Rabbah 84:1) observes on the words:

"*Vayeshev Ya'akov*,"
"And Jacob dwelt." (Gen. 37:1)

When thou criest, let them that thou hast gathered deliver thee. Unlike the usual indications that this may have expressed irony that collections of idolatry will save the people, the Midrash, with its sense of insight and examination, makes the following observation. It was this gathering, the gathering of Jacob and the gathering of his sons that saved them from Esau. "A wind and a breath shall carry them away." That is Esau. "But he that taketh refuge in me shall possess the land." That is Jacob, as it is said. *Vayeshev Ya'akov*, And Jacob dwelt.

And the *Yalkut Yehuda* suggests a fascinating speculation. He compares the word your cry, with the same root in Exodus and concludes: "When Israel will cry and pray before God, then its gathering will save them, because the prayer of a multitude united is not repudiated emptily." And hence the gathering of Jacob and his children was successful because he was united with his children and they with their father. There was neither cleavage between father and children or among themselves and hence this unity saved them from Esau.

Taking off from this point, the *Yalkut Yehuda* apparently confronts the problem mentioned before. How to explain the actions of the *shevatim*, first the plot to kill Joseph and then selling him into slavery. The commentator suggests that is because the brothers recognized that their power resides only in their unity, and their unity with their father was perhaps the one guarantee of their future survival. When they saw, as the Bible narrates, that Joseph brought evil reports about them to their father, they regarded him as a cleavage in their unity and appraised him now as someone whose actions would lead to their destruction. Hence they felt it

advisable to remove the very root of that evil to ensure their preservation. If he were removed from their midst, they reasoned he
would no longer be a menacing factor against their unity. Hence
they plan to sell him into bondage. But observe that very act now
was conducive to disunity. Because their Father Jacob, could entertain suspicions that the boy had met with foul play at their hands,
and the uncomfortable situation led to disunity among the brothers themselves.

Observe in the story of Judah and Tamar. We are told:

"*Vayered Yehuda me'et ehchav*,"
"Judah went down from his brothers." (Gen. 38:1)

One commentator explains he went from the rocky hills of
Ebron to Adullam in the valley. But why does the Torah add "*me'et
ehchav*," "From his brothers?" And the *Yalkut Yehuda* considers
the Rabbinical attitude, that the brothers removed him from his
importance, from his position as their leader, because they criticized him for not influencing them to return the boy Joseph to
their Father. This of course, led to their migrating to Egypt and the
Egyptian *galuth*, diaspora of slavery, all because of the interruption of the family national unity.

Time and again we are cautioned about maintaining the unity
of our people. Now does that imply a ban, a prohibition against
individual thinking or honest differences of opinion? Surely, anyone who has the slightest knowledge of Talmud is aware of constant interaction of differing opinions among the Sages. As we all
have been taught that *Eylu vieylu divrei Elokim chayim*, These
and these are the words of the living God (Eiruvin 13b), each opinion was really a sacred truth, both voiced with responsibility and
concern for the other.

But in our history it would seem that there has been a thread of disunity that has been more than differences of opinion. When Esau differs from Jacob, it was not simply a matter some preferred interpretation of events or convictions. It penetrated the very essence of our existence and the victory of one might have spelt the total destruction of the other. Ishmael and Isaac did not differ because of some little characteristic wherein one was violent and the other perhaps docile satisfied to continue whatever Father Abraham had initiated. Mother Sarah was frightened by the cruelty of Ishmael because she saw in this scorn idolatry, murder and immorality. Judaism proclaimed a reverence for life. We could not agree with Plato that children when unneeded should be set aside to die. Differences of opinion yes, but we did not persecute heretics such as in the history of Athens, Rome, and Medieval Europe. In certain parts of the world though it is at least publicly denied, torture is still widespread. But Judaism prohibits torture and in the Talmud the only reference made to it, is how the Roman invaders and King Herod employed these harsh, cruel, methods. Yet, we suffered fears from disunity, because of the manner in which opposition deteriorated in hatred, bestial and viciousness.

But once this disunity erupted in our ranks, we never taught our children to hate, persecute and if possible murder. The Maccabean revolt clung to the doctrine of Father Mattatathias. Let the non-Jews worship their gods, and we shall walk in the way of the Lord our God.

We have been taught about the *Mityavnim*, the assimilationist who wanted to rape the Greek manners of the enemy. Chanukah signifies a rejection of that form of assimilation but nowhere have we been taught that it was a *mitzvah* to kill *Mityavnim*. There have been dissensions in our midst, the Karaites who denied the oral law, or the false Messiah, Shabbtai Ben Zevi. But where do we find teachings that it is a *Mitvzah* to kill them? In fact, when Hitler exercised his cruelties in occupied Soviet areas, Jews went to the extreme of saving Karaite lives by denying that they had any association with Jews and claiming that they were non-Jews. Our history had the unpleasantness of clashes between *Mitnagdim* and *Chassidim*. The latter insistent upon its warmth and camaraderie and the joy of service to God, also suffered from superstitions, Charlatan *Tzaddickim*, and a bias against the erudite Talmudist. The former looked upon the movement as an aberration, wild tutored, etc. Fortunately the war between them declines as Talmudists, under the influence of the Vilna Gaon, recognized their own shortcomings and *Chassidism* understood that *Yiddishkeit*, Jewishness could not flourish without them forever. And whatever discrepancies there may exist today, the majority of Jews look with disfavor when some outlandish Jewish splinter group finds solace in attacking Israel or other *Chassidim*. But within the patterns of disunity there threatens the expressions of hatred, hatred that carries within it seeds of destruction. Let us not seek counsel of great scholars. But let us as Jews review in our minds the exercises of those expressions within modern times.

Who with any knowledge of the past century cannot understand what the *Yevsektzia* meant to our people? It was not simply a matter of leftist Jews who had decided they did not want to be kosher, keep the Sabbath, or observant in traditional Jewish life. What erupts in this break of Jewish unity was hatred. A murderous passion that excited, aggravated, encouraged and abetted the persecution, torture and murder of Jews and Judaism.

Today, apparently everyone looks back upon modern Zionist history and acclaims every leader as having played a great role in the development of that movement. But he who is knowledgeable can not deny the truth. The personality of Jabotinsky, the leader whose political visions towered over many in the opposition: the man who created the Jewish Legion for participation in the conquest of Palestine: the founder of defense organizations throughout the Diaspora, the mentor of thousands of the finest Jewish youth, the founder of the Hagannah and of the Irgun, the man who proclaimed Aliyah Beth, the so called extra legal immigration, the man whose visions and prophecies have been vindicated by time, that man was not simply opposed by those who differed with him. Rather they hated him with a murderous passion, and they taught their children to hate.

And this hatred has erupted not only on the left towards the right, but on the right towards the left. This hatred still operates against the Jewish religion and the Jewish national conceptions of freedom. It is this pattern of disunity that has been responsible for the murder of Jews. It has unleashed and continues to unleash terrible waves of hatred, which seek nothing but the death of Jews and Judaism and at times even Jewish survival.

It is also disgraceful when Religious Jews throw stones at other Jews on the Sabbath. It is also disgraceful if brethren who claim to be observant of practices and rituals deprecate the worth and accomplishments of other Jews. It is disgraceful when the hatred of the left or the right for everything that does not coincide with their opinions waxes brutally, spitefully and with murderous intent.

That earlier speculation on how the fears of disunity misled the *shevatim* to encourage and further the very phenomenon they feared is always worthy of consideration and study. Please God, let us remember that the Maccabbes were willing to die not only for the defense of ideas and ideals, but also for the welfare of fellow Jews. The intolerant manifestations in Jewish life and in Israel demonstrate small concern for our survival as Jews. Let us gird ourselves to struggle for that sacred ideal so that like the Maccabbes of old, we too may prove our fidelity to God, Torah and to the existence and preservation of the Jewish people.

ET ACHAI ANOCHI MEVAKESH, WITH MY BROTHERS WE SEEK GOD

"*Et achai anochi mevakesh*,"
"I seek my brethren." (Genesis 37:16)

I recently listened to a young non-Jewish man speaking about conditions in the Near East. I personally became intrigued when he plaintively asked, what do the Jews want? He then quickly disassociated himself from implications presented by his query and asked what do the Israelis want? Now, I know there are those among us who have insisted that there is a difference between the Diaspora Jew and the Israeli, because the latter is some kind of a Cannanite. Though we may be subjective to many interpretations, one thing is clear: we are all Jews. What do we want?

Why did I become so intrigued by this man's question? What do we Jews want? Freud was known as one who plaintively asked, what do the women want? Years ago, in a discussion on the psychological question posed by Freud, my sainted Mother quietly declared, women want men. But aside from this non-professional response, what have others wanted. Germans dreamt of a Baghdad to Berlin railway. England dreamt of an Empire upon whose flag the sun would never set. Russia yearned for warm water ports so that she, too, could penetrate into the resources of the Orient. There are many opinions on what Americans want. Once I heard a scholarly instructor declare that America wanted to be loved by the entire world, that is why America has been generous in extending assistance to poorer nations. Another historian explained what Americans want is life, liberty and the pursuit of happiness. What is it that Jews specifically have wanted? Surely, we are certain the same hopes which attract the teeming hundreds of millions of human beings some of who are assaulted by starvation, perishing from hunger, their children die from malnutrition and disease, we share their world and we react to the same pain and fears. What have we wanted? What is it that we believe will exalt us and lift us towards the realization of our sommum bonum, the best which earthly existence could offer?

Perhaps the Torah lesson senses these questions? Young Joseph was dispatched by his father to visit his brothers in Shechem and ascertain how the family interests were progressing. But when he comes to Shechem, he is disappointed that they have left the area. A strange man meets Joseph and asks:

"*Mah tevakesh*,"
"**What are you seeking?**" (Gen. 37:15)

Do we not know that Joseph had already embarked upon the road that was destined to help him attain his objectives? His dreams were of grandeur and majesty, most outstanding among his brethren. His agile mind was engrossed in the fantasies of youth but simultaneously blessed with the insight and perception of the visionary. Instead of discussing his personal search for his own identity, he answers:

"*Et achai anochi mevakesh*,"
"**I seek my brethren.**" (Gen. 37:16)

And the man informs him:

"Nasoo mizeh, nailcha dohtanah,"
"They have traveled from here and have gone to Dothan." (Gen. 37:17)

But consider the actual reply of the man, it would have been more natural to say *haulcho*, they have left or *yatzoo*, they have gone out. No, he says, they have traveled from this place. And the Midrash comments *nasoo mizeh*, they have traveled from here, *mimeedotav shel makom*. (Gen. Rabbah 84:15) From the characteristics of *makom* which in Hebrew means a place or God who is everywhere, in every place.

The *Yalkut Yehuda* commentary notes that the stranger who traditionally has been regarded as an angel, a heavenly messenger wants Joseph to understand this Shechem is the spot where Jacob erected an altar, that here is where God forgives and pardons those who sin against him. And because the brothers had decided not to forgive Joseph for any wrongs he may have committed against them, they withdrew themselves from the sacred qualities of God. Rashi, too, refers to the expression and says they removed themselves from brotherhood. And again the commentary notes: perhaps because this area of Shechem was a stark reminder of how Shimon and Levi were ready to sacrifice themselves to protect their sister Dinah from the people of Shechem, and they were all removing themselves far from the feelings of the brotherhood of Israel.

Are we speculating too much if we try to reconsider the response of Joseph? Who knew what his personal ambitions were? Rashi notes that this Joseph was a lad, a young boy and he interprets this to mean that Joseph acted like a young boy, he arranged his hair, and fixed his eyes so that he would appear handsome.

(Rashi to Gen. 37:2) But when Rabbi Bunim studies Rashi's practical explanation, he sees deeper. When the Torah refers to the *Parah Adumah*, the red heifer that was used in the ritual of purification, Rashi himself says, if there were two black hairs on this animal it was enough to disqualify it from this ritual. (Rashi to Num. 19:2) The Gemarah (Pesachim 113b) examining the idea of perfection reiterates the thou shalt be whole, perfect with the Lord thy God, examines the righteous rigidly, even imperfection as thin as a thread of hair denies him the glory of perfection. Joseph, says Rabbi Bunim, arranged his hair symbolically to demonstrate that he should not tolerate imperfections even the slightest in his personal makeup. Such a man may very well have responded with the perfection of goals which he seeks in life, instead we read: "*Et achi anochi mevakesh*, I seek my brethren."

But it is the Chidushei Harim who reveals the underlying motif of the reply, *et achi* also means "with my Brothers," "*Anochi mevakesh*," "I am looking." "I am looking for the *anochi*, not my *anochi*, not the ego of man, but the *anochi* of *anochi Hashem Elokim*, I am the Lord thy God." Some looked and saw in Joseph what Spinoza saw in our people. We are a God intoxicated nation, beyond all the goals within space and time. We have always wanted a special particular goal that has driven us in history as a people. It has made us resist all forms of betrayal, hostility, prejudice, hatred, tortures and murder. What is it that we want, what is it that has given us the ability to discover the mystical strength that renews us, regardless of the situation into which we have been hurled? Why are we so different? In this awesome historical era of mankind here on earth, in this world where man boasts with apparent justification that our advances have but pervious generations in the shade, we still see that life is not secure. The sciences which place man in space are also responsible for terrible disasters which threaten us, whether through technological accidents as that which has imposed such grief, pain, suffering and staggering fears for the future upon India or the anxieties of nuclear warfare which disturb tranquility. And where are the liberties of the world, when democracies support dictatorships? Where the presumably liberal impressive declarations marred and nullified by the lack of liberties which existed in the third world countries, the Soviet Union, India itself, Africa and the wide spread complexion of Arab governments, dynasties and territories and where is the happiness to which we are urged to hasten?

Joseph's response is precise, almost curt but profound. You say that my brethren have abandoned the spiritual qualities of Shechem. You want me to believe that my people have abandoned the brotherhood of Israel? I will tell you, that despite momentary deviations, despite the prattle of those who would have us believe that Israelis and Jews are totally different, one from the other, I tell you that we have one motivation. Basically, we shall never waver in our loyalty to the force that has created this world because of our conviction that this is not a fortuitous world resulting from some accidental combination of chemical ingredients, which produced our ability to perceive and conceive. No, with my brethren I seek *anochi*. The eternal God who is the source of all liberties, the source of all life, the source of all morality and with whose union we can find happiness, *anochi mevakesh*, I seek God. On the eve of Chanukah, we should understand that what propelled the Maccabees to war against the invader. Of Course, there is the national political moment in the struggle, yes, there is the ritual, moment that revolt against the rituals of the invader, but above all there was response, incomprehensible to the world. This response to reject anything and everything, anyone and every one who stands in the way of our march toward God. Mattathias emphasized this when he displayed sensitivity towards the other nations that they rarely have emulated in their appraisal of us.

Let every nation worship their God, but we shall walk in the ways of the Lord our God. *Anochi mevakesh*, I seek God. Because I seek God I shall always be with my brothers. That is the *shibbolet*, torrent of Chanukah. That is the fundamental explanation of Jewish history. Does the world really want to know what we want? *Achai anochi mevakesh*, with my brethren, with our Jewish brothers and sisters, anochi mevakesh, we seek God, yesterday, today, tomorrow and forever.

THE AWE OF ISAAC

The Zohar opens its comments on the Torah portion of *Vayeshev* by observing that Rabbi Chiyah opens a discussion by quoting the Psalms:

"Rabot ra'ot tzaddick umekulam yatzelehnu Hashem"
"Many evil things assail the righteous but he is rescued from all of them by Hashem." (Psalms 34:20)

"Come and see," continues the Zohar, consider how many impediments a person has from the very day that he is given breath in this world. It often seems that from the very moment we breathe the very air around us, we are subject to impulses for gratification. Instincts which resemble primitive, animalistic behavior; lusts, desires and physical passions which continue to motivate our conduct; psychological needs and compulsions, all of which have been grouped under the category of the *yetzer harah*, the evil inclination, as intimated by the verse:

"Lepetach chatat rovetz,"
"Sin couches at the door." (Gen 4:7)

Is it not so, continues the Zohar, *"Ki habeheymot miyom shenaldoo,"* "That the beasts from the very moment of their birth," intuitively understand to protect themselves and run from the flames of fire and areas dangerous to them. But humans, no sooner than they are born, quickly throw themselves, as it were, into the emotional, inquisitive, psychological fires that sear our physiques and psyche. Life is not a "bowl of cherries," as we all must learn.

The introduction to the drama of Joseph and his brothers, cannot help but remind us of the frequent observations, we, as parents, have made on sibling rivalries. So many of us realize that we are fortunate if we are not compelled to sustain these conflicts in our households. In general, our basic lives, those we must experience within the closest confines of personal relationships, in the family, cannot deny the possible potential pressures, some might claim, the probable eruptions of such relationships. Dr. Joseph H. Berke in his intriguing study, *The Tyranny of Malice* notes that the "Biblical origins of Western civilization touch Adam and Eve, Cain and Abel, Sarah and Hagar, Isaac and Ishmael, Jacob and Esau, and in greatest detail Joseph and his brothers." This scholar reminds us of the conflict between Sarah and Hagar. And even though Esau and Jacob were reconciled at the death of Father Abraham, the descendants of these two brothers, the Jews and the Arabs, remain antagonists. It is not inconceivable says this fascinating scholar, "that their feuds continue to reflect the bitter hatreds that passed between their respective mothers some thousands of years ago." Is it not a frightening idea, to confront the very thought that the differences between the Palestinians and the Israelis arise from that rivalry thousands of years ago?

Do we not understand the pain which must have assailed an aged father who sustains prophetic insight in the development of his family, which will eventually establish a people dedicated and consecrated to the eternal, only living God? A unity that they must somehow try to teach mankind and above all, integrate into their own lives.

Let us return to the very opening sentence of the Torah portion:

"*Vayeshev Ya'akov be'eretz migurei aviv*,"
"And Jacob dwelt in the land of the sojourning of his Fathers." (Gen. 37:1)

The Zohar interprets this phrase by studying the linguistics involved. It is true that the word *migurei,* sojourning is related to the Hebrew term, *garah* meaning to reside. On the other hand, the Zohar associates it with the word *magor* in the verse:

"*Ki shamati dibat rabim, magor misaviv, behivasdam yachad a'lie lakachat nafshi zamahmoo*,"
"I have heard the slander by many, the terror (magor) all around, as they take counsel against me, they scheme to take away my life." (Psalms 31:14)

The Zohar piercingly perceives that "*Kol yamav hayah mityareh vehayah bepachad*," "All his life Jacob sustained fears and anxieties."

When we who are mature review our own lives, how many disappointments, how many frustrations, how much fears, anxieties, insecurities have we all sustained? Who of us cannot sympathize with Jacob? *Vayeshev Ya'akov*, And Jacob sat. "*Bikesh Ya'akov leshev beshalvah*," "Jacob requested to sit in peace." (Rashi to Gen. 37:2) What did he want? Just to dwell in peace. An old age without turmoil, without pressures, without fears and aches. "God, after all I have suffered, let me, at least, enjoy my remaining years without problems." But what happens. *"Kafatz alav ragezo shel Yosef,"* "The ordeal of Joseph sprung upon him." (Rashi to Gen. 37:2) Instead of dwelling in peace, practically jumping at him, assailing him, threatening to undermine his old age, rises the specter of the rivalry between Joseph and his brothers. In the midst of our own insecurities, our own anxieties, where shall we turn?

One commentary reviewing the Aggadoth of the Zohar, looks at the interpretations we have just considered and says, yes, Jacob was frightened, anxious, insecure, terrified but not only by the pressures, the failures which assail us, but also by his fear of God. As the *Mitzvah* teaches us:

> **"*Et hashem Elokechah tirah*,"**
> **"Thou shalt fear the Lord thy God." (Deut. 6:13, 10:20)**

But perhaps this fear has another ingredient, not the paralyzing fear of terror, but the awe of what we may see.

Is it not clear from all the pain and agony which that unhappy man, Jacob, sustained, that he continued, because of a deep source of strength which inevitably prevailed in his life? The symbol of his belief and faith, when he called upon the *"Pachad Yitzchok,"* "The awe of Isaac," his father, the undisturbed faith in God. We who live in this strange universe, where galaxies and space become mind-boggling, where constant new discoveries only arouse new questions, when our constant addition to knowledge only reveals how little we actually know, when the magnificence, beauty, majesty, harmony and equilibrium revealed by our new advances only impel us to repeat as did our fathers, look at the heavens and the universe about us and ask with awe, *mi barah et eleh*, who created all this? In his fears, this awe bolstered Jacob in all his anxieties. Oh, if only people and leaders of the world today would sustain this awe in the midst of their own fears. We too might ask "*Leshev beshalvah*," "To sit in peace." This was denied to Jacob because as the commentary reminds us, such righteous spiritual personalities consider insufficient what is prepared for them in the world to come. (Rashi to Gen. 37:2) They may not achieve the success of all their visions now, but unto their descendants they have the awe, the "*Pachad Yitzchok*," which is our strength and also our salvation.

THE PROPENSITY TOWARDS EVIL

Several years ago, there was a very specific intent upon the part of some contemporary thinkers, to obliterate sin and evil from our vocabulary. We had embarked upon a pattern of situational ethics and people were urged to listen to their conscious without having any particular strong guide or priorities with which to compare their own urges or desires.

In fact, this tendency continues to exert strong influences over us, up to this very hour. Within this framework, we are advised that in lieu of the changing circumstances which time and history imposed upon us, we should realize that what was right once upon a time, might no longer be morally applicable for us today, and of course, the same transformation holds true with what generations before us considered wrong. In brief, we are being projected into a society which featured similarities to a period marked by the end of the Book of *Shoftim*, Judges, defined *by ish hayasher be'eynav*, right in his own eyes, namely, that since there was no King in Israel, every man did that which was right in his own eyes. If that seems startlingly intriguing, we ought to pause and remember that at that particular time because there was no King in Israel, no specific laws had to be upheld, you might say. But what of the old Torah laws? The answer might be again, that there was no King in Israel. *Avinu Malkeinu*, our Father, our King, namely God had not abdicated, but his subjects were not paying him as much attention as they should have. In this wild, primitive and unrestricted era, we also sustained a terrible civil war that erupted because of the evil of sexual abuse. In one tribe at least, Jews had forgotten the moral standards to which we have been collectively pledged by our forebear's, and the result was a war which almost erased an entire tribe from our annals.

If we are stirred by the expression of human evil of which that war gave evidence, we should recall it is a time when the concubine wife of a Levite, visiting Gibeah together with her husband, was assaulted forcibly by some men of Benjamin. She was sexually abused an entire night so that she died. The Levite sent parts of her body to the other tribes with the complaint that these men had committed villainy, an evil that had not been heard of in Israel since the time they had been liberated from Egypt and slavery. The people of Israel were disgusted and they demanded that the guilty parties be turned over to them for capital punishment, but the tribe of Benjamin foolishly refused this righteous demand, and war erupted. For several days it appeared that the battles were going in favor of Benjamin, but eventually the strategies changed and Benjamin itself sustained a horrible blood bath. What is more, the people swore, cursed be the man that giveth a wife to Benjamin. Later everyone had to partake of a fictitious ritual, whereby Jewish girls gathered to dance, attract the Benjaminites, who were then permitted to pretend that they were kidnapping or seizing these girls for wives. If not for this pretense, the entire tribe would have been erased from the Jewish people.

When we think of this narrative about evil we may compare it to some of the earlier immoral decline that emerged among our forebears, The *Shevatim*, the fathers of the tribes, as manifested in their envy, hostility and cruelty towards their brother Joseph. No one can pretend that evil and sin have no basic place in our personalities. Evil *rishus*, permission (acts) is a phenomenon we would like to believe is due to the influence of someone who forces us to do bad. Did not all the Nazis, when standing trial, defend or at least attempt to explain their cruelty and evil by insisting that they were only following orders. But as Eric Fromm, the prominent psychologist demonstrated to us in his study, "Escape from freedom," the Nazis were not Germans who were enslaved by Hitler or threatened by him. No, Fromm indicated that within German society there were cultural, social and political features that impelled the Germans to sell out to Hitler. The Nazis did not rob them of their freedom, but on the contrary, the Germans were happy to escape from freedom, its obligations, its dictates and above all its *menschlichkeit*, its humanity.

Primo Levi, an Italian Jew, a scientist, a survivor of the concentration camp, has been, as many of you probably know among the greatest of contemporary Italian writers. His books will serve as a living testament on how the human spirit can defeat evil, terror, murder and torture through significant and ethical ideals. And yet, this gentle soul, this tremendous teacher, this magnificent artist of the word committed suicide in April of 1987, because he felt we were reducing the ordeals, the horror of the Holocaust to what Hannah Arendt called the banality of evil. In Levi's last completed work, *The Drowned and the Saved*, he closed with awesome words,

"Let it be clear that to a greater or lesser degree all were responsible, but it must be just as clear that behind their responsibility stands that great majority of Germans who accepted in the beginning, out of mental laziness, myopic calculation, stupidity and national pride the "beautiful words" of Corporal Hitler, followed him as long as luck and the lack of scruples favored him, were swept away by his ruin, afflicted by death, misery and remorse, and rehabilitated a few years later as the result of an unprincipled political game."

In both our collective lives as society, nation, cultural forces as well as in our individual lives, we still retain a fearful propensity for evil.

Consider the Torah portion of *Vayeshev*, here was Joseph who undeniably has deserved the appellation with which our tradition praises him, *Yosef hatzaddick*, Joseph the righteous, the saintly. Here was a sensitive soul, a visionary, a soul infused with stirring ideals and dreams, a person who had the potential for achieving peace in his relationships with others. In fact the *Keli Yakar*, obviously is motivated by this appraisal because it comments on the phrase:

"Vehu na'ar et b'nai Bilhah ve'et b'nai Zolpah, nishai aviv,"
"And Joseph was a lad with the children of Bilhah and Zilpah, his father's wives." (Gen. 37:2)

"VeYisrael ah'hav et Yosef mekol bahnav key ben zekunim hu low,"
"But Yisrael loved Joseph from all the children because he was the son of his old age." (Gen. 37:3)

The commentary interprets the verses to signify that when Joseph was together with the other youngsters, he too pursued all the activities we associate with youth. Probably in today's age he would have avidly argued about sports, the prominent baseball, basketball or football stars, their abilities, their accomplishments, etc. He probably would have indulged in all the conversations of youth; school, girls, sex, money, ambitions, parental relations, so did Joseph act. But when Joseph was in the presence of his aged father, his conduct was that of an older, more mature person, withdrawing from less mature concerns, confronting the larger issues of our existence, moral obligations and our responsibilities toward God and Man. And yet, this magnificent youth could momentarily abandon moral posture, stance and insight and deteriorate into a pettiness that could lead only to disaster and destruction.

On one hand, the brothers could not tolerate the apparent peaceful conduct that Joseph displayed towards them. If he regarded them simply as sinful, then obviously it would be proper on his part to hate them, as an old tradition teaches, he who sees a sinful or evil act committed by his fellowman should hate him. "If so Joseph, then why continue your uninterrupted dialogues with us so peacefully. If you do insist upon pursuing this course of action, then obviously you do not consider us sinful." So they considered it as habitual on his part to slander, libel or condemn them and because of this, they hated him, with a subsequent action that led to his humiliation and historical development of the family and the nation.

We must always be alert to the vibrations of evil which have appeared in the past and which, God forbid, can appear again in the future.

The propensity towards evil is not restricted to any one group. Many honorable countries stood silently while our brethren were being massacred by the German evil. Democracies toward which we looked for help and the fulfillment of their potential, turned a deaf ear, very much like brothers who were silent and who sat eating a meal at the repulsive moment of Joseph's cries coming from the pit. When the Maccabees had to struggle for the victory which we celebrate at Chanukah, they, too, were pained by the realization that within our own ranks there were Jews who in mad haste to curry favor, obtain material advances, fulfill personal ambitions and avoid undue pressures, ran to embrace the enemy Camp. Our heroic Hasmoneans recognized that evil, armed with faith, conviction and courage changed the course of history. Chanukah should remind us today that evil still exists in our midst, whether it is due to the unprincipled politics of powers, the mad ambitions of individuals, or our own inability to maintain proper perspectives. And it is the characteristics of the Maccabees which alone can bring the fulfillment of our potential for decency, honor and humanity and justice into our own lives. May our visions be as clear as Joseph's. May we repudiate evil by uninterrupted honest concern for our brothers and sisters, here, in Israel and everywhere.

Miketz

— 10 —

וַיְהִי מִקֵּץ שְׁנָתַיִם יָמִים

"It happened at the end of two years." (Genesis 41:1)

DETERMINATION AND FAITH

In the Torah portion of *Miketz*, we read how famine assailed the land of Canaan, after Joseph's brothers were responsible for having him sold into slavery. Poor Joseph suffered loneliness and humiliation, but his abilities enabled him to advance, only to be imprisoned on a trumped up charge. Even there, he becomes popular and important, and one special day interprets the dreams of his fellow prisoners correctly. This, however, is completely forgotten by Pharaoh's butler, the very one whom should have been grateful forever, until he is reminded by the famous dream sustained by Pharaoh, the ruler of Egypt.

In these dreams the King envisioned how a group of sickly, dried up, and lean cows, swallowed juicy, healthy-looking, sleek and fat cows, and gained in neither appearance nor health. He then dreamt about sickly, wind beaten sheaves of grain swallowing healthy, sweet, tasty grain, but again nothing happened. They remained the same dried up sickly, wind beaten sheaves of grain. This dream, as you all know, is what helped Joseph get out of jail, and become Prime Minister to the Pharaoh.

However, in this act, there is one scene that we find difficult to understand. When the King awakens from these nightmarish dreams, he naturally wants them explained, and so he summons his advisors, the magic doctors of ancient Egypt, but they were unable to interpret the dreams properly. How is this so? Anyone who has studied history knows that these men were great scholars and really knew many things. For example, they possessed engineering skills, which are verified by the pyramids and the sphinx. They had absorbed agricultural talents by which they taught the people to utilize the overflow of the Nile for food planting. They studied the skies and obtained a great deal of astronomical data about the stars and celestial movements.

The Midrash does tell us that they did offer some explanations (Gen. Rabbah 89:7), but none met with Pharaoh's approval. (Sefer Hayashar, Midrash HaGadol 41:15) How was this possible? It is claimed that these scholars were quite modern in their approach to Pharaoh's dreams. Does not the Talmud (Masehchet Berachot 55a) and the Midrash (Gen. Rabbah 89:10) tell us that *"kol chalamot holichin achar hapeh,"* "Many dreams really follow their interpretation?"
The explanations actually influence the dreamer toward certain decisions and responses. This is a reaction that is recognized in contemporary psychiatry. There are certain dreams that may be due to events that really have transpired.

On the other hand, these Egyptian chartumim would probably have agreed with the Rabbis in the Talmud (Masehchet

Berachot 57b) that *chalom echad mishishim linvuah*, that a dream is one 60th part of prophecy, modern recognition that dreams are a language of themselves, as Freud and other pioneers in psychiatry have demonstrated. So why were these Egyptian scholars such dismal failures? This was due to the fact that they were totally logical. They, we are told perceived that *hakol holech lifey chukei hatevah*, everything in the world proceeds according to natural and logical developments. It certainly wasn't natural for sickly cows to swallow healthy cows and remain sickly. It certainly was not natural to expect that wind-beaten, dried-up grain would absorb healthy grain and still remain dried up. Hence, that which was not natural or emulating anticipated, regular, normal patterns could not be explained; probably, it is unimportant and meant nothing. Only Joseph could interpret these dreams for the eventual salvation of the entire land, for he sensed that the unexpected, the superficially unintelligible might contain profound implications. That is the story of all Jewish history.

Now, think of it: that is the underlying meaning of Chanukah. We recite it in our prayers of gratitude for the Chanukah victory.

Everything about our background and our people is illogical. It started with Abraham, who opposed the idolatry of the day by proclaiming the one, eternal God. Moses was just as illogical centuries later when he had the audacity, some might have said the stupidity, to stand up against the Egyptian might and declare that the Hebrew slaves must be liberated. Centuries later our ancestors pursued the unintelligent, the illogical, the superficially senseless objective of organizing a defiant revolt against that power. It was illogical for Mattathias to defy Antiochus and imagine that he could depend upon his five sons led by Judah to initiate a revolt against a world power, drive them from the temple, retake the land occupied by the invader, and win the right of people to worship God as they saw fit. A mighty empire, a superpower of its day was determined to exterminate all our associations with Torah. And what happened, the illogical resulted: "*Masartah giborim beyad chalashim, verabim beyad miatim,*" "The strong were delivered into the hands of the weak, and the many were defeated by the few." This was a tremendous victory for Jewry and all humanity. It took a long time for others to appreciate this.

Let us not forget that even in America, despite our pride in freedom and democracy, not everyone welcomed the thought of religious freedom. Peter Styvesant didn't want Jews in New Amsterdam. The Puritans were against religious freedom. Some people, who fled from Europe because of religious persecution, settled here to find their freedom, but refused to give that treasure to others. That is why it became so important for the development of our country, to have the constitution guarantee freedom of religion. When the Jews were persecuted, humiliated and tortured by the inquisition, it was illogical to hang on to their religion, when deserting it could have brought them security and prevented their goods and property from being stolen from them.

In many other areas of the world, other people confronted similar situations and rapidly accepted other faiths and creeds, just to escape sorrow and pain. This same set of circumstances pursued the Jews in every European land, but always the vast majority of Jews responded illogically, with loyalty to their faith and their God. For two thousand years, Jews were forced by the sheer weight of numbers to live in exile, severed from their ancient homeland, but illogically they refused to yield and insisted upon voicing their claim before the entire world, everyday in their prayers.

And when the world was ashamed by its betrayal of Jews during the Holocaust, and recognized that ancient Hebrew claim through the founding of the State of Israel, everyone agreed that it certainly could not be logical for the survivors of the concentration camps to become soldiers overnight and defend the new state against seven Arab armies. But that same unnatural illogical pattern emerged. The words of the Chanukah prayer were repeated. "*Masartah giborim beyad chalashim, verabim beyad miatim,*" "The powerful were delivered unto the weak, the many unto the few," and that illogical and unnatural and unintelligible response is what we need today.

How illogical it was of the Jews to raise the banner for Soviet Jewry, believing that the mighty communist empire would some day yield and permit Jews to leave? As Mr. Spock might say in a Star Trek episode, "Totally illogical" but it happened. How illogical to imagine that a comparative handful of rebellious youth could compel the British Empire to leave the Middle East. But these young Jews did just that, all because, they possessed a peculiar characteristic in their mental composition. That factor is called determination and faith. That is what we must all learn today, to expand our determination and faith.

In life, there are moments when we decide upon a course of action only because we sustain a spirit of love, devotion and loyalty to higher demands than just our immediate satisfaction. Not because of any immediate reward that we may see, but because higher goals and true objectives mean subordinating and giving of one self. It is a lesson which history teaches everywhere.

Think of the animal world about us. Large animals, powerful animals that did not learn the science of cooperation disappeared. Dinosaurs now live only in the books and toys of our children. But do you know who continues to thrive in our day? The ants, the birds and the bees. Even the cockroaches are alive because of their sense of cooperation.

In science, we read of men and women who apparently pursue illogical, unnatural studies, only to end up by being a Frenchman who cures rabies, an Englishman who defeats small pox, a Russian Jew who co-achieves streptomycin, or another Jew who establishes a vaccine against polio. Every one of these great people had a sense of determination and faith to stray from what was considered logical and normal, and thereby become great benefactors to humanity. Very often we have been told that the selfish way, worrying about no one, me myself and I is the natural way. Chanukah reminds us that we are a people who have not been afraid to follow the heart, the spirit, and the need, to recognize our inner faith and not quiver with fear, because the world says it is illogical. Of course, use and develop your brains, your reasoning power, and intelligence. But never abandon faith and spirit. This will guarantee success as a human being and a source of success and pride to our history and our people.

CHANUKAH AND UNITY

Many are the commentaries that remind us that the Torah portion of *Miketz* invariably occurs in association with The Festival of Lights, Chanukah.

There are many intimations within the Torah lesson regarding this festival, but perhaps the most obvious is the presentation of Pharaoh's dreams, in which thin, emaciated, weak looking cows emerge from the Nile river and swallow well fed fat healthy appearing cows. In another dream sequence, we read of how thin sheaves, obviously defective physically, ingest those sheaves that are full and clearly healthy and nutritious. This, as we can all immediately recognize, is representative of the great clash on the field of combat between the numerically inferior forces, the Maccabees against the better armed, superior in numbers, armies of the Hellenistic Syrians. As the Chanukah tradition reminds us, "*Masartah giborim beyad chalashim*" "The strong were delivered into the hands of the weak."

Today, we confront situations in Jewish life which bear similarities to those times, and it would do us good to consider some of the implications that the Biblical lesson contains. Once more, we are subject to great pressures by the external world, which consider reality in terms of numbers and weapons. Moral considerations are no more present than they were in the days of Antiochus and the Maccabees. Consider for example the silence that meets the constant arming by Arab lands. With an arsenal which is certainly not required for defensive purposes, yet so deeply imbedded is the avarice for profits, that neither the corporations nor the governments involved in selling these weapons to the Arab countries would think of preventing such sales. Nor does anyone have the most basic decency to inquire for what purpose are these weapons demanded.

There is much talk and expressions of sympathy for those who cry aloud for the rectification of current political and economic wrongs. The Pope in his Christmas and other messages demonstrates his concern and sympathy for those who have suffered violence at the hands of opponents. And although we all employ terms like democracy, freedom, justice and the need for reducing violence and lessening war, not everyone defines these expressions in the same way. This should not mean that powers involved should not continue genuine efforts for peace, but it certainly serves to emphasize that differences of opinion exist and should not be shrugged away.

We Jews have always found room within our community, our faith and our people for dissenting opinions. As the Sages asserted their individual analysis of Jewish history and Jewish values, they recognized, to use the Rabbinical phrase, that both *"Eylu vieylu divrei Elokim chayim,"* "these and these are the words of the living God." (Eiruvin 13b) All the positive values taught by Sephardim and Ashkenazim, Kabbalistic mystics and philosophic realists, the scholarly Mitnagdic opponents of the romantic Chassidim, the militant Zionists who wanted a homeland where Jewish creativity would preserve the nation, and the pious opponents who wanted to depend only on the benevolence of God, all these groups, while diverse, were always motivated by one ideal, and that was the survival of our people and the elevation of Jewish dignity, honor, and truth.

Rabbi Abraham Scheinberg, made reference to the *Miketz* Torah portion. He observed that the term for all of us, *"Nachnu,"* as in those plaintive words that the brothers spoke to the unrecognized Joseph:

"Kulahnu b'nai ish echad nachnu,"
"All of us are the children of one father." (Gen. 42:11)

This statement is repeated in scriptures in two other verses. The first, *nachnu peshanu umarenu,* we have all sinned and rebelled, is found in The Book of *Echah*, Lamentations (3:42) and the second, in The Book of *Bamidbar,* Numbers (32:32), *nachnu na'avor chalutzim,* we shall pass forward as scouts. The assurance given by the tribes on the other side of the Jordan to Moses, indicating their readiness to help their brethren subdue and possess the sacred soil of the Promised Land.

The entire Jewish people, no matter where they may be dispersed, are still concerned with Israel and its centrality to Jewish life. Our Sages have always reminded us what history teaches. Whenever we remember to be *"Kulahnu b'nai ish echad nachnu"* when we remember that we are members of one great, sacred, national family, the Jewish people, and we stand united, then the numerically superior forces of Antiochus in any generation must eventually fall before us and we can emerge victorious. Even when we are guilty of transgressions against our inheritance and our people, we still may be heartedness by the thought that *"Nachnu na'avor chalutzim,"* "We still go forward as victorious scouts, pioneers, whose very act of devotion bears the fruits of victory."

The State of Israel and the Jewish people still confront situations similar to the difficulties encountered during the first Chanukah. There are still the Hellenists among us, who kowtow to every whim, capriciousness, and betrayal by external forces. They split Jewish unity; they place the temporary good will of the *"poritz,"* "squire" above the true interests of the State and our people everywhere. But this treachery, this transgression and rebellion against our inheritance, our faith, our destiny can nonetheless be totally removed. And we may continue to be the *chalutzim,* front line pioneers and scouts of our people and brethren, if we only remember to be truly united in reverence, in empathy, in concern for and dedication to our brethren.

Chanukah surely provides us with a guide. We should never forget how the struggle for national security, religious freedom and the preservation of Jewish values began. It was when the elderly Priest of Modin, witnessed the act of a renegade Jew, prostrating himself before the idol erected by the pagan invader Mattathias, obviously, he did not have his cool, because he plunged a knife into the traitor and this initiated the active, violent response to Antiochus. Let us, at least, learn from Chanukah, to stand firm with our people, to demonstrate our solidarity with Israel always, and above all to live with Jewish pride and dignity, rejecting all ploys, as befits the descendants of the Maccabees. And so, we may rest assured, that despite all temporary difficulties, the Chanukah tale will be repeated again and again. The fat cows will be swallowed by the thin, the full sheaves will be ingested by the smitten, and the mighty and powerful will be delivered into the hands of the weak.

FULFILLING DREAMS

In the analysis of the Torah teaching of *Shabbat Miketz*, we find profound insight in our individual and collective lives, as well as implied guidance for our nation and its rank and file.

Once a German philosopher Ludwig Feuerbach insisted: "*Der mensch ist was er isst*," "A person is what he eats." Admittedly, there is validity to such an assertion. In recent times, we have been the target of constant campaigns regarding the foods we digest and the drinks we imbibe. Too much fat increases our cholesterol levels, too much junk food imposes added burdens on the pancreas due to an overabundance of sugars, too much alcohol pours swiftly into the blood stream and causes more accidents than many wish to admit. But to portray the human personality as the product solely of food intake without considering values, social relationships, ethical objectives, and the influences of affection and love ascribes false and intolerable attributes.

True we do find at this time of the year that millions of our fellow citizens are attracted by that perennial favorite, the narrative of a miserable, miserly person who has withdrawn from the impulses of human compassion and mercy, Scrooge. Visited by apparitions who evoke memories of his own faults and errors, and imply a resultant, unhappy ending to his life, he too first ascribes his uneasy feelings to a morsel of undigested food. But once I heard someone rationalize this narrative by explaining that the ghostly visits were obviously dreams because all of us are subject to dreams and the latter invariably are associated with deeply concealed facets of our personality, which lie interred in that strange realm called the subconscious. "*Der mensch ist was er traumt,*" "Man is what he dreams," said one teacher, and long before Freud sought the aid of magicians, religious leaders, or inspired prophets to translate the strange, confused senses into realities which the dreamer might understand.

Consider the Joseph drama as it develops in scriptures. Everyone dreams. Jacob Dreams, Pharaoh dreams, Joseph dreams, the royal butler and baker dream. Jacob dreams of a ladder which standing upon the ground, nonetheless reaches the very heavens and is transformed into a channel upon which angels move. Joseph dreams of sheaves in the field, of sun and moon and eleven stars. On the other hand Pharaoh dreams of cows swallowing other cows, fat cows. The butler dreams of cups of wine while the baker sees in his dream a basket with all kinds of food. In the book of Kings we read how Solomon also dreams and in this state he implores God to grant him an understanding heart to be able to judge his people properly, so that he could distinguish between good and evil. Yes, the Bible is full of dreams, Nebuchadnezzar also dreams of fierce images, with heads of gold, arms of silver, belly of brass, legs of iron and feet of clay. Ah what a difference there lies in these dreams even as our ancestors dreamt of heaven and earth, even as they dreamt of sun and light, spirit and wisdom, others dreamt of fierce, material powers, food and wine, all the elements to satisfy the stomach, but nothing about the soul and the spirit. "*Der mensch ist was er traumt*," "Man is what he dreams." True, there are those who have tried to dismiss dreams as some confused unimportant gyration of the brain. But today's psychiatry reminds us so often that the dream is nothing but the concealed desire of the subconscious. How great was the perceptivity of our sages when they declared that "Man's dreams include those visions or scenes which are the yearnings of his heart." How appropriate is the anecdote related in the Gemarah (Berachot 56a): The Roman Emperor Caesar said to Rabbi Joshua, they say of you that you are the wisest of the wise. Tell me, therefore, what shall I see tonight in my dreams? And he answered. In your dream you will see that the Persians have captured and enslaved you in captivity and their king will humble you and you will spearhead pigs with a golden staff. The Emperor was so perturbed by this statement, throughout the day, that at night he saw in his dream everything that had been told to him by this wise Jew. Elsewhere in the Midrash we are informed that this king had originally tended to pigs before he became ruler. He always engaged in wars with the Persians constantly suffering the anxieties produced by the thoughts of possible defeat and humiliation by the enemy. And that wise Jew knew exactly what vulnerable points to emphasize. And hence the subconscious fears of day were expressed as dreams at night.

Let us not suppose that concealed concerns that erupt during our dreams are restricted only to individuals. Large groups, masses, complete nations have their own dreams and these to, are expressed by their so-called policies and programs. Some statesmen dream that they may be recognized as the greatest personages in history, if they will speak about peace, justice, and good will and coopera-tion, where none of these exist.

It is interesting to read the verses of Joseph's encounter with his brothers, the first time they came down to Egypt to obtain food. The Bible tells us:

> **"*Vayacare Yosef et echav, vehaim lo hekeyroowho*,"**
> **"And Joseph recognized his brothers but they did not recognize him." (Gen. 42:8)**

Joseph recognized his brothers that day because he contin-ued to dream the visions of our people "*Kol Yisrael arevim zeh bezeh*," "All Jews are guarantors for each other." (Rosh Hashanah 29a) The visionary, the dreamer recognizes his brethren, the satis-fied pragmatists they do not recognize Joseph. The tragedy with all mankind has been the constantly repeated scene where vision-aries recognize their fellowmen, but the alleged leaders, the self crowned messiahs, the know everything Ebermenschen, the supe-rior masters never see the others. Spiritual leaders and preachers who scream and shout and warn and threaten the country, the en-tire populace with Armageddon's, destruction and annihilation if their views are not accepted and supported in totally. We too must be careful that we do not delude our own dreams and fail to recog-nize our brethren. "*Kol Yisrael arevim zeh bizeh*." We Jews are troubled. We are constantly discussing, appraising, evaluating and speculating on what we failed to do during the years of the *Churban* and the Holocaust. As more and more documents are released, as the data continues to grow, the evidence increases that Jewish lead-ership failed because it considered itself above the visionary and dreamer. Everyone regarded himself as most practical, officials in public office and leadership in established organizations. They too did not recognize their brethren. And today, we, the masses too often defend ourselves by claiming that the leaders did not tell us the facts. But can we continue to use this alibi?

"*Vayizkor Yosef et chalomotav*,"
"And Joseph remembered his dreams." (Gen. 42:9)

Even as his brothers bowed to him, Joseph thrilled at the fulfillment of his dreams, but the greater joy was that his Father, the source of his family lived, and that he was able to nourish and sustain his brethren. So, too, let us rejoice that our eternal Father lives forever. That the people of Israel continue to live and that we have the possibility of fulfilling our own dreams that "*Kol Yisrael arevim zeh bizeh*," "All of Israel are guarantors for each other." May the house of Jacob our Father live on. May we not fail now or ever again.

FORGIVE AND NOT BE PETTY

Rituals and ceremonies, embellishments that are both aesthetically attractive and satisfying are of course magnificent facets of religion that should never be minimized. Who can deny this when we think of the pomp and artistry which are inherent in religious ceremony, whether we view the primitive mystic rites of dance and play among various tribes in all parts of the globe, the beautiful dances among the Japanese, Hindus, other Asiatics, the American Indians, African tribes, or perhaps we may consider our own rituals like the kindling of Shabbat and Chanukah lights, the waiving of the Lulav and Etrog, the Passover symbols, etc. These aspects of religion are particularly impressive at this time of the year. The cathedrals are full of pomp and pageantry at the Christmas festival, the priesthood tries to emulate the symbolism of the *Kohen Gadol,* The High Priest among our forefathers, they stand eagerly to receive the sacrament whereby a piece of matzoh and wine are transformed into the body and blood of the Jesus.

However, observe that while we always appreciate this aspect of religion, traditional Judaism is always reminding us that no matter how significant is the *miztvah beyn adam leMakom*, the relations between man and his Creator, it is the *miztvah* of *beyn adam lechavero*, it is the relations between man and his fellow man that elevate man's sanctity, far more than does one ritual or another.

Consider the personality in Joseph's orbit who achieves a victory and a position of status, the butler of Pharaoh. Undoubtedly, it was a most uncomfortable moment for Joseph when he heard both dreams and he realized that the interpretation delivered to the butler was one of exultation, and the dream analysis for the baker was indeed, a sorry one. In Hebrew, to lift up the head, can become a play upon words. It can mean to restore to dignity and honor, or to hang in the gallows, or to decapitate a person. Whatever may have been the evaluation which others accorded Joseph, he now established his credit as a person of piety, who entertained a special communication with heaven. Even if someone could have guessed that the Pharaoh would celebrate his birthday by granting amnesty or clemency to those he had sentenced to imprisonment, and pardon one of his officers, and perhaps punish the other, but who could have possibly guessed which one would receive his favor, or that he would demonstrate his anger by hanging the dead body of the prisoner and expose it as a prey to the fowl of the heavens?

Now the butler who was restored to favor turned out to have a common character trait. He was a dishonorable person, unworthy of the respect of others. After all, he had learned that this young man had been terribly treated, brutally kidnapped, framed by a woman's passion and unjustly condemned to prison.

Joseph had not the authority to release him from prison, but how could the butler forget to be grateful and sensitive to this young man who had lifted his spirits, infused hope within his heart and encouraged him to believe that salvation would come. But unfortunately as often happens, high status often changes one's manners. One becomes inflated with his own importance, thinks of himself far above his humbler acquaintances, remembers neither kindness nor good will but is only inflated with his own petty and insignificant character. Poor Joseph had his ray of hope, his illuminations that lighted him to freedom. He could commend himself to the intercession of the chief Butler, but alas, the butler had forgotten him, and it was to the *Ribono shel Olam*, the Creator of the world alone, that he could look to for help and salvation.

In stark contrast to the butler, consider Joseph as a person when in his position, power and status. Even as he subjects his brothers who do not recognize him, to pressure, anxieties and fears, he does this not out of spite, nor out of pettiness, become some contemptible, repulsive bug who wants to get even. Ah no, he hopes to make them see how wrong they were to hate him, when he was young and full of dreams and visions. He listens to the passionate words of Judah. He sees how his brother is willing to lose his own freedom, to become enslaved just to be certain that Benjamin, his younger brother will return to their father, that their father will be spared this terrible blow of losing another child. Even before this moment, when he began to observe the doubts, concerns and the sense of remorse which pervaded the hearts of their brothers. He probably wanted to reveal himself when he heard Judah cry out, God has found out the iniquity of thy servants. This is not a reference to the accusation against Benjamin, that he stole the silver goblet, no, it is rather the recognition of the sin against Joseph and their father, Jacob. Rightly does Dr. J. H. Hertz in his commentary say the work of moral regeneration of the brothers is complete, that has been Joseph's objective.

Now Joseph is only concerned with his brothers and wishes to protect them. He orders every one to leave the room, whereupon the Midrash notes: Joseph did not act correctly, because had one of those brothers jumped or kicked him in anger, he would be dead. But the *Yalkut Yehuda* notes Joseph said, "Better I should face the danger of being attacked and even killed rather than embarrass my brothers before all Egypt." That is what the Gemarah (Berachot 43b) means when it says, sooner a man cast himself into a fiery furnace rather than shame another in public." The Ramban adds, "Had the Egyptians heard the complete story of the betrayal of the brothers of Joseph, they would have said these people cannot live in our land, because if they could betray their own brethren, what will they do against the King and the Nation?"

It is the greatness of Joseph that we see now when he does not throw up the old wrong to his brethren. He forgives them completely and totally. He strives to prevent their remorse. "Don't be angry with yourselves that you sold me here." Understand that all this was part of God's plan, because God brought me here to preserve your lives and the lives of our people"

God did this yes, in the worst hour, we Jews say a *Brechah*, a blessing, *Baruch dayan haemet*, Bless the Judge of truth, because the end of the Lord's work is salvation, and God brings good out of evil and men are only instruments in his hand, even when we cannot understand his purpose or comprehend why certain things happen. But whatever path we seek, it is Joseph who reminds us that in our relations with our brethren, we must seek to avoid being petty, and instead stand up with sensitivity and understanding.

The Rabbis who observe that whenever inner greatness emerges, invariably somewhere in God's scheme it finds its compensation. Judah who spoke so magnificently in the *Parsha*, who is ready to sacrifice himself for his brother, Benjamin, earns gratitude that is exalted in Jewish history. Centuries later when the tribe of Judah is the ruler of Israel faced with civil war, and the other tribes brake from its dominion, it was the one tribe of Benjamin that remained staunch in its loyalty to the Kingdom. Joseph is not only the record of a chapter in the beginnings of Jewish history. The story of Joseph is a profound religious instruction cautioning us not to be petty when we think we have the power to do evil against another. It is not only those whom we hate and injure who may feel bad, but also it is we ourselves who expose our own rottenness. For when Joseph is considered as to having taken a great chance being alone with his brethren, the Midrash continues that he did right, because he considered the essential righteousness of his brothers and considered God forbid they should even be suspected of blood shedding. He was so enthralled with discerning the influence of God in all this scheme of things, that he easily forgot their wrongs, that they tortured him, humiliated him, threw him into a pit, threatened him with death and then sold him into slavery.

So let us warn in these days when we are challenged everywhere. When assassins threaten our people, hypocrites menace

Israel and when we face great challenges for survival and the preservation of our heritage and values, let us learn from Joseph, so that we may be able to say to our people, I am Joseph your brother, is father still alive? Is father in heaven alive in our hearts? Do we remember his teachings? Let us therefore cling to each other and stand by each other, until God's salvation will shine and redeem us.

RELYING ON MIRACLES

"Eyn somchin al hanes,"
"We do not depend upon a miracle." (Pesachim 64b)

There are not too many references to Chanukah in the Talmud; the reasons for this differ. Some authorities once claimed it was due to the choice of Rabbi Judah, the Prince, who could not forgive the Hasmoneans for assuming royal prerogatives over the Jews, especially since they where not of the Royal House of David, from which Rabbi Judah himself descended. Other authorities contended that it was due to the fact the Hasmoneans also acted with the authority of the high priest for which they were not entitled. But despite the various reasons suggested, the people, obviously, were not that much impressed by these various analyses.

And so through the generations the Holiday attracted the broad masses. Old and young alike sang their songs and attempts to regain Jewish National Freedom always meant a comparison with the Macabbees. Hence every generation of Jews can appreciate those simple magnificent words by the immortal Jewish national leader Zev Jabotinsky, *"Al tagidu ki enenu dam avinu haMacabee, Ki shalosh tipot mimehnu nimzigu bidam leebee,"* "Tell me not that no longer is there any blood of our father the

Maccabee, because three drops of it still flows within the blood of my heart." What is it that impelled every Jew to claim with pride that at least three drops of Maccabean blood flowed within him?

The Talmud does however make reference to this day. Perhaps the Rabbis limited their explanations because they were so peaceful; they did not want to glorify a military victory. And yet, it is clear that the regulation of kindling the lights on this festival was impressed upon our consciousness. Does not the Talmud (Baba Kama 62b) declare that he who places the Chanukah lights twenty cubits or higher, does not fulfill his obligation? Rashi explains this by saying "that such a position would be too high for normal light and thus one could not see the flickering lights, the viewer therefore, would be unable to do his true obligation," which Rashi explains *Lishem pirsum hanes*, to publicize, to propagate the miracle of Chanukah.

The miracles of Chanukah are varied, as our people understood the holiday. The Talmud, of course, emphasized the miracle of the little flask of sanctified oil which should have lasted for one day and instead lasted for eight days. There is another miraculous phenomenon, namely the victory of the *Chalashim* over the *Giborim*, namely the weaker over the stronger. The *Miatim* smashed the *Rabim*, the minority thrust back a numerical majority. And so we continue to sing *"Al hanisim ve'al hapurkan,"* "For the miracles and on the salvation," and in the synagogue we recite the Hallel, the Psalms of praise and gratitude. A question that invariably arises for our consideration is, are we reciting the Hallel because of the miracle of our rescue? Why then do we not follow suit on Purim? After all, this too is a Holiday of a miracle and of a rescue. Surely, the series of incidents that culminated in the salvation of Persian Jewry from the nefarious schemes of genocide that Haman sought to materialize are miraculous. And yet on Purim we do not recite Hallel, why?

The usual response is that we need not do so, since on Purim we recite the Megilah of Esther. Yet this Megilah of Esther which contains the narrative of Purim does not make any reference directly to God. In it Mordechai simply warned Esther that if she lacked the courage to sacrifice herself in behalf of her people, help would come from another quarter. Nether the less, do we not recite the same "*Al hanisim ve'al hapurkan,*" "For the miracles and on the salvation in the *Shomoneh Esreh* Prayer on Purim as we do on Chanukah, so why the failure to recite Hallel? Do we lack gratitude to God, are we not thankful that he helped Esther? Have we not been taught one does not hit his finger with a hammer down here below, unless it has been decreed up above? So perhaps as at this moment we should consider this difference in the liturgy and ask ourselves, if there is no specific reason staring us in the face that would answer our questions, we would simply say "don't we rejoice over all miracles?" But what is it that the Talmud tells us?

"*Eyn somchin al hanes,*"
"We do not depend upon a miracle." (Pesachim 64b)

True, we are a people of miracles. Our very existence is a miracle. In the face of a hostile and belligerent world is it not miraculous to be a Jew? What is a Hebrew *ivri*? And from whence this term? The Masorah tells us, you and I, each of us are an *ivri*, because Father Abraham stood *meyver echad*, on one side, confronting an idolatrous world, and he stood up to their hatred and persecution, he was thrown into a fiery furnace and *maaseh avot siman lebanim*, the lives of our forefathers has been a guiding post to their descendants. Abraham stood in a fiery furnace, because of Numrod, and his children were thrown into the crematory ovens under Hitler. Our fathers had to cross a turbulent Red Sea, and their children had to cross many waters. Yes we crossed oceans running away from persecutions, we crossed the Mediterranean to escape Arab persecutions and violence in the times of Rambam, we crossed the Atlantic trying to escape the pogroms of Russia, we crossed the pacific after trying to find shelter in Asia from the Nazis: we wandered in the desert and how many deserts have our people crossed?

But we learned to be miraculous, like Abraham our Father like Moshe, like Rambam, like our own parents and grandparents we learned that we had to do our best to stand up to the enemy, to the entire world. And we did it, with whatever energies we could muster. Hiding in broken ships on the Danube, crossing the seas in poor freighters while the British war ships fired their cannons upon the survivors of the camps. Yemenite Jews marched on foot on the hot burning sands that seared their feet, but they walked determined to find shelter in Zion. And always we learned "*Eyn somchin al hanes*," "Do not depend on miracles." Yes, even when the Jews crossed the Red Sea, they were afraid at first, they were sure they would drown, but Nachshon said do not depend on miracles, let us throw ourselves into the waters. And this they did. And what does the Midrash tell us, only when the water came up to their very nostrils, only when the world could see that Jews did not depend upon a miracle, only then did the miracle take place, and the waters parted and Israel walked on dry land.

On Purim, our forebears waited for a miracle, we all fast, we all pray, we shall cry, and maybe a *nes,* miracle will occur. Brave Esther will save us, Achashverus, de Narisher Koenig, the foolish intoxicated King, sensuous, hedonistic, concerned with the beauty of his Vashti and bereft of shame and dignity. Let us hope for a miracle. God we thank thee for saving us, "*Al hanisim ve'al hapurkan,*" Esther manifested *gevurah*, bravery, she was our heroine, but on Chanukah we did not just wait for a miracle.

The Maccabees went out and fought, the old father as not deterred from his activism, he actually stabbed a traitorous Jew who was ready to betray our God, our people, our land, our freedoms, our convictions and our faith. Perhaps this was the greatest miracle. Jews who were ready to fight when the entire world considered it unthinkable that a little group should stand up to a great military machine. A miracle that women would join the struggle. A miracle that children should offer their lives for *Kiddush Hashem*, the Sanctity of God, a miracle that Jews should learn that even the sacred Shabbat may be violated when we just fight for our lives and for Jewish survival. Yes, we recite Hallel because our forefathers did not just depend on a miracle, they knew the truth. God helps those that help themselves. Or as the Talmud declares, "He who acts to purify himself, is helped from heaven." (Berachot 17a) We face so many challenges today. A tremendous battle against assimilation, the struggle against ignorance upon which cults who come to prostitute the holy word of our God.

Let every Jew recognize that spark within us, as the Rabbis taught, every Jew has *nitzutz* of Moshe Rabbanu within him, we all have a spark of the heavenly flame that animated Moses.

And what about our moral standards which we must uphold against an idolatrous world which plays about with unprincipled games. For this we need courage, determination and faith. And that calls for the real miracle. The miracle of the Jew to make his will that of God's will. Now we understand why the Gemarah

(Shabbat 23a) tells us that he who kindles the Chanukah lights must recite his thanks to God who makes miracles. Yes, the great miracle of being inspired to stand up and labor, struggle, suffer and serve until the *Yeshua,* Redemption arrives. That is what the Maccabbes taught us and that is why Chanukah merits the Hallel, a full Hallel, an outpouring of the Jewish heart. We thank thee heavenly Father for that miracle of divine inspiration to stand up for thy truths. May we meet all our challenges. May we become transformed into modern Macabbees, may we all feel *ki shalosh tipot memenu nimzigu bidam leebee*, as long as three drops of their blood flow in our veins, in our hearts, in our *neshama,* our soul then we shall be victorious. We shall earn the respect for all future generations, and of us they will say, this was a generation that deserved the privilege of having the Hallel proclaimed.

Vayigash

— *11* —

וַיִּגַּשׁ אֵלָיו יְהוּדָה

"And Judah came near unto him," (Genesis 44:18)

BROTHERHOOD AND SINAT CHINOM

Today we realize that we stand upon the threshold of a new civil year. With the passing of time, we all become aware that this element in our existence accelerates with its every measurement that we recognize, minutes, hours, days, months and years. There are those of our people that reject the civil calendar, as it constitutes a Christian calendar and therefore; not one appropriate for the Jewish people. On the other hand, we may yet find that recognition in a civil New Year is not too difficult, in as much as we have a tradition of many new years.

We are reminded of this when we bring our attention to the Hebrew calendar new year, which starts with the Hebrew month of Nissan. Then there is a moral New Year that begins with the Hebrew month of *Tishrei* and the *Rosh Hashanah* Holiday. In addition to this there is the *Rosh Hashanah lailanot*, the New Year of trees, which takes place on *chamishah asar Beshvat*, the fifteenth day of the Hebrew month of *Shvat*. And of course, the King and his government had their own financial year. Our government like the old Hebrew Kingdom has its own fiscal year that runs from July first to June 30th.

What has always been interesting, because it reminds us of the sentiments which many share, is the fact that January is probably derived from a mythological God, Janus who had two heads, one looking forward and the other looking backward. If we discard the drinking, dancing and noise of New Year celebrations, we might notice that there are those who utilize January first as a day on which they look backward, consider the failures and victories of the past, and upon analysis, attempt to discern some guidelines which might illumine the roads of the twelve months ahead.

We have learned that if anyone wishes to be righteous in his life, he should try to fulfill the teachings of the Avoth, the Ethics of our Fathers because they teach us how to avoid injuries, and living such an ethical life means that we can rectify and improve our actions and attain a life that will be good to our fellowmen, and also good to ourselves. Whether we had victories in the past year or look forward to greater accomplishments in the year ahead, there is one thing that is startlingly clear:

"*Al tifrosh min hatzibur,*"
"Do not separate yourself from the community,"
(Ethics of the Fathers 4:7)

"*Shekol haporesh min hatzibur ayno roeh binechemat hatzibbur,*" but participate in their problems and troubles, because "Everyone who separates himself from the community will not be privileged to see the comfort of that community."

It is a stark reminder that decent human beings ought to resolve to stand with their fellowmen. If you follow the practice of making New Year's resolutions, those resolutions should incorporate your determination to stand loyally by and with your people, until our many handicaps and pressures are solved. This great truth is asserted immediately in this Torah lesson, when we read the eloquent words of Judah as he intercedes in behalf of his brother, Benjamin. It would appear that Judah was the most articulate among his brothers. When Joseph's brothers in their first explosive expressions of anger spoke about killing Joseph, it was Judah who eloquently spoke to the brothers and asked:

> **"Mah betzah key naharog et achinu, vechiseenu et damo,"**
> **"What profit is there in this action if we slay our brother and we shall hide his blood?" (Gen. 37:26)**

Come let us sell him to the Ishiaslites and let not our hand be upon him, for he is our brother, our flesh. It was the same Judah who articulated his request so well to old Father Jacob, that he send Benjamin to Egypt with them. And it is the eloquence of Judah that we hear again as he rises to his potential greatness here. Because he does not act like an ordinary lawyer insisting that his brother is innocent, that none of them stole anything, instead, he personally fulfills the tradition, *"shekol yisrael arevim zeh bizeh,"* "All of Israel is responsible for the other."

Every Jew is responsible. He is a guarantor for every other Jew. Judah generously declares that he is willing to serve in stead of Benjamin. His words strike deep into the heart of Joseph. More than his own life, Judah loves his father. He has mercy. He realizes that his word is more important than his own life and that he has promised to return Benjamin to his aged father. In addition

Judah piercingly understands that no Jew can live in isolation, unconcerned with another member of the tribe. Even as he prepares for his defense when the trumped up charge of theft is revealed in the sack of Benjamin, it is Judah who inaugurates the response by addressing the Egyptian officer and saying:

> *"Ma nomar la'adoni, mah nidaber, umah nitztadok, haelokim matzah et avon avadechah,"*
> **"What shall we say, what shall we speak, how shall we clear ourselves, God has found the sins of your servants." (Gen. 44:16)**

He represents the conscience of the brothers who now know that their entire lives have been marred and profaned by their terrible sin against their brother and their betrayal of their father.

Joseph can no longer control himself and reveals himself to his brothers. And what a tremendous hour of emotion that is, especially when he looks upon his younger brother, Benjamin.

> *"Vayipol al tzavarei Binyamin achiv, vayevk, uBinyamin bachah al tzavara,,"*
> **"And he falls upon the neck of Benjamin and he cries, and Benjamin cries on the neck of Joseph."**
> **(Gen. 45:14)**

Now the Talmud is alert to the peculiar spelling in the verse, superficially the verse reads that Joseph fell upon the necks of Benjamin. How many necks did Benjamin have? Rabbi Eliezer comments, *"Bachah al shney mikdashim sheatidim lehyhot bechayleck shel Binyamin viatidim lichare,"* "His prophetically insight impelled Joseph to weep, because he foresaw the two temples which would arise in the territory of the tribe of Benjamin, and also that both temples would be destroyed in the future.

Rashi quotes the other side of the prophecy, namely that Benjamin wept because he foresaw that the *Mishkan beShiloh*, that the sanctuary at Shilo which would be established in the area of Joseph's portion would itself be destroyed. (Rashi to Gen. 45:14) Each wept over the catastrophe that would befall our people in the future, each wept for the pain and agony the other would yet sustain.

Rabbi Yechezkile Kuzmirer, looking at these interpretations was moved to say that basically, there is a question here. How does it come about, that during this great joyous moment, when the two brothers are united that they should weep about future distractions? And how come they wept because of the distractions which would occur to the other, rather than weep for his own personal loss? Well, as our tradition often reminds us, both temples were destroyed because of *Sinat Chinom*, unjustified hatred. When Joseph and Benjamin drew near to each other and both felt that the cleavage within the family had emerged because of *Sinat Chinom*, unjustified hatred among the brothers, they both immediately foresaw future distractions and ruins which would be the result of this same *Sinat Chinom*. Hence unjustified, undeserved hatred and hostility between brothers which produce such horrifying results would still be operative in the future and cause disruption, destruction, dispersal and ruin among Jewish brethren. Both cried realizing that even as they had sustained so much personal tragedy because of hatred between brothers, that very same hatred would infect their descendants in the future, resulting in such disastrous consequences.

Of course, added Rabbi Kuzmirer , the rectification of *Sinat Chinom* is to increase the mutual affection, true love to such an extent that the others sorrows and troubles will cause you more

348

grief, pain, and anguish than the suffering that you would sustain from your own grief. This indicates that each was more concerned with the destruction that faced the other.

Historically speaking, we understand that the temples in the area of Benjamin could not be established until the destruction of the *Mishkan Yosef*, the Sanctuary of Joseph. Yet Benjamin wept so piteously, because in his heart he prayed that the temples in his area should completely not be constructed and thereby Joseph's Sanctuary would not be disrupted. They could very well weep, when they realized how far they had wandered from their father's teachings.

The Torah tells us that when Laban pursuing Jacob and his family on their way to Canaan, finally made a peace covenant symbolized by a pillar of stones, we read:

"Vayomer Ya'akov le'echav liktu avaneem,"
"And Jacob said to his brothers, gather stones."
(Gen. 31:46)

And in the Midrash, (Gen. Rabbah 74:13) the discussants are surprised. Jacob spoke to his brothers? How many brothers did he have? He only had the one, Esau from whom he had to flee. But because Jacob experienced that pain, of fleeing from a brother, fearing for his family when he had to meet that brother again, Jacob knowing that agony, spoke to his children regarding them as brothers. Brothers to love, brothers to confide in, brothers to share sorrows and joys, brothers in whose progress we should share vicariously and proudly, brothers with whom we stand in the vicissitudes of life with affection, with unity, with unmitigated love. It is the essence of brotherhood to stand by each other when in distress. (Ibid) Such unselfish love, such totally free and unrestricted affections are the only effective manner in defeating the ugly mani-festation of *Sinat Chinom.*

The teaching of concern for the other is again emphasized and highlighted as it were by a third incident in the Torah portion.

The Torah tells us that after the revelation of Joseph unto his brothers and their reconciliation, Joseph dispatched them home-ward with many gifts. And the Torah notes that when Jacob heard this miraculous news of his son's progress and above all the miracle of his being alive:

"*Vayafag libo key lo heh'ehmin lahem,*"
"His heart stood still unable to believe them."
(Gen. 45:26)

And he did not believe them. But when he saw the wagons that Joseph had sent, then the spirit of their father revived.

Rashi explains that when Jacob saw the wagons he jumped for joy because Joseph had placed special signs on these wagons. Joseph put signs on the wagons with reference to the Torah lesson his Father Jacob had been teaching him before his being betrayed and sold by his brothers. (Rashi to Gen. 45:27) Jacob immediately understood that Joseph was alive. He had indeed sent these wag-ons with their inscriptions as his evidence to verify the claims of the brethren. So once again we are witness to a profound lesson, indeed, in the weekly portion, the Holy Torah projects guidance for all of us to live our lives.

For our own sakes, as well as for the sakes of the entire Jew-ish people, let us resolve to live with Jewish ethics. Let us, too, like Joseph stand firm with loyalty and compassion for others sor-rows. Let us see to the suffering of brother and sister. Let us do away with *Sinat Chinom*, unjustified hatred by pouring forth un-restricted affections and unlimited love for our own people. Let us vow that we shall not stand idly by when others are placed in dangerous situations. Let us be like Judah, Benjamin and Joseph. Let us live with sensitivity for others.

For centuries our Rabbis have taught us that no vessel contains blessings as does peace. *Ahavah veachava*, love and brotherhood depend on peace. Let the chorale of Beethoven resound throughout the world, let all mankind truly be brothers. And that can be and shall be when those who profess to pray for peace will find it in their hearts to paraphrase the brethren as they first stood before Joseph:

"Avdecha achim, kulanu b'nai ish echad,"
"Your servants are brothers, we are all the children of one man." (Gen. 42:13)

Then we all shall be privileged to enjoy prosperity, peace, good health and good will. Our people shall be privileged to participate in the comfort of Zion, Jerusalem and the entire Jewish world. And together with all our brothers we shall drink of the cup of salvation and glad tidings.

BLOOD LIBELS

There is a fact which so many of us refuse to acknowledge, namely that apparently nice people may lie to interpret facts to their own satisfaction rather that expand their perspective to include the truth, even if that validity is not to their own liking. For example, in an issue of *Lamishpachah*, a most enjoyable Hebrew publication, there was an interesting review of a volume devoted to the historical development of the Hebrew-Israeli fighting forces.

Reference was made to Joseph Trumpeldor who was active in the Zion mule corps at Gallipoli, and Ze'ev Jabotinsky of the Jewish Legion. References were made to Hashomer, the early defenders of Palestine Jewish settlers. Other names noted were those who had fought in the British units in the Second World War, and of course, as we should anticipate, most studies of this nature invariably speak with pride of the Palmach and the Hagannah. Those defenders, who fought against the occupant but for whatever reasons, opposed the establishment, are usually ignored or grudgingly recognized by an insignificant line or meager paragraph.

Of course, nowadays, that falsehood and distortion has been rather effectively shattered by books like *Exodus* by Leon Uris, whose readers and viewers at the cinema, were amused by the weak attempt of the author to conceal the fighters of the Irgun. Other works like Gerold Frank's, *The Deed* which introduced the daringness of the Lechi, and the Stern Group which broke away from the Irgun in their execution of Lord Moyne, naturally awakened an interest in that group's struggle. Mr. David Ben Gurion who had fought these groups bitterly, however, as Prime Minister admitted, his reverence for the dedicated patriots, such as the men who were hanged in Cairo for the assassination of Lord Moyne. Although he declared that he did not accept the philosophy of the poet, Abraham Stern who was the mentor of that group, he did say, that Stern "was one of the finest and most outstanding figures of the era."

In a recent discussion of this item, I remarked how sad has been the distortion of history, by those who pretended that they did not know that Jabotinsky, was the founder of the Jewish Legion during the First World War. That following the war, he was also responsible for the Haganah, and later the Irgun. Whereupon someone remarked that at their last visit to Israel, they were astounded to discover in Jerusalem, a plaque on the front of a building, announcing to the whole world, "*Babayit zeh gar uhvo ne'esar*

Zev Jabotinsky magen Yerushalayim," "In this house lived and was arrested (by the British) Ze'ev Jabotinsky defender of Jerusalem." At that announcement, someone, obviously upset, joined the conversation to deplore the truths of history, which are not always to our liking.

How could a founding father of the United States, John Quincy Adams proclaim that the Bible contains the revelation of the will of God, the history of the most extraordinary nation that has ever appeared on the face of the earth? An inexhaustible mine of knowledge and virtue. Or those personalities like Samual Coleridge, Johann Wolfgang Von Goethe, Roger Bacon or George Herbert, etc. should have been so overwhelmed by its volumes, that they overlooked terrible reports by that same Bible.

For example, that David, the sweet singer of Israel, from whose lineage so many of us say the Messiah will spring, was a fierce warrior, barbaric was the term used by the young man, because to demonstrate his bravery, he fought philistines and cut off the foreskins of one hundred and displayed them to King Saul. Well, let us admit it, the Hebrew Bible does not conceal the truth, and its heroes are presented as they appeared in their times, with real human characteristics. But, argued another, David is supposed to be a redeemer, someone who will bring peace to the land and the nation, and here we find a bloodthirsty warrior. But the fact remains, whether you like it or not, David was a warrior.

A situation emerges from this portion of the Torah. The Alshich in his great commentary arrives at a conclusion that demands consideration today. He observes that Rashi, regarding the opening verse of the Torah portion:

"*Vayigash elav Yehuda*,"
"And Judah came near unto him," (Gen. 44:18)

the unrecognized brother standing before him as a domineering and threatening figure. Rashi notes, *Diber elav kashot*, Judah now began to speak with harshness, with rigidity, with a determination that apparently had not been present at the beginning of this final encounter. The Alshich suggests that when the accusation of robbery and the theft of the Egyptian lord's goblet was hurled against them, Judah perceived this as a devastating blow against the family, as a punishment for the sale of Joseph and the failure of brotherly love to have prevailed. Therefore, he is quoted as saying,

> **"*Ma nomar la'adoni, mah nidaber, umah nitztadok, haelokim matzah et avon avadechah*,"**
> **"What shall we say, what shall we speak, how shall we clear ourselves, God has found the sins of your servants." (Gen. 44:16)**

By this, Judah meant, the terrible sin of selling Joseph years ago into slavery. But when Judah realized, that the Egyptian was freeing all the brothers, but that Benjamin, who had not participated in that dastardly deed was being held as a slave, he then understood that the situation was not due to an actual historic experience, (*Yalkut Yehuda*) but it was nothing but a lie, a blood libel against Jews. And then Judah's anger explodes and he speaks eloquently but firmly, with dignity but with truth, with a defensive action but with no cowardice.

We who cling to the truth must follow the example of Judah. *Diber elav kashot*, yes we must speak firmly. We must stand alert and vigilant, we must solidify our ranks, we must unite in a struggle not only against the external lie but also against the enemy within. Ignorance, false and pernicious doctrines, rebellion against the word of God, and the assurances of the eternity of our people. When falsehoods of people voiced, then we must again and again repeat the slogan of Mattathias in the attainment of truth, justice and peace.

"Mi lashem elai,"
"Whosoever stands with God, let him join me."
(Exodus 32:26)

REMEMBER THE STAKES

Everyone who has understood the various components of the Joseph narrative has always been sensitive to the stirring, dramatic facets of this scriptural tale which reads, rather naturally, as several acts of a tremendous play. The actors, their roles, the words they say, the actions they pursue, the background which is of a vigorous character, sweeping as it does from the pastoral setting of Canaan, to the Egypt of intrigue, licentiousness and the advanced administrations of state affairs and economy. The psychological explosiveness is evident in the climax that occurs in the recital of the Biblical portion of *Vayigash.*

Harassment, cunning strategy, betrayal, calumny, slanders, outright prevarications have all combined to entrap the innocent Benjamin, and now in a show of magnanimity the strange viceroy says unto the brothers. "I wish to be fair, go in peace and return to your home, only Benjamin, who has repaid my hospitality with theft, must remain here in bondage to me."

"Vayigash elav Yehuda,"
"And Judah came near unto him." (Gen. 44:18)

Self protection and self rescue aside, he stands forth to approach this Egyptian official, in all his glory and power, and in forthright terms. He hopes his eloquence will be aided by his sincerity and convictions, to the end that Benjamin will be returned to their aged father, and that Jacob will be spared further grief in his advanced years.

The Midrash analyzes this scene and several Sages differ in their conclusions and evaluations. Rabbi Yehuda declares "*Hagasha zu lamilchama*," "His approach can only be interpreted as an acceptance of war." (Midrash Lekach Tov) Look at it from this point of view. This strange official, a man of prominence and power who provides food for the entire country, attacks them with harsh words, utters libels and slander against them. He accuses them of being spies, yet returns their money in their sacks so that they would be framed on false charges as though they really were thieves, and finally after pretence of hospitality conceals his divining cup within the sack of Benjamin. All this scheming to confuse and entrap them. Under such circumstances there can be no counsel, no recommendations, no logical approach except to engage in war. What are we taught by tradition: "*Habah lihargichah hashkem lihargo*." " When some one comes to kill you, rise earlier and kill them first." (Numbers Rabbah 21:4)

Rabbi Nehemiah considers the *hagashah* approach to be a strategy towards peace, to continue to appease the Egyptian until he finally yields. Because argues this Sage: "*key eyn lichah adam sheyuchal la'amod neged haemet*," "Because no one can stand always against the truth." But the other Rabbis apparently differ, "*Hagashah latifilah*" *omrim Rabbanan*, Judah's approach was focused upon prayer, the Rabbi's say. They felt in such difficult hours we can rely upon no one but our Father in heaven. But along came Rabbi Eliezer who believed that there actually was merit in all three propositions, since to effect rescue, we are obligated to be active and labor in every possible manner. Hence, if it is war then I am ready. If it is peace then I am ready and if we need prayer, there too I stand ready. The vibrancy of Judah, is the representative of all of us. For we stand here before a stranger and opponent, as one man with one heart and we possess a unity of opinions. And here the personality of Judah emerges.

As Rashi explains: "*Veani nitcashartee leheyot menudeh beshney olamot,*" "I Judah, guaranteed the safety of the lad. I am bound with tremendous bonds, and I may thereby lose both worlds, this world and the world to come," (Rashi to Gen. 44:32) and therefore I must enter the fray, I must meet the challenge more than do the rest of my brothers." You see Judah felt impelled to go beyond any activity that might be contemplated by his brothers, because he felt the stakes were so high for him. Perhaps that is what complicates matters for us today, that is what increases our confusions, that is what causes us to fail in responding properly and honorably to the challenges of our times. Our failures to realize how high the stakes really are. So high that we may be losing our stability today and abandoning our future world as well. When we accept certain phrases, or insist that we agree on certain policies which arouse controversy within the gates, I fear that we say and do certain things, simply because we forget to evaluate the stakes and see how high they really are.

Centuries ago we had an activist who was acclaimed by our tradition, namely Pinchus who killed a traitorous Jew who was carrying on with an immoral woman of Moab. The Torah puts it bluntly. The Israelites went whoring after the Moabite women. And so Pinchus put an end to it by slaying both the Jew and the woman. Our tradition approves of Pinchus because he realized the stakes were high. They spelt the defeat of Israel in the wilderness and the defeat of its future. Mattathias went to war because he considered that the future of our people as well as their contemporary lives demanded that they emulate Pinchus and strike physically at the enemy. There have been scholars who looking backward at moments of terrorism in our history, feel that Sicari and Kanaeem who went to war with Rome might have been better advised to labor unceasingly through peaceful means, because Judaism was an attractive religion in those days and millions might have joined it. But the revolts against Rome and the eventual defeat of the Hebrews led to a condition whereby Jews were suspect, feared and disliked, and millions of our people were slain or sent into slavery.

And incidentally, not only we but all mankind. Wars of religious hatred, prejudice and violence that culminated into the nefarious Hitler years which not only decimated our people three times over but was responsible for wholesale slaughter of millions of other human beings. That the stakes for them have been so terribly high has been overlooked

We must remember our priorities. We must never refuse to see the stakes involved and never forget just how high the stakes are. Stakes so high that they may include threats against our *Olam Hazeh* and our *Olam Habah*, the two worlds, the world of here and now, and the world of the future. Of course, we should study and explore those channels that might lead to peace, real peace. Of course we should rally our people to prayer, and by that I mean, rally our people to the heritage hallowed by centuries. But we must also stand ready for activist deeds and militant expressions of our claims. We must learn from Judah. "I have guaranteed the safety of Benjamin." And I stand to lose worlds, my present one and the future. We Jews today must realize that we too are responsible for the safety of generations yet unborn. We too, are responsible for actions that may thwart our futures. Direct your energy against the real enemy, because two worlds have become our responsibility, the world of today and the world of tomorrow.

THE CHOSEN PEOPLE

Few concepts have been so fatally misinterpreted as the idea of Jewish chosenness. As most of you recall the Bible speaks of us as having been chosen by the Lord to be His elect people, and that we are to be a nation of priests and a holy people. Most non-Jews see in the Jewish claims to the title, the chosen people an obnoxious affront of arrogance. This is very strange indeed, since most of our Christian friends in their own faith try to claim that the chosenness of their religion is the truth, because it has inherited it from Judaism. Jews who are ignorant of the real meaning of the chosen people rest satisfied in the smug and complacent delusion that they are really very important because God has chosen them to be superior to others.

This confusion regarding Jewish chosenness is not only limited to the man in the street. Intellectuals and writers, from the early Roman historians and satirists to such contemporary literature as George Bernard Shaw and H.G. Wells have proven themselves to be equally uninformed. During the height of the Hitler atrocities, Shaw and Wells seem to go out of their way to find what they considered similarities between the Teutonic dogma of Aryan superiority and the Jewish belief in Divine election. Yet the idea of Jewish chosenness has as little in common with the Aryan racial fancy as the God of Israel has with Wotan, the Warrior of the Germans.

In the first place the doctrine of Israel's Divine election has no racial basis whatsoever. It is not a claim of those of Jewish blood to be racially superior to the rest of mankind. Jewish chosenness rests solely on Israel's spiritual treasure. Since the Torah is accessible to all men, everyone is potentially chosen. It does not matter whether one is born into a family of the people i.e. the Jews or whether he be a convert. Jewish chosenness is not racially limited. All who desire may enter the Jewish fold and thus be chosen. The Nuremberg Laws on the other hand excluded even those with a mere trickle of non-Aryan blood from the community of the general people. No matter what a non-Aryan might do, he could not become a German, for according to the Aryan racial theories, character is contingent upon the blood. This is why the Nazis proclaimed "It doesn't matter what the Jew does, he belongs to the other race."

Judaism never endorsed the fatalistic view that a man's soul is the result of his physical-racial traits, for this would be tantamount to the denial of the freedom of will, one of the cardinal convictions. Judaism emphasizes that a wicked father may sire a pious and righteous son. It is man's ethical choice and not his blood or a gene that makes him good or bad, the ideas of Jewish chosenness is altogether free from notions of racial exclusiveness. All authoritative Jewish teachers stress that racial-religious choice and not racial heritage makes the Jew. Judaism emphasizes that all mankinds are descended from the same Adam. As a result, there are no chosen, those claims to superiority are often based on quack biological facts, and the Rabbis guarded the idea of Jewish chosenness from racial biological justifications by stoutly asserting that Jews and gentiles alike are descended from Adam. The same universalizing tendencies motivated Rabbi Meir's statement "Adam was created from dust collected from all four corners of the earth," which precluded the possibility of a notion claiming the distinction of having cradled mankind.

Israel was truly a chosen nation when we realize that throughout the centuries doctrines have been preached regarding racial superiority, doctrines which were exceedingly popular in the 19th and 20th centuries, doctrines which are so in vogue amongst many. The Sages taught us that if a gentile practices the Law he is equal to the High Priest, therefore, all men could attain chosenness by accepting the law. The election of one nation does not imply the rejections of the rest of mankind. Judaism emphasizes that God does not reject anybody. He receives them all. The doors are always open, and everyone who so desires, can enter.

Although products of its role, Israel does not exclude the rest of mankind from serving in God's vanguard. All men are potentially eligible to serve God. Israel's ancestors Jacob, and Esau the progenitor of the gentiles were twin brothers of the same family of sons, born in the same hour and brought up in identical surroundings. It was not race that made Jacob serve the Lord and Esau serve his instincts. Jacob's free choice and equally free decision determined their paths. Jacob's chosenness was within the grasp of Esau as well, even as it is still accessible to his descendants.

A patriot always considers his country and his people to be the best. Patriotism is normal and becomes a menace only when it claims a priority or superiority. The Aryan racial theories were of this kind. Of the same class were the ancient Greeks claim that only the Hellenes were true human beings, while all others were barbarians destined to be slaves to the superior master nation of the Greeks. The confidence in the racial national superiority was so deeply rooted in the Greeks that even philosophers of Plato's and Aristotle's standing endorsed it as indisputable. They were firmly convinced that mankind was to be divided into two groups.

The Greeks and the barbarians, the former chosen to rule and the latter condemned to be ruled. A barbarian was forever excluded from the Greeks, no matter what he contributed to Greece race or its culture. His blood and race disqualified him.

When a Jew prays in the morning and renders thanks to God for having been born a Jew and not a gentile he does not therewith say that a Jew is by destiny superior to a gentile. He merely rejoices in the fact that he is enjoined to observe six hundred and thirteen Divine commandments. While the righteous gentile in order to qualify for future bliss need observe only seven commandments. Socrates and Plato are said to have rendered thanks unto the gods for having been born Greeks and not barbarians. Their benediction however was not motivated by gratitude for added obligations but by the proud joy in being members of the ruling nation and the caste of the privileged few for whom other men must toil. In the final analysis there is no difference between the Greek attitude towards non-Greeks, later adopted by the Romans as well and the frame of mind which gave rise to the perversion of the Nuremberg laws. Both spring from the vaunted and stubborn delusion of preordained national and racial superiority. To the Greek, the barbarian was always a slave, to the Roman, others were weaklings to be mistreated, and to the Nazi the non-Aryan was inferior.

It is most pitiful that as a result of such fallacious misconceptions broadcast with convictions by peoples of high cultural attainments, many students have failed to see that the idea of Jewish chosenness is free from perverted claims of predestined superiority. It has always been the great tragedy that Judaism has been interpreted in terms of fiction rather than fact. When men like a Shaw or Wells profess to see in the doctrine of Jew chosenness nothing but arrogance, it is of misinformation or perhaps just a reflection of the idea which lies within our own souls as Britishers. Our people have never interpreted Jew chosenness as anything other than a regimen of sacrifice and service. The law and ethics of the sea ordain that the captain of a sinking vessel be the last to abandon ship, as the highest-ranking officer. The chosen one must excel his crew in sacrificial courage and self-discipline. Israel too has conceived of its role as stewardship to the nations who, as yet, have not advanced to the full knowledge of the Lord as revealed in the Torah. As guardians of the Torah, the Jews are keenly recognizant of their obligations to the rest of mankind. That is why all Jewish sacred writings stress Israel's obligation wherever there is a reference made to its divine election.

As the Midrash says before our acceptance of Torah we were called Israel just as other nations are called by their names, but after our acceptance of the Torah, God refers to Israel as my people. Thus we see that the meaning of Jewish chosenness means to be the servant of he Lord and the servant of mankind, in spite of hardship and suffering to never stop trying to lead mankind to God.

Now how did that chosenness, that mission, express itself in ancient days unto the nations. First and above all there was the doctrine of God. At a time when all the peoples of the world were steeped in idolatry, Israel was chosen to spread the greatest ideal in the history of mankind, that of one God. When mankind was steeped deep in anthropomorphic confusions, when the planets and natural manifestations were worshipped simply because they were not understood, when people worshipped rulers such as did the Egyptians and the Babylonians, when animals were considered holy, the Jew appeared in the arena of history, elected to preach the doctrine of one God, the creator of Heaven and earth. This at a time when Israel was chosen to preach that God is not bloodthirsty nor does He posses the evil attributes of man. How important that was could be seen from a study of the worship of Moloch wherein children were sacrificed or burnt alive on the stone altars of the god Moloch. In fact it was most radical that God should chose his prophets to protest against this aberration of man's sense of worship. Our very term for hell, *gehinnon* came from the valley where wicked kings pursued this horrible rite. Through the Bible story of the binding of Isaac where God intervenes and says unto Abraham do not stretch forth your hand to do evil to this boy we learn, martyrdom for ideals-yes, but the wanton murder of one of our own children for idolatry-no.

Again, Israel became a chosen people in its concept of human holiness. Whether this referred to parent-child relationship, husband and wife relationship, man to fellow man relationship, Israel was chosen to preach the holiness of humans to humanity. When Israel preached such doctrines, the world was unable to conceive of it, the human beings and the justice to each. The King as the King and law applied only to the subject. The slave was less than human being, he could be beaten tortured and even murdered and nothing or no one could go to his defense. Israel was chosen to protect the sanctity of the human being. Torah taught the man that he was a human being. He is to go free for the loss of an eye or even a tooth at the hands of his master. The Babylonian code, a product of an intricate civilization that tightly industrializes a commercial city, closes with a case of a slave whose ear is to be cut off for desiring freedom. The Mosaic Law opens with a case of the servant whose ear is to be bored as a mark of disgrace because he refuses to go free when his six years of servitude are ended. When for men to starve, for the poor to perish like beasts of the field was considered normal, the Torah taught Jewish laws of Sabbath which provided for the poor, where the state had to think in terms of the jubilee which would free all slaves, where redivision of the land secures again to the poorest his fair share into the bounty of the common Creator. As Henry George spoke more than a half century ago, the dominant idea in Jewish chosenness centuries ago was to teach humanity, live and let live.

Israel was a people chosen to preach the doctrine of peace when war was the dominant theme in the life of every nation. In our faith the Rabbi's found no ideal as glorious as peace. They never tired of singing its praises. Peace among men is considered to be the goal of the Torah. Even Maimonadies, paraphrasing the Rabbis of old, declares that the Torah came down to earth only to establish peace in the world, this at a time when all the nations pressed their ideals only in terms of war. Greek, Roman, or earlier Egypt, all history was conceived only through the eyes of the warrior. And history was looked upon as the record of war, their defeats and victories. And Israel was chosen to reach the doctrine of peace.

Israel was chosen to be what the Mohammedans called us, the People of the Book. People devoted to study. A people to be different from all other people in that we would build an aristocracy not of money, not of title, not of family background, but an aristocracy of the intellect. When great philosophers and thinkers of other nations insisted that only a few select ones had the intelligence to learn, to understand and that the rest must be submissive to them, it was the Jew who was chosen to say to the world that every man was born with a free will, that every human being could think and what was more should do so. Contemplate the

Creator, his manifestation, his nature, his creatures and by seeking to do his will, develop thinking powers and abilities. In this manner did Israel show that it was chosen.

But today when we have made so much progress and we hear other peoples use the terms we first used, can we still maintain we are the Chosen People, or have the others completely displaced us from that exalted title? Are we still the chosen people? If by that title we mean the great Jewish tradition to teach the world and lead mankind onward to its union with God and his justice, righteousness and peace, then we still continue to be the elect and must maintain that mission. Not too long, it was Arthur Schopenhauer, the German Philosopher, notwithstanding his frequent outbursts versus Judaism, who appreciated the true nature of Jewish monotheism when he stated "Judaism still cannot be denied the glory of being the only genuine monotheistic religion on earth." That is still true today. Here we are in this modern era and yet in the dominant faith, our neighbors still deify the human being. What is more is a great sect of that faith in addition to its founder has decided that his mother is likewise to be deified and regarded as having ascended to heaven like him. He in this modern day superstitions are still popular among masses the world over, still great areas of the world regard beasts as divine and sacred, only the Jew still remains the unique people with a mission to teach the world the One God.

We have watched a modern world glibly speak about the necessity of making the cultural, spiritual lag catch up with the technical advancement and yet the entire world is saturated with injustices. What is a modern dictatorship but not the failure of the world to catch-up with the doctrine preached by God's elect. If the ancient king was above the law, is this not true of the modern tyrannies. Israel is still chosen to teach that which the Gerrer Rebbe has expressed, "If a person rears anything besides God, he is guilty of idolatry, as fear is a tribute related to worship and only God should be worshiped." The dictator is above law and is feared above everything, and is looked upon with great tribute, a form of idolatry. And what is the war-like totalitarian doctrine, which still sweeps over the world if not a modern version of the Moloch religion that still demands sacrifices of our children? And when we think of Israel's uniqueness in teaching the holiness of the human being, can we deny the need for that teaching today? Here and there it is true we find others apparently mimicking some of our words, but what do the real facts show us? A world in which youth is sinking into the snares of immorality and wrong doing, shocking revelations of our young joining clubs devoted to immorality, juvenile delinquency reaching astounding proportions. Dry statistics speak to us about thousands of children being brought annually before the court bench in this country, sooner or later becoming a problem for the police. For years we insisted as moderns that poor material conditions, lack of nourishment were the great if not the only factor in creating delinquents. And now along come those prominent sociologists Sheldon and Eleanor Gluck, Sheldon Gluck is a professor of criminology at Harvard, while Dr. Eleanor Gluck, his wife, is an outstanding research associate at the Harvard Law school, and they have published a startling thesis on unraveling the threads of juvenile delinquency. And we learn that contrary to accepted beliefs, the delinquent is not weaker than the good boy is. And once again we begin to stir uneasily in our consciences at the realization that it is not the physical factors as much as the spiritual character forming traits that is most important. Subject to so many pressures we still remain a chosen people when we realize that material influences of the environment notwith-standing, is the modern trends so many of us seek to follow. The spiritually Jewish child is still free from the delinquent trend only because of our past religious backgrounds of a generation and two ago. The world is still sacrificing its children to Moloch and Israel is still elected the chosen people to preach the road back to the one God who wishes to see children live for ideals and not be mur-dered for perversions.

Nor is it in the field of social thought that Israel has lost his sense of election. In spite of our many social reforms, all of which incidentally since the days of the Gracchi brothers in Rome, the Elizabethan poor laws in England and our New Deal and the sub-sequent social legislation in our own country all owe their incep-tion purely to Jewish influence. And yet how unhappy is the lot of economic justice in our own country? The rightful association of laborers is still fought in many parts of the United States. Jim Crow laws are still in existence. Discrimination because of color and when we think of how much of the worlds fears today origi-nally began because masses were denied economic and social jus-tice, the chosenness of Israel in preaching this doctrine as a people still holds true. For other nations can boast of individuals who are inspired with that vision of such righteousness, but no nation as an entirety can speak as does Israel of its passion for social justice. Judaism has not only implanted in the conscious of the Jew a deep rooted interest in the laborer which was responsible in large mea-sure for his unbounded zeal in every social and economic forward looking movement, but Judaism also offers a definite view. It of-fers a clearly defined conception of the whole economic problem of man. A great teacher Rabbi Simeon ben Eliezer expressed this view in a beautiful though naive fashion: In all my life, I have never seen a deer engaged in gathering fruits, or a lion carrying loads, or a fox acting as a shopkeeper. And yet they seem to find sustenance for themselves without pain or sorrow. They were created only to be of service to me. I, then, who was created to serve my Maker, ought surely to be able to support myself without any anguish or trouble. But I find it difficult to support my actual needs and gain my daily sustenance because my deeds were filled with evil as it is written; your iniquities have turned away these things. To what depths does this simple comment reveal the evils of our social and economic life? This is a beautiful world in which we live, offering enough for each and all. Nature is bountiful. With honest labor and just regard for toil, there would be sufficient for the needs and wants of all. But, alas, man has by his unbridled corruption turned the economic system into a mad whirlpool, bringing destruction and misery into the lives of vast masses of man. Judaism pleads for the higher ethical law in all relationships that affect the life of man. It has still, much to offer for the well being and happiness of mankind. For the very problems that present themselves in the fields of labor, capital management, economic competition, Judaism even in our day still offers living wholesome vital solutions. As in ancient days, so also in our own, Judaism can be a tree of life to us, if we but grasp it in the spirit of the mission to which we have been selected.

Finally, however, there is one aspect of our existence, which was always underscored years ago, but which in these days have been forgotten. We are alive. In spite of all the persecutions to which we have been subjects, for the past two thousand years, we have managed to survive because of our optimism and faith. And we have managed not only to survive but also to recreate. A stubborn hard-necked people we were called by the Bible and to a certain extent a stubborn people we are even today. But in the light of our past and our present, does anyone who claims to be a thinking Jew deny our future and its potentialities? Our very survival today proclaims to the world that we are still God's elect, that we are still the chosen people. These are the simple things and in our hurry of daily life, in our many discussions on various aspects of Jewish life, let it be certain that we do not forget this outstanding feature of the world Jew. A people chosen by God to be his servants, to teach and preach his ways, to bring light unto the world and as such to live forever.

AL TIRGIZU BADERECH, DO NOT QUARREL ALONG THE WAY

"Al tirgizu baderech,"
"Do not quarrel along the way." (Gen. 45:25)

In the dramatic Torah portion of *Vayigash*, we reach a climax when Joseph reveals himself to his brothers and demonstrates his great character. Instead of seeking revenge upon them for the mistreatment that they accorded him when he was a mere lad, instead of holding it over them and saying, "I told you so, I am better than you. Here I am Joseph, the boy whom you sold to slavery and now you must come to me, bow down, beg that I give you food and that I permit Benjamin to return home to the aged father." He instead is full of forgiveness, weeps at seeing his brothers and upon hearing that his father is alive."

He sends them back home to get Jacob and bring him back to Egypt and as they go he shows that he is still the great wise Joseph. He gives them a bit of advice by saying:

"*Al tirgizu baderech*,"
"Do not quarrel along the way." (Gen. 45:25)

The Rabbis in their Talmudic discussions interpret this to signify that Joseph gave his brothers three principles which their descendents might well follow if they seek to attain success as they go on the road of life.

The first principle Joseph gave his brothers was "Do not become to deeply engaged in the law." This may be interpreted to mean, in your daily lives and relations with others try to avoid too much technicality. Law, of course, is a complicated system and naturally must be composed along technical lines. The same is true of other arts and sciences. Medicine does not mean writing a simple prescription, it is science which is the most complicated. It requires a great deal of knowledge of human anatomy, physiological and mental functions, herbs, roots, and chemicals, etc. The painter is not a man who daubs a brush into paint and streaks a line across a canvas. He must study many technicalities, the composition of paints and color schemes, the various materials he may handle, the rules of beauty, perspective, harmony and symmetry, etc. The architect likewise is a person who must first study the art of making blueprints, the composition of slate, lime, marble, wood and metal. He must deal with legal regulations regarding the erection of buildings in the community he works, etc. Even the smallest businessman and worker in our midst will find that his work is actually very technical. The operator must understand his machine, how to cut a proper design, what materials he must use and which will sell best.

But in the fields of human relations, as each of us walks on the road of life, we can not permit ourselves the luxury of getting too technical. Throwing up recriminations, "your mother is to blame, your brother is to blame, your sister annoys me, I can not stand your cousins," etc. Awakening quarrels at home, at business, at the club with your friends because of various loopholes, viewpoints, in short technicalities upon which we can each dwell is bad. It does not lead to happy living. It means taking much joy out of life. And so Joseph warned his brothers, on the road do not become too immersed in your technicalities, do not be touchy and sensitive to every little detail.

The second principle Joseph gave his brothers was "Do not take big steps on the road." That is a problem that is always annoying us throughout our lives. Every one of us without exception is always trying to take big steps, get far ahead of the other man. Of course, no one should cast away his ambition, nor has anyone the moral right to overlook his natural capabilities and talents in creating things and attaining goals that are superior to the average. But must we all be in such a hurry to get ahead of the other man? We run and as the Talmud says; running deprives a man of his eyesight (Berachot 43b), we run so fast and so furious that we forget where we are running and end up by getting lost. Perhaps the best advice that we can give to modern society today is stop taking such big steps, slow down, stop raising the statistics of heart attacks, nervous disorders and ulcerated stomachs. Psychiatrists tell us we rush so much today because we are driven forty percent by worry over past sins, and sixty percent by worry over future troubles. Take slow steps. Try to keep in Rhythm with your fellowmen. Practice good humor. Think a little more about God and the good he has given you. Try to share some of your good with others. Don't be in such hurry and you will see how much happier you will become.

And finally, Joseph's third principle to his brothers was "Bring light into the city." Whatever community of men you enter, whether it is the city wherein you live, the office or shop where you work, or the associations wherein you seek fellowship, bring light therein that will warm as well as dispel darkness. Do not be an ignoramus. Try to read more. Listen to words of wisdom whenever you can. Try to improve your knowledge and thereby your mental powers. In this manner you will bring light into your communities, light which must dispel the darkness of ignorance, light which will help fight prejudice, light which will combat anti-Semitism, light which will preserve democracy, light which will bring peace unto the world.

Bring light into the community, the light of brotherhood that warms. Can you deny that a soft word will turn away wrath? Don't we all admit that when we feel blue, the comfort and consolation which others show us can change our entire attitude almost immediately?

As we go through this short path called worldly existence, do not get too engaged in technicalities. Do not be in such a hurry. Bring some light into the lives of others and you will find that Joseph's advice will make you healthy, happy, wise, and bless you with inner and outer peace.

Vayechi

— *12* —

וַיְחִי יַעֲקֹב

"And Jacob lived." (Genesis 47:28)

OLD AGE AND VALUES

T he Torah portion *Vayechi*, evokes some tough questions for us, about our lives, longevity, purpose and activities. These are problems that will always confront us, and as long as we continue to exist on this planet, possess the same ambitions, needs and desires. They will continue to intrigue, irritate, aggravate and perhaps comfort us.

"Vayechi Ya'akov,"
"And Jacob lived." (Gen. 47:28)

And dreamt, hoped, struggled, and died, and his entire pattern of life demands our examination. The other day, I listened to a discussion about longevity and our own hopes. Reference was made to three prominent personalities who have all passed away: Andrei Sacharav, the Russian scientist, Rabbi Aron Zlotowitz, who at ninety-two was a Dean of the American Rabbinate, and the

Bluzever Rebbe, who was the oldest living Chassidic Rebbe and who attained the age of one hundred. Naturally, admissions were made about the desire of everyone to reach a ripe old age, and I suddenly remembered a family incident, when my oldest brother of blessed memory, declared that he would be satisfied to obtain the proverbial seventy years of life. This evoked the displeasure of our mother who criticized him, and who lectured us on the necessity of praying to God for the gift of life and that we use it wisely, for as long as it is bestowed upon us. Furthermore, when my brother attempted to defend his viewpoint by quoting the ancient prayer,

> *"Al tashlichenee leate ziknah, kichlot kochee al taazveynee,"*
> **"Cast us not aside in our old age, do not abandon us when our physical strength weakens." (Psalms 71:9)**

Old age is something which most of us can never appreciate until it is granted to us, but as we do get older, we become sensitive to its many implications. Once, primitive tribes compelled the elderly to climb trees, which were shaken by the family in an attempt to dislodge the parent. If he or she were able to hold on, they were granted a respite and could continue living until they were subject to this test again. If they were not killed when they fell, they were executed by the family and then were proceeded to be eaten by them. Not only was this a gourmet banquet, but it also represented a ritual whereby the positive assets, the knowledge, the experience and the former physical strength of that elderly person was now ingested by the family, adding to their own physical prowess.

True, it has often been claimed that the Chinese and our own people have been both considerate and respectful towards the aged. Are we not taught that the commandment:

"*Kavaid et Aveechah ve'et Emehcha*,"
"Honor thy Father and Mother" (Exodus 20:12)

this also includes respect for all the aged, since they are the possessors of experiences and knowledge we have yet to attain?

An evaluation of contemporary life reminds us that advances in civilization do not guarantee that we behave civilly towards each other. The daily headlines bemoaning the cruel abuse of children, the horrendous penetration of our lives by the drug epidemic, the hypocrisy prevalent in social, political and economic life, racial and religious bigotry that was responsible for the Holocaust, and the violence of war, terror, and murder support that philosopher's assertion.

On the other hand, all that should not be misconstrued to mean that previous days were always better than the present. More than one hundred years ago, Rabbi Nachman of Bratslav, the fascinating Chassidic leader, cautioned his followers: "do not say things were better in the "good old days," because now you have more money, and often live so much better. The evil one wishes to confuse us and overwhelm us with doubts, fears and insecurity, so that we might lose all our hope. When people complain that the past was better, we should remember the words of *Koheleth:*

**"*Al tomar meh hayah shehayamim harishonim hayu*
tovim mayaleh key lo maychachma sha'alitah al zeh,"**
"Do not say the first days were better than these, for it
is not out of wisdom you say this." (Ecclesiastes 7:10)

We all want to get old but as every person knows, it is not easy. Hence our forefather Jacob standing before the Egyptian ruler Pharaoh was probably impressed by this ancient wise man. But, when he asked for Jacob's age, he answered sadly, the days of my years are few and evil. At one hundred and thirty I do not expect to live as long as my Father and Grandfather. Everything is called living. Have not our people often insisted, in the light of their own unhappy experiences, "as long as you live, live!"

But consider Jacob's life: in the very womb, he struggled against his twin brother; a brother who later threatened his life. To escape that terror he left home and had to live with Laban, the arch hypocrite and vile schemer. Returning to his homeland, his beloved Rachel died on the way. He was menaced, oppressed by his neighbors, he suffered the terrible and shameful relationship imposed upon his daughter, Dinah, and even in his old age, could not obtain the peace of the golden years, because of the enmity that existed between Joseph and his brothers. Material and financial prosperity is significant, but poor old Jacob felt at one hundred thirty years old, that his very days remain few and evil. Jonathan in *Shir Hashirim Rabbah* notes the way of the world.

When Solomon was young he wrote the *Shir Hashirim*, Song of Songs, when he matured he authored *Mishle*, Proverbs, but when he became old, he composed *Koheleth,* Ecclesiastes. When we are young we sing songs. As life pushes us along, we become wiser and voice many appropriate thoughts. But when we are old and realize our errors and failures, we cry vanity of vanities. Jacob has left such an impress upon his descendants and we hear many references to his relationships with his children.

The Torah portion of *Vayechi,* preserving for us his last benedictions and evaluations of his children are overwhelming and yet, this great father undoubtedly shared the experiences of other old fathers. I do not remember exactly where I heard this inference, but the Torah does tell us that Jacob lived in the Egypt of his son's great success for seventeen years. But apparently, there is more to this story. Was this old father surrounded by the love of his children? Was he bolstered by their respect for him? Did they take time to ensure that he would not remain alone? I have no doubt that he did not lack any money and he may have had a servant or two. But did they visit him themselves? Apparently not, because:

"Vayomer le Yosef,"
"And it was said to Joseph" (Gen. 48:1)

someone had to tell Joseph that his old father was very ill,

"Vayaged le Ya'akov,"
"And it was told to Jacob" (Gen. 48:2)

and someone had to tell Jacob that he should expect a visit from his son. I am aware of the accounts that his grandchildren once studied Torah in his presence, although we read in the Torah portion that he did not recognize Joseph's children, poor Jacob with his prosperity and his magnificent children. This old man was alone. And yet, we cannot escape the feeling that Jacob did not measure his life in that context. We have always felt that even as Jacob spoke to his children on his deathbed, he speaks to all his descendants.

We know how peculiar and turbulent are our times. We know how there are voices uplifted in the nation, which are not enthralled by the prospect of the aged. A prominent biomedical ethicist, Daniel Callahan, writes in his book *Setting Limits*, on the limits of medical progress. He is not saying, God forbid, that euthanasia should be practiced upon the elderly, but he would like to forbid some life saving care to be given to some people in their late seventies or older. I wonder how Callahan will feel when he gets older and needs some assistance. There are certain tendencies in today's society to perceive of the old as stumbling blocks, impediments for which material assistance should be withdrawn for the benefit of others. I say that I for one would certainly never place Daniel Callahan in the category of the accursed Nazis, but who can be so certain that as the aged become scapegoats, other segments of the population will not someday be held responsible for all the other ills of society.

When we read of Jacob, we witness the spirit that thrives despite the years, the decrease of physical energies, the spirit that thrives because of spirit. We have often heard of those who despite their advanced years continue to be productive and creative. There is much to be said in behalf of a campaign that was waged by the Lubavitcher Rebbe that the elderly be inspired to study our sources. Adult education is nothing new to our tradition. Dr. Sidney Wolf the activist who continued to press Washington in behalf of the nation's needs for health maintenance it would seem, had received much inspiration from his own parents, who in their eighties enroll every summer in college courses.

Jacob's faith is what encouraged his own determination to recognize the evil, and get through the pain and the difficulties in life. But the very words to his children give evidence of alertness, courage and vitality. May we be inspired by that same faith so that of us it may be said, as it is of him by the commentary:

"*Ya'akov Avinu lo met, mah zaro bechayim af hu bechayim,*" " Jacob our Father did not die, for as long as his children live by his values, he will live." (Ta'anit 5b)

PARENTS AND GRANDPARENTS

"*Kachem nah ayilie, va'avarchem,*"
"Bring them to me and I will bless them." (Gen. 48:9)

Let us look to the Biblical lesson of *Vayechi*. When Joseph realizes very clearly that his Father Jacob's life is drawing to an end, he brings his sons into the presence of Jacob to obtain the Patriarch's blessings for his children.

It is natural for parents to have much of their lives rotate around the happy progress of their children. But sometimes grandparents lose their perspective when the young are regarded. Oh, of course, grandparents want to rejoice in the pride and joy that the young provide. But here and there, we are told with regard to grandparents, "you have done your share. You have provided and taught dignity, integrity and honor to your children. Now, go and take it easy. Enjoy your well deserved advancing years. Let your children break their heads over their own kids. You did your share of worrying, of sleeplessness, of fears and anxieties. Enough is enough. Now grandparents take it easy, sit back and relax, and let your children do the work."

But this mood is not truly Jewish. In fact, we have guidance from our parents and grandparents who declared, *kleine kinder, kleine tzores, groise kinder, groise tzores*, little children little headaches, big children big headaches. And apparently Grandfather Jacob adhered to that line. When Joseph brings his sons into the presence of Jacob to obtain the Patriarch's blessings for his children, the Bible tells us,

"*Vayar Yisrael et b'nai Yosef vayomer mi eleh,*" and
"Jacob saw Joseph's sons and said, who are these?"
(Gen. 48:8)

Naturally, Joseph told him that they were his sons, Ephraim and Menasshe who were born to him in Egypt. And so old Jacob said:

"*Kachem nah ayilie, va'avarchem,*"
"Bring them to me and I will bless them." (Gen. 48:9)

"*Veaynie Yisrael kavdu mizoken lo yuchal lirot,*" but
"Jacob's vision was dim from age, he was unable to see." (Gen. 48:10)

Consider this. First we are told that Jacob saw the young men, but a moment later we read that his eyesight was poor, because of his old age. The question that should invariably press upon us is, could Jacob see or couldn't he? Is it not one or the other? Then why is there this peculiar wording in the Bible? He saw them and asked who they were and then we read his vision was bad and he couldn't see. Which is it? But the Torah may be trying to tell us a startling and vital observation.

Jacob looked at his grandchildren and asked who are they? Who are they really? Of course Joseph answers, they are my sons, your grandchildren who were born here, in Egypt. There may be a generation gap here. They dress differently; they talk a jive that sometimes creates an impediment towards easy communication between one generation and another. They speak, act, and respond differently to the gals than you did towards mother. Their entertainment, their games, their relaxation, their priorities differ, because they were born here in Egypt, where I am a most prominent, successful personality. Their social development, their economic and educational opportunities have been different, but you should know that they are your grandchildren.

And Jacob replies bring them to me. Let us establish the necessary rapport, let us have the opportunity to exchange our ideas, let them hear from elders' explanations, interpretations and factual data. Let them not be ignorant, but help them know and be aware of the experiences prior to their growth, the factors of yesterday which make for the realities of today. Bring them to me, to the Torah of Israel and I shall then wield an influence in the formation of their characters that will do all of us proud.

There is a startling and fascinating episode recorded by the Torah when it speaks of the meeting between Jacob and Joseph after a long separation of twenty-two years. The Torah speaking of that moment tells us that Joseph fell upon his father's neck and wept. At that moment Jacob whispered *"Shema Yisrael."* (Rashi to Gen. 46:29) The incident has the best minds of our people who were concerned with homiletic interpretations asking, why this particular verse?

Actually, the Gemarah of Brachot (13b) tells us that the first verse of the Shema is that of *kavanah*, intent of entire concentration and meaning. How long does it take to mutter this little verse? And why? After all, this is a tremendous moment in their lives, tremendous for Joseph who has achieved great personal attainments, a man of note, family etc. At his age he has the great privilege of seeing his father alive. He can embrace, hold and love him. It is no wonder we see the tears pouring forth from his eyes. And what about Jacob? The pain of all these years, the mourning, the blind hopes, the sorrow and the anguish, and now to behold this great scene, and all you can think of Father Jacob is *Shema*?

The fact is that this father met his child, and at that great moment whispers, what do I want from you child? What do I want from life? What are my concerns? *"Shema Yisrael,"* "Listen to the

God of your father and his philosophies of life. Listen for the Lord God one." A great moment in Jewish history with a lesson clear for all generations.

Now at the time when Jacob is about to bless the Sons of Joseph, Jacob tells Joseph, you know these two sons, who were born to you in Egypt before I came down here, Ephraim and Menasshe, they are to me just like my older sons, Reuben and Simon. Yes your two boys:

"Li hem,"
"They are mine." (Gen. 48:5)

And Jacob blessed the boys. Now, Joseph knowing his Father had poor vision tried to manipulate his right hand as was expected, on Menasshe the elder. But the old man who couldn't see well, said, never mind Joseph, I know what I am doing, because henceforth, that is how our people will bless their sons for centuries:

"Yesimchah Elokim ke'Efraim uMenasshe,"
"God should make you like Efraim and Menasshe."
(Gen. 48:20)

And we want to ask, Grandpa Jacob, why only these two kids? Why? But old Grandpa Jacob, with poor vision, he saw. He saw with an insight and a prophetic intuition into the future, that the others with their 20/20 vision could not see. He was saying look at these boys, the first Jews really born in a Diaspora, youths that were born in a different culture subject to a diverse heritage, speaking another language. But *"Li hem,"* "They are mine." They recognize the integrity, the honor, the glory, and the truth of the Jewish heritage. They read the lips of their contemporary world and they recognize its moral bankruptcy, its bestiality, its shallowness, its hypocrisy, its duplicity, its chicanery, its lies and distortions, its drugs, and the fraudulent politicians who pretend they are statesmen. The phonies who profess they are concerned with justice and decency, but are ready at any moment to betray humanity and deny us our rights, our abilities, our contributions to the advancement of all mankind in fields of science, education, medicine, religion, literature and art. In every field of human endeavor they intend, pledge and are determined to live and grow and create as Jews. They are as loyal and faithful to the greatest expression of the human soul before God and man, as resolved and loyal as Reuben and Simon.

Now, we know why all our children require and merit the total, undisguised, and forthright concern of parents and grandparents. That is why we must not shirk our responsibilities. Each child must learn and each parent and grandparent must teach, to think what it means to be a Jew, what Jewishness can mean to the world, to our people, and our very lives. Let each child deserve and revere that magnificent summons. May God make you like Ephraim and Menasshe.

JOY AND DIVINE PRESENCE

In the Torah portion of *Vayechi*, the old Patriarch Jacob our forefather senses that his long and intriguing life is drawing to a close. He summons his children to his bedside, so that he may charge them on their conduct and moral behavior.

The Rabbis note that Jacob was so prophetically intuitive at that moment "*Shebikesh legalot et haketz lebanav*," "He wanted to reveal the end of days, the climax of a long and turbulent future to his children." (Gen. Rabbah 96:1) As he sought to achieve this, "*Venistalkah mimenu shechinah*," "The Divine Presence withdrew from him and he was unable to continue his prophecy." Rashi again reveals the influences of the world and the manner which the present may cast its shadows over the future. Rashi notes that Jacob seeing the children of Joseph dimly wanted to bless them but the Divine Presence was withdrawn from him, because that in the future Jereboam the rebel against the Solomonic Kingdom and Achab the sinner, would come forth from Ephraim, and another disappointment would emerge from Menashe. (Rashi to Gen. 48:8)

One Chassidic leader asks why was this? Why did the Lord suddenly interrupt his musings and prevent his intended revelations? The answer he suggests deserves our consideration. He says that Jacob's prophetic ally reviewing the future, perceived how the decades and centuries would impose disappointments, hardships, suffering, persecutions, humiliations, terror and often despair to his own descendants. And that humanity partaking of these outrages would not only bear the responsibility for this miscarriage of justice and indecency, but would itself be the victims of its own barbarism. And the tongue of Jacob faltered, his heart palpitated, his eyes grew glazed and he was totally embraced by sadness, sorrow, tears, depression and unhappiness. This commentator continues. It is well known in our Chassidic tradition that *aiyn hascheniah shurah lo mitoch aatzevoth*, the Divine Presence does not rest upon him who is immersed in sadness. It is written:

> **"*Ivdu et hashem besimchah*,"**
> **"Worship the lord with rejoicing, serve God with joy."**
> **(Psalms 100:2)**

Our ancestors discovered that joy not only exalted their spirits but also provided an inner strength, courage and determination that enabled them to survive incredible hardships and achieve those victories which preserved us to this very day. Perhaps we need to repeat that admonition.

We too should turn or better said return to those sources of strength and faith. Bolstered by the spirit of God and Torah, we too may not only confront our problems successfully, but also emerge with the knowledge that victory and progress will crown our efforts in behalf of our brethren and also guarantee our contributions to a happy, peaceful and righteously redeemed mankind.

THE WORLD IN WHICH WE LIVE

Controversies abound within the gates of our people, despite the fact that we achieved tremendous heights at Sinai, where our unity enabled us to enjoy the great treasure of revelation and the Ten Commandments. Unity is not always the badge of our people. Discord, disunity, disharmony and dissension, often replace devotion, dedication and decency. These negative forces particularly come to the fore whenever we are subject to the influences of the external world. Just as I have heard Italian neighbors bemoan the influence of the La Strata; we too hear similar echoes in criticism from our parents who worry about such influences. "The influence of the street," which simply means a recognition that we are all influenced by external standards and thus face the danger of assimilation and the loss of our own pristine values.

No one really suggests that all of us follow the example of small minorities in our midst who would escape these problems by isolating themselves totally from the world, but neither does it mean that we can afford not to realize the dangers which are inherent from the external influences. We are happy that democracy makes for an open society in which we may strive towards higher, progressive material objectives, as well as absorb the best in the culture that characterizes that society.

The Biblical lesson of *Vayechi* introduces us to the end of that fascinating epoch which Israel descended to Egypt and brings us to the brink of the radical changes which inaugurated the never to be forgotten dimensions of the Egyptian bondage for Israel the Nation. We also witness the mortal end of the Patriarch Jacob.

> **"*Vayechi Ya'akov be'eretz Mitzrayim*,"**
> **"And Jacob lived in the land of Egypt." (Gen. 47:28)**

Rashi notes that this particular portion is known as *Parshat Stumah*, a closed portion, without any space between its beginning and the final words of the previous Torah portion. Rashi's words of explanation are mournful. The fact is that,

> **"*Lefee shecayvan sheniftar Ya'akov avinu nistimu eyenehem velebam shel Yisrael mitzarat hashi'ebud shehitchilu leshbdam*,"**
> **"No sooner did Jacob pass away that the eyes and the hearts of Israel were closed because of the hardships and bondage which then began." (Rashi to Gen. 47:28)**

However, in another verse, we find that the same commentator, Rashi, observes, "*Shelo hitchil hashi'ebud elah achaare mot Levi shehachaharon b'nai Ya'akov*," "The bondage began only after the passing of Levi who was the last of Jacob's sons to die." (Rashi to Exodus 6:16) "*Kol zeman shehachad min Hashevatim kayem, lo hitchil hashi'ebud*," "As long as any one of the *Shevtaim*, the founders of the tribes, lived, the slavery did not begin." The *Al HaTorah* anthology naturally comments; if that is so, then it would appear that these two Rashi commentaries contradict each other. This same observation was noted by the Sfat Emet, Rav Yehuda

Aryeh Loeb of Gur, the Gerer Rebbe, who then attempted to explain the differences by teaching that there are two kinds of *galuth*, bondage, a *galuth haguf*, a bondage of the body, and a *galuth haneshamah*, a spiritual bondage or a bondage of the soul.

Galuth haguf signifies the physical body. The physical homelessness of the Jew, his constant wandering about the world, the oppression he sustained, the persecutions, the pressure of the *galuth*, their property to be seized and their very lives to be abandoned. One need only think of that prominent study by David S. Wyman, *The Abandonment of the Jews* to appreciate the essence of this observation.

The *galuth haneshamah*, the spiritual bondage, the exile of the soul is also characterized by attributes that we all recognize, idolatrous cultures penetrating our ranks, the alien non-Jewish traits with which our education becomes contaminated, the strange and conventional practices the non-Jew pursues and the spiritual and cultural assimilatory influences.

Hence the Sfat Emet; explained, "the physical servitude did not really begin until only after Joseph and all his brothers, and all that generation died." Only then do we read:

"*Vayamut Yosef vechol hador hahu*,"
"and Joseph and all his generation died" (Exodus 1:6*)*

"*Vayakam melech chadash al Mitzrayim asher lo yadah et Yosef*,"
"and there arose a new King who did not know Joseph." (Exodus 1:7)

It was Achad Haam, the Hebrew philosopher who used that magnificent phrase, "*Avdut bitoch herut*," slavery in the midst of freedom. That first exile, the *galuth haneshamah*, the spiritual exile was an *avodah bitoch herut* that began to develop with the death of Jacob. With the departure of Father Jacob invariably the eyes and hearts of Israel became closed, the heart and eyes, these two organs of sin and transgressions. These two organs, the heart which lusts and lures, the eyes which see and prods us to follow, and thus was the evils of Egypt learned. Hence we learn that our future salvation will require the conquest of both exiles, to lead the Jews out of *galuth*, and also to take the *galuth* out of the Jews, the latter is more difficult than the first.

When we scrutinize that *galuth*, when we regard its shocking immoral overtones, the abuse of children, the corrosion of the nuclear family, the shocking lack of self-discipline within the portals of educational edifices, the lack of respect shown to instructors, parents and authority, we are perturbed for the future of mankind and certainly for the future of our people. We are surrounded by a world which admittedly pours forth without cessation, a flux of scholarship and knowledge in the sciences, humanities, various capabilities of human thought and philosophy, and yet all these organized accomplishments are frustrated by the failure to meet our expectations.

Probably such emotions and problems pressured the hearts and minds of our people as they increased and prospered in Goshen, Egypt. The pomp and tinsel of Egyptian civilization, culture and philosophy undoubtedly made its inroads in the hearts of our people and probably many parents wondered what to do.

Scriptures intimate a solution when Israel saw the sons of Joseph and he asked:

"*Mi eleh*,"
"Who are these?" (Gen. 48:8)

And after hearing Joseph's response, he continued:

"Kachem nah ayilie, va'avarchem,"
"Bring them unto me and I shall bless them."
(Gen. 48:9)

The Midrash Tancumah comments on this conversation by wondering why did Jacob ask "Who are these?" Rabbi Yehuda ben Shalom asks how is it that Jacob did not recognize them? A tradition has it that they sat with him daily and studied Torah from his lips, and now he asks, who are these? After they were in his attendance for seventeen years?

What happened was that through prophetic insight, Jacob foresaw Jereboam the son of Nabat, and Ahab the son of Omri, Ephraim's descendents who would worship idolatry. Because Jacob was so shocked by this traumatic perception, the *Ruach haKodesh*, the Holy Spirit withdrew from him. (Pesachim 56a) The *Pesikta Zutratha* explains that this is why he questioned them, because he asked: "Who are these who will in the future lead Israel astray." Whereupon Joseph witnessing this transformation in his father, immediately lowered himself upon the ground and implored divine mercy, "Master of the universe, if these boys deserve blessings, do not let me be shamed today."

The *Yalkut Yehuda* recalls that despite Ephraim's future, idolatrous descendants nonetheless, now he is still a son and even when such descendants are bad, we must not overlook the good within them. For example the Gemarah asks, why was Jereboam privileged to achieve Kingship? (Sanhedrin 101b) Because there was still good within him. He originally rebuked Solomon for the sake of heaven. He attacked Solomon by saying that David had opened many entrances in the walls leading to the city of Jerusalem to enable more Jews to come and worship God in the Sanctuary on the festival, but Solomon closed them and left only a few openings as so that he could control the visitors and pilgrims to Jerusalem and tax them. In fact Rav Nachman said that just as a new garment has no defect, so was Jereboam's teachings without defect. (Ibid).

A similar comparison can be made with the story of Ahab, (Sanhedrin 102b) the King who did bear the burden of wrong doing but nether the less, he too had his good points. The Sages recognized this in the Biblical narrative of Ben Hadad, the Assyrian who contemptuously said to Ahab, "Your silver and gold are mine, your wives and children are mine, and I shall send my servants to you and they will search your houses and the homes of your people and whatever is good in your eyes they will take." But Ahab listened to council of those elders who were scholars in Torah and although he regarded Ben Hadad as more powerful, militarily his superior, he rejected the Syrian conditions and defied the tyrant. The Bible notes that he replied, "I shall accede to your original demands for the gold and silver, but the women and children, this I cannot do." Ahab went forth to war and was victorious.

Yes history reminds us that even in the days of evil men, there were still righteous men among our people. We must never forget the spirit of Jacob, the spirit of our ancestors who stood at Sinai, who taught us to proclaim *"Shema Yisrael Hashem Elokeinu Hashem echad,"* "Hear o Israel the Lord our God the Lord is one." That which forms our spiritual countenance will never disappear from our hearts and souls.

Rashi intimates that Jacob was concerned that they were not worthy of the blessings. From whence came the idea these young men were not worthy of benedictions? Perhaps in spite of his physical difficulties with sight that was dimmed by age, Father Jacob had not lost that inner vision, his ability to grasp and comprehend the reality of the life and influences which surged all about him.

He could see by their dress, perhaps speculate at their semantics, the language they used, topics they discussed, the emphasis which they assigned to certain objectives that impelled him to wonder, "If these grandchildren had not become totally subject to the influences of the street, the external culture characteristic of Egypt, then they are worthy of the blessing." Joseph tried to clarify the situation by saying, "Look Father, what do you expect, look at all the young people and for that matter the older ones, too what is it that we want? What is it that we consider important? It may be true that sometime in the future, evil will emerge from my children, but do not forget their good points either."

Recent studies show that everything we hear about magnificent Jewish philanthropy and sensitivity, our people are nonetheless influenced by the ideals of the prevalent culture. We still spend far more at entertainment, self indulgence, cosmetics, luxuries and good times than we do for charities, religious needs or great social objectives. Why should we be in a hurry to be critical of younger people when we ourselves are no less impressionable to the mores and culture around us? Joseph said to his Father, "These are the children which God has given me here in Egypt, in a land deluged by immorality, deceit and hypocrisy, therefore, they are somewhat alienated, removed from the House of Jacob, from the ideals you profess because the spirit of the locale and the environment can influence them. Do you expect that my children should not have some stains upon them, living in such an environment, influenced by this pagan culture? Therefore, I beg you, please consider their good points, even if they are not entirely perfect." When Jacob heard this statement, "These are the children God gave me here in Egypt," he replied in order to bless them:

> ***"Kachem nah ayilie, va'avarchem,"***
> **"Bring them to me and I will bless them." (Gen. 48:9)**

Bring them closer to me, to the Torah of Grandfather Yisrael, closer to my ideologies and I shall then have the opportunity of influencing them, so that they may be worthy of the blessing. Joseph reminds his father that despite our failures, our lack of unity, our discord within the ranks of our people there still is a tremendous reserve of goodness, a reserve which has to be released so that its inherent decency and loyalty and faith may burst forth and show its redeeming qualities. Upon hearing such words, Jacob recognized their truthfulness and he said to Joseph, I did not think that I would see your face again , and now I have even seen your children. Reb. Moshe Leib of Sassov says that Jacob is saying to Joseph, "I was afraid that your own countenance, your own face, your own basic personality, the image of God within you would be corrupted, marred, defaced, disfigured and spoiled by the uncleanness of Egyptian influences, but God has shown me even your children though born here and subject to all those constant pressures, nonetheless, they too, still maintain upon their faces, their spiritual countenance, the *tzelem Elokim*, the image of Godliness."

The *Yalkut Yehuda* takes an intriguing observation on this event by turning to Rashi. Rashi reminds us that when Joseph said "These are the children God gave me here in Egypt," he produced before his aged father two documents, his engagement (Kedusha) and his marriage certificate (Ketubah.) It seems that Joseph sought his Father's compassion at Jacob's premonition says the *Yalkut*, the aged Father feared that someday evil would emerge from these children, because they were born without the benefit of sacred Jewish marriage, and hence he feared there was no hope for their improvement or remedy for their progress. But when Joseph proved that he was married according to Jewish Tradition with the proper sanctification and document, Jacob recognized that these children were *zera kodesh*, sacred seeds. Then Jacob knew that even if they would sin, they would be able to repent and make amends and thus, were deserving of the blessing.

As foretold by the Prophet (Isaiah 6:13), when the trees are felled, the holy seed, the remnant, the stock, the vital element from which the tree obtains its life will be left, thus the tree in the winter is beret of leaves, but when spring returns the tree will sprout leaves and fruits. Hence even when descendants will shed their loyalty to God and our heritage and our faith nonetheless, there always remains the hope that with spring, with the propitious moment, they too recognize their errors, rectify their lives and spout fruits, in the action of good children always perform good deeds.

Our forebears believed that in every Jew there is a *nitzutz*, a spark of Moses our Master. The Talmud (Moed Katan 9a) recalls when Reb Shimon bar Yochai says to his son, go with Reb Jonathan ben Asmai and Reb Yehuda, son of Gerim (proselytes) "Because they are men of countenance," i.e. they are men of importance because they too have the *tzelem Elokim*, the image of God stamped upon them, it is this characteristic which is basic to our people.

We must continue to be strong, faithful and pledge ourselves and not to forget either the countenance of Jacob or the *tzelem Elokim* which has forged our spiritual countenance and which eventually will bring the fulfillment of God's promise to our people.

Our response to inner weakness and external betrayal must be the words of our Father Jacob, the words of Yisrael:

"*Leyeshuatchah kiviti Hashem*,"
"For your salvation God, have I hoped," (Gen. 49:18)

because that salvation which guaranteed our past will always insure our future.

Glossary

SECULAR AND MODERN NAMES

Achad Ha'am, (1856-1927) Pen name for Asher Ginsburg, Writer and Philosopher, published on modern Jewish times.

Aristotle, (384-322 BCE,) Greek philosopher and naturalist, his *History of Animals* shed light on ancient processes.

Berke, Joseph, Author of *The Tyranny of Malice*, exploring the Dark Side of Character and Culture.

Bernoulli, Johann, (1667-1748,) Studied and refined theories of calculus, his lectures were published as the first calculus textbook.

Braun, Wernher Von, (1912-1977), Rocket engineer, leading authority of space travel, directed teams that built rockets sending man into space, helped develop V-2 rocket used by Germany to bomb allied cities.

Carlyle, Thomas, (1795-1881) Scottish essayist and historian, great philosopher of Victorian England.

Cervantes, Miguel De, (1547-1616) Outstanding writer of Spanish literature.

Cohen, Hermann, (1842-1918) Philosopher of Religion, Lecturer, studied at Jewish Theological Seminary of Bretslau. Exponent of Kantian system, modeled works after Maimonidies Guide to the Perplexed.

Coleridge, Samual Taylor, (1772-1834) Poet, philosopher, critic of English Romantic Movement.

Dante, Alighier, (1265-1321) Italian author and great poet. Published *The Divine Comedy*, one of finest works of world literature.

Darwin, Charles, (1809-1882) British naturalist, explored the theories of natural selection.

Davies, Paul, Professor of mathematical physics. Studies in physics and cosmology.

Einstein, Albert, (1879-1955) One of the greatest scientists of all time. Formulated Theory of Relativity.

Fackenheim, Emil, (1916-) American philosopher. Leading figure in the thought and literature of American civilization. Jewish Philosopher, educator, Reform ordination after concentration camp release, explored religious implications of Holocaust.

Feinberg, Gerald, With Robert Shapiro, Authored *Life Beyond Earth: The Intelligent Earthlings Guide to Extraterrestrial Life.*

Feuerbach, Ludwig Andreas, (1804-1872) German philosopher, stressed scientific study of humanity.

Fischmann, Nachman Isaac, (1809-1878) Hebrew writer, poet, playwright, member young Haskalah Movement, left many unpublished works at death.

Freud, Sigmund, (1856-1939) Austrian Physician. Revolutionized ideas on how human mind works.

Fromm, Eric, (1900-1980) German Philosopher, Psychoanalyst, said "Human behavior is learned from social conditions."

Galilei, Galileo, (1564-1642) Astronomer and Physicist. Founder of modern experimental science. English author, wrote essays on popular subjects of his time.

George, Henry, (1839-1897) Economist and social reformer. Analyzed the workings of capitalism. Published *Progress and Poverty*, "Economic progress greatly increases value of land."

Gould, Stephen J., (1941-) American scientist and educator. Professor of Zoology and Geology at Harvard University.

Haeckel, Ernst, (1834-1919) German Zoologist, first to draw "family tree" of animal life.

Herberg, Will, Sociologist, authored *Judaism and the Modern Man* (1959), writings on Martin Buber.

Humbolt, Alexander, (1769-1859) German scientist, founder of modern geography, writings include 5 volume work on cosmos (published 1845-1862), popular account of the physical universe.

Jabotinsky, Vladimir, (Zev), (1880-1940) Jewish patriot and statesman, founder of Zionist Revisionist Movement, Irgun and Hagannah.

Jung, Carl Gustav, (1875-1961) Swiss psychiatrist, developed field of analytical psychology.

Kant, Immanual, (1724-1804) German philosopher, established main lines for philosophical developments.

Kepler, Johannes, (1571-1630) German astronomer and mathematician, discovered 3 laws of planetary motion.

Kook, Rabbi, *Avraham HaCohen Issac* (1865-1935) 1st Chief Rabbi of Yishuv (Zionist Settlement that preceded State of Israel). Mystic and theologian known for his charismatic outreach to non-observant Jews.

Levi, Primo, (1920-1987) Jewish chemist, survivor of Auschwitz, wrote memoirs on the Holocaust period.

Mendel, Gregor Johann, (1822-1884) Austrian Botanist and Monk, formulated basic laws of heredity, experiments led to development of the science of genetics.

Millikan, Robert, (1868-1953) American Physicist, Nobel Prize for physics 1923. Known for isolating electron and for research on cosmic rays.

Moyne, Lord, (1880-1944) British lord high Commissioner of Egypt during World War II, declined to save Hungarian Jewry, assassinated in 1947 by Jewish Underground.

Oppenheimer, Robert, (1904-1967) American Physicist, "Father of Atomic Bomb."

Pagels, Heinz R., Physicist, author, *The Cosmic Code.*

Philo, Judaeus, (20 BCE-50 CE) Jewish philosopher, leader of Alexandria Community.

Plato, (427-347) Philosopher and educator of ancient Greece, one of the most important thinkers and writers in history of western civilization.

Pliney the Elder, (23-79) Gaius Plinius Secundus, Roman polymath, works on natural history.

Ptolemy, Clauius, (100-178) Mathematician, astronomer and geographer, writings are source of information on ancient world.

Rabelais, Francois, (1494-1553) French humanist, used laughter to question most important intuitions of his time, practiced & lectured on Medicine.

Ranke, Leopold Von, (1795-1886) German historian, examined history scientifically, introduced seminar method of teaching, published nine volume *World History*, 1881-1888.

Royce, Josiah, (1855-1916) American philosopher, leading representative of "Idealism" Movement, emphasized religious aspect of philosophy, published *The Problem of Christianity* (1913).

Schopehauer, Arthur, German philosopher, known for pessimistic views and fine prose style.

Shapiro, Robert, with Gerald Feinberg, authored *Life Beyond Earth: The Intelligent Earthlings Guide to Extraterrestrial Life.*

Spengler, Oswald, Author *The Decline of the West.*

Spinoza, Baruch, (1632-1677) Dutch philosopher, strong supporter of religious liberalism, unorthodox views of religion, philosophy and politics.

Steiner, George, (1929-   ) Scholar, authored works on Holocaust, *Language and Science.*

Thomas, Lewis, (1913-1993) U.S. physician and author of books on medical and biological issues for the lay leader.

Toynbee, Arnold Joseph, (1889-1975) British historian, published study of history, divided world into 26 civilizations tracing their rise, decline and fall.

Turnbull, Colin, Anthropologist, author, *The Human Cycle* and other works.

Velikovsky, Immanual, Author, *Worlds in Collision* and other works of science.

Vesalius, Andreas, (1514-1564) Flemish anatomist and physician, contributions to study of human anatomy.

Weber, Carl Maria Von, (1786-1826) Composer of German romantic opera.

Westfall, Richard S., Author, *Never at Rest: A Biography of Isaac Newton.*

Wheeler, John Archibald, Physicist, writer and educator, studied atomic energy.

Whitehead, Alfred North, (1861-1947) English mathematician and philosopher, writings narrow gap between philosophy and science.

Wolfe, Sidney, Dr., Physician, established and Director of Public Citizen Health Group, pressed Washington for need in health maintenance.

BIBLICAL SCHOLARS AND COMMENTARIES

Abarbanel, *Rabbi Yitzchok ben Yehuda* (1437-1509) commentary to the Torah, leader of Spanish Jewry at time of 1492 expulsion, assorted works on discussing philosophical and theological issues.

Abayai, Rabbi, Also known as *Abba* and *Nechmani,* child prodigy, Rosh Yeshiva in Pumbedisa, great Talmudic Scholar, many debates with Rava in Talmud.

Aggadat Bereshit, Midrash of Genesis compiled from ancient sources around 950.

Akedat Yitzchok, *Rabbi Yitzchok ben Moshe Arama,* (1420-1494) Rabbi in Spain, after 1492 went to Naples, philosophic commentary to Torah.

Akiva, *Rabbi (ben Yosef),* Mishnaic sage, (40-135) leading scholar of his generation, a central Rabbinic figure of the Talmud, strong supporter of Bar-Kochba rebellion against Romans.

Al Hatorah, *Rabbi Mordechai Cohen,* Torah commentary.

Alshich, Moshe, *Rabbi Moshe ben Chayim,* (1521-1593) Authored Torat Moshe, Torah commentary, preacher in Safed, 1879.

Amshinov, David of, Rabbi, (1814-1878), Founded the Amshinov dynasty, born in Zarek, pupil of Menachem Mendel of Kotsk. Leader of large group of Chassidim in Amshinov.

Annopoler, *Rabbi Meshulam Zusha ben Rabbi Eliezer Lipman of Hanipoli (Annopol)* Early Chassidic leader, disciple of Dov Baer (the Maggid of Mezhirech), attained merit because of his innocence and personal righteousness.

Arama, Rav Yitzchok ben Moshe, *Akedat Yitchock,* (1420-1494) Rabbi in Spain, after 1492 went to Naples, commentary on Torah.

Ba'al Haturim, *Rabbi Ya'akov ben Asher,* (1268-1340) Commentary on Torah, printed in Constantinople, 1514.

Ba'al Shem Tov, *Rabbi Israel ben Eliezer,* (1700-1760) founder and leader of Chassidic Movement in Eastern Europe, studied Kaballah.

Bechor Shor, *Rav Yosef ben Yitzchok,* French Commentator on Torah, Student of Rav Ya'akov Tam, member of school that completed Tosefot.

Bertinoro, *Rabbi Ovadiah ben Yare,* (1445-1515) Commentary on Mishnah (1548), Italian, later settled in Holy Land.

Ben Bag Bag, Convert to Judaism, disciple of Hillel, early Talmudic Sage.

Bereshit Rabbah, Midrash Rabbah, collection dealing with Bereshit.

Bet Halevi, *Rav Yosef Dov Bar Soloweszcik,* (1820-1892) Child prodigy, Rosh Yeshiva Volozhin Yeshiva, Lituania.

Bialik, Chayim Nachman (1873-1934), Co-author with Yehoshua Hana Ravnitzky (1859-1944) of *The Book of Legends* (Sefer Ha'Agadah) text classifying Midrashic material according to subject matter.

Bunim, *Rabbi Simcha Bunim*, (1762-1827) Outstanding Talmudist, prominent Chasidic leader, taught Chasidim to place great emphasis on introspection, self-examination and Torah Studies.

Chafetz Chaim, *Rabbi Israel Meir HaCohen Kagan*, (1838-1933), Leading figure in ultra-Orthodox world, founder of Agudat Israel, anti-Zionist Orthodox Movement.

Chatam Sofer, *Rabbi Moshe Sofer*, (1762-1839) Toras Moshe Commentary, Halachic scholar, Pressburg.

Chidushei Harim, *Rabbi Yitzchok Meir Alter*, (1799-1867) Chassidic Rebbe, author of Talmudic Commentaries, Gur Poland.

Eicha Rabbah, Midrash Rabbah, collection dealing with Eicha, Lamentations.

Eliezer, Disciple of Rabban Yochanan ben Zakkai, Master of Haggaddah.

Epstein, Baruch Halevi, R., (1860-1942), Bible commentator, also commentary on prayer book and Avot, authored Torah Temimah, published in Tel-Aviv, 1955.

Etz Chaim, Major classic of Kabalah based on teachings of *Rabbi Yitzchok Luria* (1534-1572), written by his disciple, Rabbi Chaim Vital (1542-1620).

Ginzburg, Louis, (1873-1953) Rabbinic Scholar, compiled *The Legend of the Jews* in 7 Volumes.

Gur, Aryeh, *Ravi Yehudah Liva ben Betzalel,* The Maharal of Prague (1525-1609) Commentary on Rashi's Torah Commentary.

Ha-Gra, *Vilna Gaon, Rabbi Elijah ben* (1720-1797) Leader of Mitnagdim, opposed to Chassidic Movement, Child Prodigy.

Hannina, Rabbi, *bar Papa,* Palestinian Aormara of 3rd Century.

Hertz, Dr. J. D., (1872-1946) Chief Rabbi of British Empire, Biblical commentator, author of *The Pentateuch* and *The Haftorahs*.

Hillel, Sage of early Rabbinic period, number of disputes with colleague Shammai, great figure of the Mishna.

Hirsh, Simshon Raphael, (1808-1888) Commentary to the Torah, great thinker and philologist, spiritual leader of German Jewry.

Honi Hama'agal, Honi the Circle Maker, "The Rip Van Winkle of the Talmud."

Ibn Ezra, *Rabbi Avraham Ibn Ezra,* (1080-1164) Spanish Biblical commentator, philosopher, poet, wandering scholar.

Kaplan, Aryeh, (1934-1983) Torah scholar, produced over 50 books, force behind the Teshuvah Movement, trained as physicist.

Keli Yakar, *Rabbi Shlomo Ephraim of Luntschiz*, (1550-1619) Homiletic Torah commentary, Rabbinical leader in Poland.

Kossover, The, Reb. Baruch, Reb. Baruch of Kossov, Chassidic leader.

Kossover, The, Reb. Mendel, Reb. Mendel of Kossov, Chassidic leader.

Kuzari, *Rabbi Yehuda Halevi's*, (1074-1141) Work on Jewish philosophy and theology, poet and philosopher in Spain.

Kuzmirer, Yechezkile, Reb Yechezkile of Kuzmir (of Russia.)

Lekach Tov, *Rabbi Tovia ben Eliezer Hagadol*, (1036-1108) also known as the Pesikta Zutratha, Midrashic work incorporates many earlier works, author lived in Bulgaria and Serbia.

Leibowitz, Nechama, (1905-1997) Bible Scholar, taught at Mizrahi Women Teachers Seminary in Jerusalem, and at Tel-Aviv University, published weekly Parshat HaShavuah Commentary, Israel prize for Education (1957).

Lubavitcher Rebbe, *Rabbi Menachem Schneerson*, (d. 1994) Leader of Chassidic Movement, "The Rebbe."

Maharal (of Prague), *Judah Loew Ben Bezalel*, (1525-1609) Theologian and mystic, translated Kabalistic ideas. Author of Netzach Yisrael. Also known as Gur Aryeh.

Maharsha, *Morenu Harav Shmuel Eliezer ben Yehuda Halevi*, (1555-1631) Rabbi and Talmudic Scholar in Poland, Talmudica commentator.

Meir, *Rabb*i, Tanna of 2nd Century, 1st disciple of Rabbi Ishmael, then of Rabbi Akiva, scribe by trade, phenomenal memory (wrote Megilat Esther from memory).

Melechet Machshevet, (1663-1711) Torah Commentary of Italian Talmudist *Reb. Moshe ben Gershon Hefetz* (Gentili.)

Mendel, Menachem, Reb Menachem Mendel of Kotsk, The Kotsker, Chassidic leader, (1789-1859) "True Chassidism feared God."

Midrash, non legalistic teachings of the Rabbi's, interpretative study of the Bible.

Midrash HaGadol, Midrashic collection used mostly by the Yeminite Community, written by *Rabbi David ben Amram Adani*.

Midrash Rabbah, Major Midrashic collection on Torah, early Gaonic period. First printed in Constantinople 1512.

Nachman of Bratslav, Rav, (1772-1810) Leader of Chasidic Movement, descendant of Ba'al Shem Tov, one of greatest thinkers in Chassidic movement. Authored Likutey Moharan, Mystical, Chassidic work.

Nodeh BeYehuda, *Rabbi Yechezkiel Landau*, (1713-1793) Traced roots to Rashi, Rosh Bet Din in Brody (1954) Rabbi in Prague, eminent scholar and peacemaker, author *Noda BeYehudah*, guide to Halachic problems.

Onkelos, (1st century) Palestinian convert, wrote Aramaic translation of Pentateuch.

Pesikta Zutratha, *Rabbi Tovia ben Eliezer Hagadol,* (1036-1108) also known as the *Lekach Tov,* Midrashic work incorporates many earlier works, author lived in Bulgaria and Serbia.

Radak , *Rabbi David Kimchi* (1157-1236) authored one of most important commentaries on Bible, sought precise meaning of scripture.

Rambam, Maimonidies, *Rabbi Moshe Ben Maimon,* (1135-1204) Commentary on Mishna, one of Judaism's leading Torah authority and philosopher.

Rashbam, *Rabbi Shmuel ben Meir* (1880-1174) Commentary on Torah, grandson of Rashi, and elder brother of Rabbenu Ya'akov Tam.

Rash, *Rabbi Shimshon ben Avraham Sens,* Commentary on Mishna, brother-in-law of Rabbenu Ya'akov Tam.

Rashi, *Rabbi shlomo ben Yitzchok Yarchi,* (1040-1105) Author of most important commentary on Torah and Talmud, headed Yeshivot in Troyes and Worms France.

Rava, Great Talmudic Scholar, Rosh Yeshiva in Machoza, many debates with Abayai in Talmud, interpretation of Rava usually prevailed.

Ravnitzky, Yehoshua Hana, (1859-1944) Co-author with Chayim Bialik (1873-1934) Yehoshua Hana Ravnitzky (1859-1944) of *The Book of Legends* (Sefer Ha'Agagadah) text classifying Midrashic material according to subject matter.

Rogachover Gaon, *Rabbi Joseph Rozin (Rosen)* (1858-1936), Polish genius, Rabbi of Chasidic Community of Dvinsk, Commentary on Maimonidied Mishneh Torah in 5 vols., knew Jerusalem and Babylon Talmud.

Sassov, Reb. Moshe Leib of, *Reb. Moshe Leib of Sassov, the Sassover Rebbe.*

Scheinberg, Abraham, Rabbi, Rabbinical scholar, child prodigy in Warsaw, settled in United States, Jewish Press columnist, author, *What is the Halacha?*

Schneerson, Menachem Mendel, (1902-1994) The Rebbe Shlita, 7th Lubavitcher Rebbe, author of Likkutei Sichos, Basi Legani and other works.

Sefat Emet, *Yehuda Aryeh Lieb of Gur,* the Gerer Rebbe (1847-1905), collected writings, Polish Jewish leader and head of Chassidim of Gur.

Sefer Hayashar, Halachic work on 613 Commandments, written in story form, first printed in Venice 1525.

Shaagat Aryeh, *Reb. Aryeh Leib Ginzburg,* Born Weisun Russia, (1695-1785), great Talmudist.

Shem Mishmuel, *Reb. Shmuel Bornstein,* (1855-1926) Rebbe of Sochaczev, Poland. Giant of Torah and Chassidus, The Admor of Sochaczev.

Soforno, *Rabbi Ovadiah be Ya'akov,* (1470-1550) Italian, author of Torah commentary, physician, Talmudist.

Shammai, Mishnaic sage, many disputes with Hillel, opposed innovation in Judaism adopting stringent viewpoints in Jewish law.

Shimon Ben Eliezer, Rabbi, Tanna of 4th generation, disciple of Rabbi Meir, engaged in polemic debates with Samaritans.

Shpetivka Sage, *Rav Ya'akov Shimshon of Shpetivka.*

Simeon the Just, Cohen Hagadol at Temple, during his time seven miracles took place, most pious.

Simcha Zissel, *The Alter of Kelm,* (1824-1898) Descendant of the Maharal of Prague, disciple of Rabbi Yisrael Salanter (founder of Mussar Movement), keen insight and devout piety, knowledge of Talmud and Codes, taught Mussar, founded Yeshiva in Kelm.

Soloveitchik, Joseph, B., (1903-1992) Leading Halachist, theologian and teacher of modern Orthodoxy in America, author of Halachic Man and other works. Rosh Yeshiva of Yeshiva University Rabbinical Program, known widely as The Rav.

Talmud, Jerusalem, Oral Torah, basis for all Jewish Law practice and theology, Rabbis of Palestine.

Talmud, Babylonian, Oral Torah, basis for all Jewish law practice and theology, Rabbis of Babylon.

Tanchuma, Rabbi Tanchuma bar Abba. Early homiletical Midrash on the Torah.

Toldot Yitzchok, (1458-1535) Commentary by *Rabbi Yitzchok ben Yosef Caro.*

Toldot Ya'akov Yosef, *Rav Ya'akov Yosef of Polnoye, (1710-1864).*

Torah Anthology, *Rabbi Aryeh Kaplan*, Translation of Meam Loez, *Rabbi Ya'akov Culi*, (1689-1732).

Torat Moshe, *Alshich, Moshe, Chayim, Rabbi Moshe ben* (1521-1593) authored, Torah Commentary, preacher in Safed, 1879.

Tosafot, Midrashic Commentary on the Torah, Edited by *Rabbi Yehuda ben Eliezer*, product of Yeshiva academis of France and Germany, printed in Livorno, 1783.

Vilna Gaon, *Rabbi Elijah ben* (1720-1797) Ha-Gra, Leader of Mitnagdim, opposed to Chassidic Movement, child prodigy, modern scholar of Chassidic Rabbinic tradition in Eastern Europe.

Ya'akov of Sadigurer, *Rabbi Avraham Ya'akov of Sadigurer.*

Yalkut Shimoni, *Rabbi Shimon Ashkenazi HaDarashon* of Frankfort, early collection of Midrashim to the Bible.

Yalkut Yehuda, *Rav Yehuda Leb bar Ginsburg,* Torah Commentator, Rav in Yaroslavl (Russia).

Yehuda ben Shalom, Rav, also referred to as *Rav Yehuda HaLevi ben Shalom,* mentioned in Talmud and Midrashim particularly Tanchumah. Argued with Rav Matanya in Midrash, and Rav Pinchus in Aggadah.

Yitev Lev, *Reb. Zalman Leib Teitelbaum,* The Sigheter Rav, Chassid of Reb. Chaim Halberstam of Sanz, Grandson of Reb. Moshe Teitelbaum of Ujhely.

Yochanan ben Zakkai, *Rabbi,* gained permission of Rome to start academy and new Sanhedrin after Jerusalem and Temple were destroyed.

Zohar, Main work of Kabalah, written as Aramaic Midrash on the Bible, written by *Rabbi Shimeon bar Yocahi.*

Bibliography

JUDAISM

Buber, Martin, *Tales of Hasidim*, Schocken, 1991

Cohen, Hermann, *Religion of Reason: Out of the Sources of Judaism*, Frederick Ungar, 1972

Cohon, Samuel S., *Judaism, A Way of Life*, Union of American Hebrew Congregations, 1948

Donin, Hayim Halevy, *To Be a Jew: A Guide to Jewish Observance in Contemporary Life,* Basic, 1972

Encyclopedia Judaica, Editor, Cecil Roth, Individual volumes, Keter, 1972

Epstein, Isidore, *Judaism,* Pelican Books, 1959

Fackenheim, Emil L., *What is Judaism? An Interpretation for the Present Age*, Summit, 1987

Glatzer, Nahum M. Edited by, *The Judaic Tradition*, Behrman House Publishers, 1969 (Revised Edition)

Greenberg, Irving, Rabbi *The Jewish Way,* Summit, 1988

Heschel, Abraham J., *Between God and Man: An Interpretation of Judaism*, Rothschild, Fritz A., edited, Free Press, 1959 (pbk)

Holtz, Barry W., Editor, *Back to the Sources, Reading the Classic Jewish Texts,* Summit , 1984

Jewish Encyclopedia, The, Individual Volumes, Funk and Wagnalls, 1904

Levinthal, Israel H., *Judaism, An Analysis and an Interpretation,* Funk and Wagnalls, 1935

Louis, Jacob, *A Jewish Theology,* Darton, Longman, Todd, 1973

Neusner, Jacob, Editor, *Understanding Jewish Theology, Classical Issues and Modern Perspectives,* KTAV, Anti-Defamation League, 1973

Prager, Dennis and Telushkin, Joseph, *Why the Jews; The Reason for Anti-Semitism,* Simon & Schuster, 1983

Sarna, Nahum M., *Understanding Genesis, The Heritage of Biblical Israel,* Jewish Theological Seminary, 1966

Silberman, Charles E., *A Certain People, American Jews and their Lives Today,* Summit, 1985

Soloveichik, Joseph B., **Rabbi,** *The Rav Speaks,* Tal Orot Institute, 1983

Steinsaltz, Adin, Rabbi *Biblical Images; Men and Women of the Book,* Basic Books, 1986

Ullman, Dr. S. B., *Culture and Judaism,* Lieberman's Jewish Book Centre, 1956

Universal Jewish Encyclopedia, The, Individual Volumes, The Universal Jewish Encyclopedia Co., 1948

Wouk, Herman, *This is My God,* Doubleday and Co., Inc., 1959

HISTORY

Carlyle, Thomas, *On Heroes, Hero Worship, and the Heroic in History,* University of Nebraska, 1966, (original Pub. 1841)

Dimont, Max I., *Jews, God & History,* Simon & Schuster, *1962*

Frank, Gerold, *The Deed,* Simon and Schuster, 1963

Fromkin, David, *Peace to End all Peace, Creating the Modern Middle East* 1914-1922, Henry Holt, 1989

Gilbert, Martin, *Churchill: A Life,* Henry Holt, *1991*

Grayzel, Solomon, *A History of the Jews*, Jewish Publication Society, 1947

Johnson, Paul, *A History of the Jews,* Harper & Row 1987

Oswald Spengler, *The Decline of the West,* Knof, 1945

Toynbee, Arnold Joseph, *A Study of History, Oxford,* (1934-1961)

Uris, Leon, *Exodus*, Doubleday and Co., Inc., 1958,

HOLOCAUST

Dawidowicz, Lucy, *The War Against the Jews*, Holt Rinehart & Winston, 1973

Levi, Primo, *The Drowned and the Saved*, Summit, 1988

Morse, Arthur D., *While Six Million Died: A Chronicle of American Apathy*, Random House, 1967

Shirer, William L., *The Rise and Fall of The Third Reich*, Simon and Schuster, 1960

Wyman, David S., *Abandonment and the Jews: America and the Holocaust 1941-1945*, Pantheon, 1984

CLASSIC TEXTS AND COMMENTARIES

Alshech, Rav Moshe ben Chaim, *Torat Moshe*, Rubin Mass, ltd., 1988 (English), Munk, Eliuyahu, translator

Arama, Rav Issac, *Akedat Yitzchok*, Printed in Israel, 1990 (English,) Munk, Eliuyahu, translator

Bergman, Rav Yesachar Dov, *Haderash Vehara'ayon*, Shulsinger, 1951

Bosniak, Jacob, *The Commentary of David Kimhi on Psalms*, Bloch Publishing, 1954

Bunim, Irving M., *Ethics from Sinai*, Vol. 1-3, Feldheim, 1966

Elezri, Rav Chaim Moshe Reuven, *Nitevai Chaim*, Printed in Israel, 1980

Freidman, Alexander Zusha, *Mayana Shel Torah,* Printed in Israel, 1956

Gerona, Rav Yonah of, *Gates of Repentance,* Feldheim, 1967

Ginsburg, Rav Yehuda Leb bar Dov, *Yalkut Yehuda,* Printed in Israel, 1966

Greenberg, Rav Aaron Ya'akov, *Eturai Torah,* Yavneh Publishing House, 1973

Hadarashan, Rav Shimon Ashkenazi, *Yalkut Shimoni,* Jerusalem 1980 (orig. pub. 1521-1527)

Halevi, Judah, *Ha-Kuzari,* Yehuda Ibn Shmuel, editor, Printed in Tel-Aviv, 1972 (orig. pub. 1506)

Hertz, J. H., Dr., Chief Rabbi, Editor, *The Pentateuch and Haftorahs,* Soncino, 1963

Joseph, Jacob, of Polnoye, *Toldot Ya'akov Yosef,* Jerusalem, 1967

Kaplan, Aryeh, Editor, *The Living Torah,* Moznaim Press, 1981

Leibowitz, Nehama, *Studies in Genesis,* World Zionist Organization, Jerusalem, 1981

Luntschiz, Rav Shlomo Ephraim, *Keli Yakar, (orig. pub. 1602)*

Meir, Jacob B., *Sefer Hayashar,* Seymour Cohen, Editor and Translator, KTAV, 1973

Miller, Rabbi M., *Shabbath Shiurim,* Gateshead Foundation for Torah, 1969

Miller, Rabbi M., *Shabbath Shiurim, Second Series*, Gateshead Foundation for Torah, 1979

Orenstein, Rabbi Abraham, *Haderosh VeHaneum*, Printed in Israel, 1964

Soloweszcik, Rav Yosef Dov Bar, *Bet Halevi*, Feldheim, 1990 (English)

Starkmen, Chaim Ya'akov ben Shmuel Halevi, *Otzair Chaim*, Printed in Israel, 1966

Talmud, Babylonian, Isidore Epstein, Editor, Individual Volumes with Commentary, Soncino, 1935-1950

Talmud, Jerusalem, Jacob Neusner, Editor and Translator, University of Chicago, 1983-1984

Zlotowitz, Rabbi Meir and Scherman, Rabbi Nosson, *Bereishis*, Mesorah Publications, Ltd., 1977

SCIENCE

Asimov, Isaac, *Chronology of Science and Discovery*, Harper & Row, 1989

Broad, William and Wade, Nicholas, *Betrayers of Truth; Fraud and Deceit in the Halls of Science*, Touchstone, 1983

Davies, Paul, *The Cosmic Blueprint*, Simon & Schuster, 1988

_____, *God and the New Physics*, Simon & Schuster, 1983

_____, *Superforce; The Search for a Grand Unified Theory of Nature,* Simon & Schuster, 1984

Einstein, Albert, and Infeld, Leopold, *Evolution of Physics, From Early Concepts to Relativity and Quarto,* Touchstone, 1967

Eldredge, Niles, *Time Frames: The Rethinking of Darwinian Evolution and the Theory of Punctuated Equilibria,* Touchstone, 1986

Feinberg, Gerald, Shapiro, Robert, *Life Beyond Earth: The Intelligent Earthling's Guide to Extraterrestrial Life,* Morrow, 1980

Gould Stephen J., *Ever Since Darwin: Reflections in Natural History,* Norton, 1977

Heisenberg, Werner, *Physics and Philosophy: The Revolution in Modern Science,* Harper and Row, 1962, [pbk]

Holton, Gerald and Elkana, Yehuda, *Albert Einstein, Historical and Cultural Perspectives,* Princeton University Press, 1983

Morris, Richard, *Dismantling the Universe, The Nature of Scientific Discovery,* Simon & Schuster, 1983

Ornstein, Robert and Sobel, David, *The Healing Brain,* Simon & Schuster, 1987

Pagels, Heinz R., *The Cosmic Code: Quantam Physics as the Law of Nature,* Simon & Schuster, 1982

Schroeder, Gerald, *Genesis and the Big Bang,* Bantam, 1990

Velikovsky, Immanual, *Worlds in Collision,* Doubleday & Co.,
1950

Westfall, Richard S., *Never at Rest: A Biography of Isaac
Newton,* Cambridge University Press, 1983 (pbk)

Whitehead, Alfred North, *Process and Reality,* Macmillian,
1929

Woolf, Harry, Editor, *Some Strangeness in the Proportion, A
Centennial Symposium to Celebrate the Achievements of
Albert Einstein*, Addison-Wesley, 1983

Young, Louise B., *The Unfinished Universe*, Oxford University Press, 1993

RELIGION AND PHILOSOPHY

Berkovitz, Eliezer, *God, Man and History*, Jonathan David,
1959

Durant, Will, *The Story of Philosophy,* Touchstone, 1961 (Orig.
pub. 1926)

Egner, Robert and Denonn, Lestor, Editied by, *Basic Writings of Bertrand Russell,* Touchstone, 1967 (pbk)

Emerson, Ralph Waldo, *Divinity School Address*, 1838

Frankel, Viktor E., *Man's Search for Meaning*, Simon and
Schuster, 1984

Feuerbach, Ludwig Andreas, *The Essence of Christianity*, Harper & Row, 1958, Original Pub., 1841

Friedman, Richard Elliot, *Who Wrote the Bible*, Simon & Schuster, 1988

Heschel, Abraham J., *The Prophets*, Vol. I and II, Harper and Row, 1962

Pagels, Elaine, *Adam, Eve and the Serpent*, Random House, 1988

Rosten, Leo, *The Religions of America*, Simon & Schuster, 1975

Royce, Josiah, *The Problem of Christianity*, University of Chicago Press, 1968, (Orig. Pub. 1913)

Russell, Bertrand, *Philosophical Essays*, Touchstone, 1984 (pbk)

Russell, Bertrand, Edwards, Paul Editor, *Why I am not a Christian, and other Essays on Religion and Related Subjects*, Touchstone, 1963 (pbk)

Spinoza, Baruch, *The Ethics*, Philosophical Library, 1958

Tillich, Paul, Braaten, Carl E. Editor, *A History of Christian Thought: From its Judaic and Hellenistic Origins to Existentialism*, Touchstone, 1968

CONTEMPORARY ISSUES—MEDICAL

Callahan, David, *Setting Limits*: *Medical Goals in an Aging Society*, Simon & Schuster, 1990

Jakobovitz, Immanuel, *Jewish Medical Ethics*, Bloch Publishing House, 1959

Scully, Thomas and Celia, *Playing God, the New World of Medical Choices*, Simon & Schuster, 1987

Wingerson, Lois, *Mapping our Genes: The Genome Project and the Future of Medicine*, Dutton, 1990

ANTHROPOLOGY, PSYCHOLOGY, SOCIOLOGY

Berke, Joseph, *The Tyranny of Malice: Exploring the Dark Side of Character and Culture*, Summit, 1988

Freud, Sigmund, *The Basic Writings of Sigmund Freud,* Modern Library, 1938

Myerhoff, Barbara, *Number Our Days*, Touchstone, 1980

Turnbull, M. Colin, *The Human Cycle,* Touchstone, 1983

OTHER

Bar-Levan, Reuven, *Thinking in the Shadow of Feelings*, Simon & Schuster, 1989

Schopenhauer, Arthur, *The World as Will and Representation*, 1844 (Orig Pub. 1819)

Gombrich, Ernst H., *The Story of Art*, Prentice Hall, 1990